به آب چشم اسیران به اهل بیت پیغمبر
به خون و خاک شهیدان به عشر ماه محرم

*By the captives' tears, by the Holy House of
Him who brought God's Law*
*By the dust and blood of the martyred on the
day of 'Ashura!*

—Falaki of Shirvan

*That the dead may arise it well may be,
even if this be so*
*Can the wise expect a friendship new with
an ancient foe?*

زمرده زنده شدن ممکن است و ممکن نیست
ز دشمنان کهن دوستی نو کردن

LETTERS FROM TABRIZ

THE RUSSIAN SUPPRESSION OF THE
IRANIAN CONSTITUTIONAL MOVEMENT

Translated from the Persian
with introductory & explanatory matter by

EDWARD G. BROWNE

Edited from Browne's manuscript by

HASAN JAVADI

MAGE PUBLISHERS
WASHINGTON, DC
2008

Library of Congress cataloging-in-publication data

Letters from Tabriz : the Russian suppression of the
Iranian constitutional movement / translated from the Persian
with introductory & explanatory matter by Edward G. Browne ;
edited from Browne's manuscript by Hasan Javadi.
p. cm.
Includes bibliographical references and index.
ISBN 1-933823-25-9 (pbk. : alk. paper)
1. Iran--History--1905-1911--Sources.
2. Russia--Foreign relations--Iran.
3. Iran--Foreign relations--Russia.
4. Browne, Edward Granville, 1862-1926.
I. Javadi, Hasan. II. Browne, Edward Granville, 1862-1926.
DS313.L48 2008
955.05'1--dc22

2008019273

ISBN 1-933823-25-9
ISBN 13: 978-1-933823-25-6

Printed and manufactured in U.S.A.

MAGE BOOKS ARE AVAILABLE AT BOOKSTORES,
THROUGH THE INTERNET
OR DIRECTLY FROM THE PUBLISHER:
MAGE PUBLISHERS, 1032-29TH STREET NW
WASHINGTON, DC 20007
202-342-1642 • AS@MAGE.COM • 800-962-0922
VISIT MAGE ONLINE AT
WWW.MAGE.COM

CONTENTS

FOREWORD

HASAN JAVADI

Edward Granville Browne was born on February 7, 1862, at Uley in Gloucestershire. His father, Sir Benjamin Browne, was the head of a shipbuilding firm in Newcastle-on-Tyne. The young boy went to various private schools, of which he gives a very dismal picture, saying: "The most wretched day of my life, except the day when I left the college, was the day I went to school. During the earlier portion of my school life I believe that I nearly fathomed the possibilities of human misery and despair."[1] His father wanted him to study engineering, but Browne preferred medicine and after leaving Eton went to Pembroke College, Cambridge. Despite his studies in medicine and natural sciences, he was able to devote some of his time to the languages of the Middle East. Turning to the East proved to be a turning point in his life and an important preoccupation ever after. He began to learn Turkish, which was not taught at Cambridge at that time, and studied Arabic and Persian in order to broaden his knowledge of Turkish. He writes in his *A Year Amongst the Persians:*

---

1   E. G. Browne, *A Year Amongst the Persians* (London, 1959), 7.

It was the Turkish war with Russia in 1877-8 that first attracted my attention to the East, about which, till that time, I had known and cared nothing. To the young, war is always interesting, and I watched the progress of this struggle with eager attention. At first my proclivities were by no means for the Turks; but the losing side, more especially when it continues to struggle gallantly against defeat, always has a claim on our sympathy, and moreover the cant of the anti-Turkish party in England, and the wretched attempts to confound questions of abstract justice with party politics, disgusted me beyond measure. Ere the close of the war, I would have died to save Turkey, and I mourned the fall of Plevna as though it had been a disaster inflicted on my own country. And so gradually pity turned to admiration, and admiration to enthusiasm, until the Turks became in my eyes veritable heroes, and the desire to identify myself with the cause, make my dwelling amongst them, and unite with them in the defense of their land, possessed me heart and soul.[2]

Browne learned Turkish from an Irish clergyman who had served in the Crimean War as a private and had later been driven away from his parish because of defending the Turks publicly when they were most unpopular. Browne's Arabic teachers were such eminent scholars as William Wright and E. H. Palmer, who combined the learning and the enthusiasm of good teachers. But he was not so fortunate with his Persian teachers. One of them was "a very learned but very eccentric old Persian, Mirzá Muhammad Báqir, of Bawánát in Fars, surnamed Ibráhim Ján Mu'attar." His pupil writes of him: "Having wandered through half the world, learned (and learned well) half a dozen languages, and been successively a

---

2   Ibid., 8.

Shi'ite Muhammadan, a dervish, a Christian, an atheist, and a Jew, he had finished by elaborating a religious system of his own, which he called 'Islamico-Christianity,' to the celebration (I can hardly say the elucidation) of which in English tracts and Persian poems, composed in the most bizarre style, he devoted the greater part of his time, talents, and money."[3] Whenever Browne tried to read the *Divan of Hafiz* or the *Masnavi* with him, after a while he would push them aside, saying: "I like my own poetry better than this, and if you want me to teach you Persian you must learn it as I please... You can understand Háfiz by yourself, but you cannot understand my poetry unless I explain it to you."[4]

Thus, alongside his medical studies, Browne learned Turkish, Arabic, Persian and Hindustani. In 1884, two years after passing his second M.B. examination, he received a First Class in the Indian Languages Tripos, which at that time was equivalent of a B.A. in Oriental Languages. Then he left Cambridge to work at St. Bartholomew's Hospital in order to pass his third M.B. and to receive his license to practice as a physician. This end was achieved in 1887, and it was during his stay in London that he would snatch an occasional leisure hour from his medical studies for a chat with his Persian friends (among them were such well-known figures as Jamálu'd-Dín of Asadabad and Mirzá Malkum Khán), or would take a quiet communing in the cool, vaulted reading-room of the British Museum with his favourite Sufi writers, whose mystical idealism had long since cast its spell over his mind. It was in May 1887 that Pembroke College elected Browne as a Fellow to teach Persian and Arabic and encouraged him to spend the first year of his fellowship in Persia "in

---

3   Ibid.
4   Ibid., 13-14.

the way which would best qualify (him) for this post". The adventures and experiences of this long-desired journey are charmingly described in A Year Amongst the Persians.

Browne traveled on the old caravan route from Trabzon to Iran and stayed in Tabriz, Tehran, Isfahan, Shiraz, Yazd, Kerman and many other places. Unlike most of the Europeans who often did not go out of their own circles, he preferred to mix and make friends with Persians and did not shun the company of the strangest and wildest of men whom he came across. We see him conversing with Dervishes, Sufis, religious leaders, free thinkers, Bábís, Ezelis, and many others of different beliefs and creeds. Browne set out in his journey to explore the mind and spirit of the Persians and his book is an interesting guide to their literature and thought. The narrative of the traveler provides many opportunities for discussions of the poetry, metaphysics and philosophy of the Persians. The record of his conversations with various classes of people is interspersed with poems given in admirable translations. "Notwithstanding all her faults" he loved Persia "very dearly". Leaving the country on board a Russian steamer, he wrote: "For the first time for many months, [I] felt myself with a sudden sense of loneliness, a stranger in the midst of strangers."[5]

After returning from his travels in 1888, Browne became the Persian lecturer at Cambridge, where he stayed until his death in 1926. But it was not until 1902, after the death of Charles Rieu, the eminent scholar of oriental bibliography, that he was elected to the Sir Thomas Adams Chair in Arabic. Shortly before going to Iran, Browne, by reading the Comte de Gobineau's *Les religions et les philosophies dans l'*

---

5 Ibid., 620.

Asie Centrale (1865) had become interested in the history and doctrine of the newly established sect of the Bábís. During his stay in Iran he had met with a number of its members and their devotion, steadfastness and bravery, while being persecuted by other religious groups, had aroused his sense of admiration and he had decided to devote some of his time to this sect and the matters related to it. In 1889 he contributed two monographs on the Bábís to the *Journal of the Royal Asiatic Society*, and in 1891 he translated and published *A Traveler's Narrative* written to illustrate the *Episode of the Báb*. Browne displayed his lifelong interest in Bábísm and other Persian heresies in a number of works such as *The Translation of the New History of Mirzá 'Alí Muhammad the Báb*, by Mirzá Husain-i Hamadání, the edition of the *Kitab-i Nuqtatu'l-Kaf* by Hájjí Mirzá Jání, and *Materials for the Study of the Babi Religion* in 1893, 1910 and 1918, respectively.

The Bahá'í Faith—an outgrowth of the Bábí religion—disappointed most of the Persians who looked for a strong opposition to their autocratic government and some kind of social reform in every heretical movement. Some Bahá'ís sided with Muhammad 'Alí Sháh and opponents of the Constitution, and moreover, the attitude recommended by 'Abdu'l-Bahá himself, was one of complete abstention from politics.[6] In fact, the very universalism of the Bahá'í Faith did not tend to encourage a passionate patriotism of any kind. As a result, because of its lack of involvement and sympathy with the national cause in the most critical period of Persian history, the Bahá'í Faith has evoked many criticisms, and Browne has not been spared from such charges because of his writings on the subject. On the other hand, some Bahá'ís

---

6   *The Persian Revolution* (Cambridge, 1910), 425.

believe that Browne was not objective enough and did not express their point of view sufficiently. But one has to bear in mind that he was neither a Muslim nor a Bahá'í, and his aim was purely academic and non-partisan. In a letter to a Bahá'í friend, Browne explained his own point of view: "Let us suppose that someone could give us more information about the childhood and early life of Jesus. How happy one would be to know this! Although this is not possible for us now, it is still possible in the case of the Báb to collect first-hand materials." [7]

It was for this purpose that Browne gathered a valuable collection of Bábí and Shaykhí manuscripts, which forms more than one-fifth of his collection of oriental manuscripts at the University Library of Cambridge. The most important work of Browne is his well-known *A Literary History of Persia*, which embodies the major part of his life-long researches about Persian history and literature. When the first volume of the work was published by T. Fisher Unwin in 1902, the aim was "to set forth in a comprehensive yet comparatively concise and summary form the history of that ancient and interesting kingdom." [8] Browne further explains his purpose in the introduction: "It was the intellectual history of the Persians which I desired to write, and not merely the history of the poets and authors who expressed their thoughts through the medium of the Persian language; the manifestations of the national genius in the fields of Religion, Philosophy, and Science interested me at least as much as those belonging to the domain of Literature in the nar-

---

7   H. M. Balyuzi, *E. G. Browne and the Bahá'í Faith* (London, 1970), 50.
8   *A Literary History of Persia*, I (reprint, Cambridge, 1964), vii.

rower sense."[9] A second volume subtitled "From Firdawsi to Sa'di" was published by the same firm in 1906, but as the project was still half-finished, Browne had to turn to the Cambridge University Press for the publication of the two remaining volumes. The two sequels on The Tartar Dominion (1265–1502) and Modern Times (1500–1924) came out in 1920 and 1924 respectively.

The publication of this huge work of over two thousand pages is truly a landmark in Persian studies and, in spite of the many works which have appeared since then, it is one of the most comprehensive and standard works on Persian Literature. It is true that Persian studies have greatly advanced in the last century, and there are some errors and omissions in the work of Browne, yet the breadth of his scholarship and his understanding and his appreciation of Persian taste and mind have not been surpassed by any other Western scholar in a work of similar scope. *A Literary History of Persia* is replete with illustrative extracts from the prose and poetry of Persian authors in remarkable translations, which are extremely helpful to the uninitiated reader. Browne made a selection of his verse translations and it was published as *A Persian Anthology* in 1927.

During the twenty-four years that Browne was engaged in writing his literary history, he brought out a number of other works, of which one could mention the following: three volumes of the catalogue of the oriental manuscripts in the University Library of Cambridge; the translations of the *Chahar Magaleh* by Nizami 'Arudi and *The History of Tabaristan* by Ibn Isfandiyar; and the critical editions of *Lubab al-Albab* by 'Awfi, the *Tarikh-i Guzideh* by Hamdullah

---

9   Ibid., viii.

Mustawfi, and the *Tazkirat ush-Shu'ara* by Dawlat Sháh. Meanwhile, Browne made use of his medical training and gave a series of lectures at the Royal College of Physicians in 1919–20, of which he had been elected as a Fellow in 1911. These lectures were published as Arabian Medicine in 1921.

Another significant contribution of Browne to oriental scholarship was the completion of *A History of Ottoman Poetry* by his friend, E.J.W. Gibb, who had died in 1901, when only the first volume had been printed out of the total of six. Second and third volumes were almost complete, but the three others were put in order and completed by Browne after the notes and outlines left by Gibb. The help of Browne's Persian friend from Istanbul, Husain Danish, was valuable in preparing the remaining volumes. The fifth volume, on "The Modern School" was mostly written by the Turkish poet and philosopher, Reza Tewfiq. The Gibb Memorial Series was founded by Gibb's mother under the direction of Browne, and by the help of Muhammad Qazwini and other scholars, numerous Persian, Arabic and Turkish works were published.

Another phase of Browne's activities, which is directly related to the subject of the present work, is his involvement with the cause of the Persian Constitutional movement. As it was mentioned earlier, it was the Turco-Russian war of 1877-8 which made him interested in the East, and until the end of his life, academic activities did not keep him away from politics. During his travels Browne witnessed the growing spirit of democracy and longing for freedom among the Persians and hoped that one day it might bear fruit. In his numerous works on the subject, he tried to publicize the imperial policies of Russia and Great Britain towards Iran, and to voice the rights of the Persians for independence. The dedication of his *Persian Revolution of 1905-1909* (Cambridge, 1910) displays his sentiments:

> To all who by their thought, or word, or deed
> Have aided Persia in her hour of need,
> Whether by tongue, or pen, or sword they wrought,
> Whether they strove or suffered, spoke or fought,
> Whether their services were small or great,
> This book of mine I humbly dedicate,
> May these approve my poor attempt to trace
> This final effort of an ancient race
> To burst its bondage, cast aside its chain,
> And rise to life, a Nation once again.

Browne believed in the genuineness of the cause of the Persian Constitutional movement and opposed some superficial observers in Europe "who were apt to treat the idea of a Persian Parliament as a mere whim of Muzaffar ud-Din Sháh, a novelty imported from Europe along with motorcars, gramophones, and other Western innovations". He says, "To take this view is entirely to misjudge the importance and misunderstand the nature of a movement which, whether it be approved or deplored, had behind it the whole-hearted support of all the best elements of the Persian nation, including even so essentially conservative a class as the *mullás*, or so-called 'clergy.'"[10] According to him, the support of some of the religious leaders was an interesting feature of this movement. Regarding the reasons for the Persian revolution, Browne says, "My own conviction is that the mere tyranny of an autocrat would hardly have driven the patient and tractable people of Persia into revolt had tyranny at home been

---

10 E. G. Browne, 'The Persian Constitutional Movement', *Proceedings of the British Academy (1917–18)*, 342.

combined with any maintenance of prestige abroad or any moderately efficient guardianship of Persian independence. It was the combination of inefficiency, extravagance, and lack of patriotic feeling with tyranny which proved insupportable; and a constitutional form of Government was sought not so much for its own sake as for the urgent necessity of creating a more honest, efficient, and patriotic Government than the existing one."[11] Browne believed that the policies of Russia and Great Britain had never given the Persian Constitution a fair chance of success, and in a lecture given to the British Academy in 1918 he made a passionate plea not only for Persia, but other non-European nations, saying, "And if the reign of Peace and Righteousness for which a tortured world prays is to come, it must be based on a recognition of the rights of all nations, and not merely of the nations of Europe." In the same lecture he reminds his audience of the lack of Western support displayed in the lonely and hard struggle of the Persian people. He draws an analogy between Iran and Greece and Italy: "Politically both Greece and Italy profited much from a sympathy largely based on recognition of what human civilization owed them for their contributions to art and literature. It is my contention that Persia stands in the same category, and that her disappearance from the society of independent states would be a misfortune not only to herself, but to the whole human race. Unhappily there are a hundred scholars to plead the claims of Greece and Italy for one who can plead the not less cogent cause of Persia." [12]

The Persian Revolution is an important and contemporary record of the constitutional movement from 1905-09. It not only gives a detailed analysis of the events of these

---

11 Ibid., 324.
12 Ibid., 320.

years, but also discusses the circumstances from which they resulted. The book is mainly based on the reports sent by W. A. Smart, a former student of Browne working at the British Legation in Tehran, and the accounts given by Hasan Taqí-záda and other Persian Constitutionalists who had escaped to England after the bombardment of the Parliament by Muhammad 'Alí Sháh. There was going to be a sequel to the book to continue the history of the events up to the outbreak of the First World War and to concentrate on the sufferings and despair of the Persians, but this project was never fulfilled. The publication of *The Persian Revolution* was meant to produce some sounder effects on British foreign policy in Persia. C. B. Stokes, a sympathetic friend from the British Legation in Tehran, wrote to Browne on October 8, 1910, "I think it most important that your book should be in the hands of the public by November 1, and if you could make sure of any M.P.'s interested in Persia having it by that date, they might find material for questioning Grey and, if possible, demanding a debate on our present policy in Persia. All this is, of course, strictly private."[13]

It is an unfortunate fact that oriental scholarship has at times been associated, whether rightly or wrongly, with the imperial policies of the great powers. Edward Said's version of Orientalism cannot be applied to every scholar of the East. But as a result, a feeling of distrust has tended to overshadow the works of sincere and dedicated scholars in the minds of the people of the East. Though some unfounded allegations of such kind have been brought against Browne,[14] there is not

---

13   Cambridge University Library, MS. Add. 7605.
14   Cf. Ismá'íl Ra'in, *Húqúq bigírán-i Ingilís dar Iran* (Tehran, 1969), 434. Also see Mehdi Shamshiri, *Asrar-i qatl-i Mirza 'Alí Asghar Khan Atábak,* (Houston, 2003), 327.

a shred of evidence to support them. In fact it is ironic that the man who taught so many of the "proconsuls" and servants of British imperialism should become, in his own way, an anti-imperialist. Browne was not the only British radical to oppose the injustices of his government abroad. Another example was Wilfred Scawen Blunt whose *Atrocities of Justice under British Rule in Egypt* (1906), with special reference to the Denshawi incident, created quite a sensation in Britain. Browne was an active supporter of the Irish cause and stood strongly for the Irish Home Rule, and apparently it was for his involvement in this matter that the British government refused him permission to wear his Persian order.[15] He also had an important place as a leading anti-Tsarist propagandist in the period 1907-14.[16] George Raffalovich, the head of the Balkan Committee, which was formed in 1914 to free the Poles and the Ukrainians from Russian oppression and of which Browne was a member, referred to him as one whose "name has never been associated with any unfair or 'silencing' treatment of any subject race." [17]

Browne's extensive correspondence with his friends clearly reveals that he was a fearless supporter of the weak against the strong. In December 1908, he wrote to Denison Ross, who was at the time in India:

> You are wasted in India, and I doubt if even you,
> the least officially minded of men by nature, can

---

15 Information from Browne's granddaughter, Mrs. J. Crawford, of Little Triplow, Trenton.

16 In an unpublished thesis by Ronald Grant of Glasgow University entitled "British Radicals and Socialists and their Attitudes to Russia, 1890–1918," Browne is treated as a leading radical at the turn of the century.

17 Cambridge University Library, MS. Add. 4251 (1158).

permanently withstand the demoralizing influence of
Anglo-Indian environment. Your lack of sympathy with
the Persian Constitution distresses me a great deal, and I
ascribe it to this cause; but of course you do not know
Taqí-záda and the other leaders of the popular party,
and cannot therefore realize what fine and capable
and honest men they are. I saw a horrible and most
misguiding and misleading article on Persia in the
Englishman (Calcutta) ... and I suppose that represents
the view amongst Anglo-Indians. However, the Turks
have given the lie to the old myth about Asiatics being
incapable of representative government, and, please
God, the Persians will emphasize what the Turks have
declared, let the *Englishman* eat dirt as it will. Anyhow
Lynch and I are doing all we can to secure the Persian
Constitutionalists fair play and to enlist sympathy on
their side in this country. This has been an arduous
business, and things are going ahead now, but I won't
enter into details, as I do not know whether I should
find in you a sympathetic listener on this subject, which,
however lies very close to my heart. I cannot understand
how any one who feels that the Persians are a great and
talented people, capable of doing much in the future
as they have in the past for the intellectual health of
the world, can fail to be wholly with them in this great
crisis.[18]

In another letter (September 23rd, 1908) he writes to
Mrs. Ross:

I am very miserable about Persia, and utterly
disappointed with Sir E. Grey and the present
government. You will see other articles by me in the
Fortnightly Review for October, an answer to one by
Angus Hamilton... If Russia were prevented, she would
withdraw Colonel Liakhoff and the other Russian

---

18 Sir Denison Ross, *Both Ends of the Candle* (London, n. d.), 62.

officers, and prevent their massacring the poor Persians. But I think Sir E. Grey, like Mr. Gladstone, is infatuated about Russia. I have the most miserable letters from my friends in the British Legation in Tehran, who tell acutely the humiliating position in which they have been placed, unable to do anything for those who looked to them for help.19

In another letter to her, Browne further voiced his disappointment over British foreign policy, and said that he thought that the Muslims had never had greater need to be prepared to defend their liberties against the "insatiable greed and mischievous oppression of the so-called 'civilized Christian powers'. And if the British did not stop Sir E. Grey and his evil counsellors, it would be impossible for any nation–Muslim or non-Muslim– "to contrive to regard England as in any sense friendly to Islam." [20]

In middle life, Browne inherited considerable wealth and was able to help generously both the Persian refugees abroad and those who were fighting for the cause of Persian freedom. It was because of his valuable help and sincere feeling that, when Tabriz was occupied by the Russians in 1911, the Constitutionalists sent telegrams to him and asked for help. It is interesting to note that the people of Tabriz made a ditty, which equated the efforts of Browne to the services of Sattár Khán, their great national hero:

What the sword of Sattár did to us,
Browne accomplished with his precious pen.[21]

---

19 C.U.L., MS. Add. 5605 (118).
20 Ibid.
21 'Abdu'l-Husain Navá'í,'Fa'álíyyát-I Mashrúti–Kháhán dar In-gilís", *Ittilá'át-i máháneh*, No.9 (1948), 18.

Browne's friends were of great help in providing him with necessary materials. H. L. Rabino, the British Consul in Rasht, had collected a valuable collection of various newspapers and periodicals published during the Constitutional period, and Mirzá Muhammad 'Alí Tarbíyat had made a study of the Persian press. Browne began his *Press and Poetry of Modern Persia* (1914) as a translation of Tarbíyat's work, but added a second section to it which included translations from various contemporary poets. In the Persian introduction of the book, Browne calls it "a versified history of the revolution", and in fact it is the first important study of modern Persian poetry and its connection with the political and social life of the country. Browne also says in the introduction that his "aim was to show to the Western scholars that the poetic genius of the Persians has not died out, and it has gained extra brilliance by the revolution and will have a significant effect in the future of this nation". [22]

The collection of Browne's private correspondence at the Cambridge University Library, which is mainly related to the years 1909–13, and numerous letters kept by his family, are of special interest for the historian of the British policy in the Middle East. Besides W. A. Smart, he had other friends in the British Legation in Tehran. These were C. B. Stokes, G. P. Churchill, and W. A. Moore. Though they often disagreed with him, their help was valuable in procuring necessary information. Morgan Shuster, the author of *The Strangling of Persia* (1912) and the American adviser who had been invited to solve the financial problems of Iran, was another helpful friend. The three early chapters of *The Letters from Tabriz*, as well as Browne's other works on the Persian Constitution, were based on the materials sent by friends.

---

22 E. G. Browne, *The Press and Poetry of Modern Persia* (Cambridge, 1914), Persian introduction.

As a publicist for the cause of Persian freedom, Browne had enlisted the help of several members of the British Parliament, through whom he would make his political activities more effective.

There is an interesting letter from Major Stokes to Browne, dated January 7th 1911, which further illustrates the methods adopted by Browne and his friends:

> Under a separate cover I am sending you a typewritten account of some recent incidents here and of their bearing on the situation. I have written it rather in the way which—were I today an M.P.—I would wish to attack Grey and his policy. The main thing about it is that it has been written with the assistance of Husayn Qulí Khán and indeed that is evident from the account itself—for who else can say what Poklevski said about various matters mentioned? H.K.K. knows that it is going to you. My own idea in sending it is that—if possible—you should get some M.P.s to insist on a debate on Persia when the house meets and one of them should use the information contained in the account for the purpose for attacking Grey's policy.
>
> The less the actual words of the account are used—the less will be the chance of my share in the matter becoming known—and this is of importance to me. [23]

Moore and Stokes were apprehensive of the possible reprisals by the Legation and the Foreign Office on account of the information they were sending out. According to Stokes, the Foreign Office had made an "effort to find out who it was in the Legation who held views hostile to the policy of the F.O."[24] Naturally the fear of reprisal was more justified for the Persians who were sending letters from Tabriz

---

23 Add. 7604.
24 Ibid.

during the Russian occupation. For this reason, Browne has omitted the names of his correspondents in his book.

Browne's relationship with the Persian revolution began in 1906 when the revolt against Muzaffar al-Din Sháh led to the granting of the constitution and the opening of the first National Assembly. When the *Majlis* was in 1908 bombarded and forcibly dissolved by Colonel Liakhoff, the Russian commander of Muhammad 'Alí Sháh's Cossack Brigade, Browne became more actively involved in the cause of Persian freedom. His activities extended well beyond the period known as the "Lesser Autocracy" which ended with the victory of the Nationalist forces and the deposition of Muhammad 'Alí in 1909, the opening of the Second Parliament on November 15th 1909, and its forcible dissolving as a result of the Russian ultimatums and invasion in December 1911. Browne and H. F. B Lynch formed "The Persia Committee", which included several members of the House of Lords and House of Commons, and rendered valuable services for Iran during the critical years of 1908-12. The main objective of the Persian Committee was to oppose the 1907 Anglo-Russian Agreement to divide Persia into two spheres of influence and fight against pro-Russian policies of Sir Edward Grey. Browne and Lynch were part of a liberal group of British Liberals that vehemently opposed the policies of Sir Edward Grey, who mostly out of fear of Germany acquiesced to every demand of the Russians and tolerated their atrocities in Persia. It was through the pressure of the British dissenters that Grey publicly guaranteed the safety of Iranian refugees at the British legation in Tehran after the 1908 coup. Lynch, who headed the Lynch Brothers Navigation Co.—one of the main trading companies in the Middle East with steamers in the Tigris and Karun gave a personal loan to Bakhtiari chiefs enabling them to campaign against Mohammad ʿAlí Mirzá.

After the bombardment of the *Majlis*, a number of the Constitutionalists, such as *Muaʿzid us-Saltana*, Taqí-záda and Dehkhoda came to Paris. Dehkhoda, whose biting satire in the journal *Sur-i Israfíl* had annoyed Muhammad ʿAlí Sháh beyond measure, began to publish the journal again in Yverdon. Browne was anxious to bring these prominent Persians to England, and eventually Taqí-záda, Muhammad ʿAlí Tarbíyat and two other friends accepted his invitation. The Persians gave speeches and Browne translated them. They managed to get the support of forty-five M.P.'s for their cause and to enlist the help of several papers. The *Times*, which unlike *The Manchester Guardian* and The *Daily News* was not cooperative at all, at last, changed its policy. Browne spent a considerable amount of time in these activities and felt that his literary endeavors had been disrupted by the Persia committee, but, expecting a brighter future for Iran, he had no regrets.[25] After a few months, Taqí-záda was urgently asked by the Revolutionary committee in Baku to join its members. He traveled to the Caucasus and cooperated with the Constitutionalists of Tabriz. He was then elected as a member of the Second *Majlis* for that city and stayed in Tehran until December 1909. Because of some political disagreements and accusations made by his opponents that he was aware of the assassination of Ayatollah Behbahani, Taqí-záda was forced to leave Iran, and he stayed for about two years in Istanbul. The Russians occupied Tabriz in December 1911, and the persecuted liberals in that city, and their friends in Istanbul and other places, more especially

---

25 Browne to Denison Ross, November 15th 1908, Add. 7605 (120).

Taqí-záda, sent letters to Browne, which have been collected by him in this volume.

The Persia Committee, in whose January 15, 1912 mass meeting more than 3000 people were present, and which had 43 M.P.s among its executives members, brought together many individuals of very different political views on foreign policy. They were Irish Nationalists, Radicals, Liberal Imperialists, Unionists, Social Democrats and many others who were united in their opposition to the pro-Russian policy of Sir Edward Grey. After the Russian-backed royalist coup of 1908 in Tehran, a number of Unionists aligned themselves with the opposition against the unqualified support of their party towards Russia. Most of these dissenters were against the foreign policy of Grey from their own point of view. Some Imperialists believed that too much concession to the Russians weakened the hand of the British in Iran. Some feared Russian dominance in Persian markets. H. F. B. Lynch, though being of the same party as Sir Edward Grey, had commercial interests in mind as well. There were some other members like Browne, Blunt and John Dillon, who were for a peaceful and progressive foreign policy, and they wanted the rights of weaker nations for self-determination. Browne, who was in fact the driving force of the Persia Committee, loved Persia and her culture, and did not want her to end up in Russian hands or as a colony of Britain. In a letter to Akhund Mulla Muhammad Kazem Khurasani, the progressive Mujtahid of Najaf, he says: "If anarchy prevails in Persia, on the pretext of safeguarding the roads of the South, the British forces from India will come in, and it is obvious that they will not leave easily."[26] Some British

---

26 This letter is dated October 29, 1910, see *Siyasat-nameh-yi Khurasani*, edited by Muhsen Kadivar, Tehran 2006, 319. In

statesmen and orientalists did not consider Persians able to be united or capable of a constitutional government. Some even ridiculed Browne for his wishful thinking. Sir Arnold Wilson, the eminent British officer and scholar who spent many years in Persia, wrote in 1911:

> I see *The Guardian* declares that Professor E. G. Browne is perfectly familiar with Persian ways of thought because he has read, written and spoken Persian (in Cambridge) for thirty years and lived in Persia for one year. [27]

Browne in his letters to Taqí-záda time and time again shows his frustration, and complains: "What can a man without influence do against the policies of kings, ministers and autocrats? The ministers are after their own affairs and do not care for others. With much difficulty I managed to get to Sir Edward Grey and talked to him."[28] Grey did not change his policy, but Browne and the Persia Committee's efforts were not in vain. They managed to stop the British government from extending a loan to Muhammad 'Alí Sháh, and Lynch even provided a small loan to Sardár Asa'd, the leader of the Bakhtiari tribe, who went from Paris to Persia and marched from Isfahan to Tehran to join the forces coming from the north. In raising public awareness and keeping the discussion of the Persian crisis alive the Committee played an important role. In 1912 Sir Edward Grey could no longer associate himself with Russian actions in Iran in the light of

---

the same letter Browne calls the ulema of Najaf to unite Persians against foreign aggression.

27 Arnold Wilson, *A Political Officer's Diary* (1907-1914), (Oxford University Press, 1941), 136.

28 *Nameh-ha-ye Edward Browne beh Seyyed Hasan Taqí-záda*, ed. Iraj Afshar and Zaryab Khoi, (Tehran, 1975), 9.

protests in England.[29] He went to the extent of warning the Russian ambassador to England that he would be forced to resign if Russia did not moderate its policy in Iran.[30] This was after the Russian atrocities in Tabriz, when Browne had published his two small booklets about these events.

Letters from Tabriz can be divided into two parts: the introduction by Browne and the translation of the letters sent to him. The second and third sections of the introduction were both privately printed for The Persia Committee in 1912 as *The Persian Crisis of December 1911: how it arose and whither it may lead us,* and *The Reign of Terror at Tabriz: England's Responsibility,* respectively. Letters Nos. 3, 4, 6, 7, 9, 11, 14, 17 and 21 are from Taqí-záda, who is mentioned as "a well-known citizen of Tabriz". In the third letter Browne wanted to give the actual initials of Taqí-záda (H.T), but later on changed them to S.M.T. in order to conceal the identity of his friend. No.11 was originally written by Taqí-záda to Muhammad Qazwini in Paris, who, after omitting all references to the writer, sent a copy to Browne and also published it in the Calcutta journal the *Hablul-Matin*[31] *(No.39, Vol.19).* No.15 is a letter by Husain Kázim-záda Iranshahr, who was another member of the Persia Committee in Paris. The originals of

---

29 Mansour Bonakdarian, *Britain and the Iranian Constitutional Revolution of 1906-1911: Foreign Policy, Imperialism, and Dissent,* (Syracuse, 2006), 382. Since I published the Persian version of *Letters from Tabriz* thirty-seven years ago Dr. Bonakdarian has made the Persian Constitutional Revolution and Britain the subject of his doctoral thesis and has offered a very comprehensive study of Browne and the Constitutional Revolution in his book.

30 Ibid., 382.

31 See the review of the *Nama–hayi az Tabriz* by Iraj Afshar in *Rahnemayi-Kitab,* Vol.15 (1973), 856–9. Also see *Nama-haye Qazwini beh Taqí-záda,* ed. Iraj Afshar, (Tehran, 1974), 1-4.

these letters were in the possession of Browne's granddaughter, Mrs. Crawford, who was kind enough to allow me to publish them in the Persian version of the present work. [32]

In a note left on the manuscript, Browne says that *Letter from Tabriz* was prepared for the press, and accepted, in 1914, "[But] the outbreak of the war in August of that year rendered their publication inexpedient for the time being."[33] During the war, Browne devoted his time mainly to Bábí materials, and in the last years of his life the completion of the fourth volume of *A Literary History of Persia* claimed his attention. After his death, *Letters from Tabriz*, along with some of his private papers, went to the Cambridge University Library; thus the manuscript was never published.

The letters contained in the present volume cover but a short period in the history of the Persian constitutional movement, and being reports sent out under the most difficult conditions by various nationalists, they sometimes repeat the same incidents; however, they are extremely revealing as records of one of the most critical periods of Persian history. The description of the horrid condition of the prisoners, cruelties and barbarism of the Russians and the reactionaries, and the sufferings of common people are rarely found in contemporary records. On the one hand, these letters reveal the true character, steadfastness and incredible valor of the Constitutionalists; on the other hand they show that the revolution was a popular and deep-rooted movement. The lives of the victims of the Russians and *Shujá'u'd-Dawla* display an interesting range of people, from the intellectual *Ziyá'u'l-*

---

32 See my edition of *Nama-hayi az Tabriz* (Tehran, 1973), 22.
33 C.U.L., MS. DE3.

'Ulamá to the great *mujtahid Thiqatu'l-Islám*, from the young sons of Karbala'í 'Alí, Monsieur to Hajji Samad the tailor and the Assistant-Commissioner of Police Ghulám Khán. Each and everyone's life and his devotion to the cause of freedom is a reflection of the revolutionary times in which these men lived.

I would like to thank Ms. Farinaz Firouzi and Dr. Willem Floor for their help and suggestions in preparing this book. I would also like to thank Dr. Rahim Raisniya and Dr. Mansour Sadr Seghatoleslami for providing the pictures of Ziya ul-ulema and Thiqatu'l-Islam respectively.

INTRODUCTION

I. Sir Edward Grey as the Guardian of British Honour [1]

It cannot be doubted that the majority of the people of Great Britain, to whatever political party they may belong, sincerely desire that the honour and fair fame of England should be jealously preserved, and that she should continue to be regarded as the opponent of tyranny and cruelty and the protector the weak and the oppressed.

It is time, then, that they should realize that, since Sir Edward Grey assumed the office of Foreign Secretary, and especially since six years ago, he completely reversed the traditions of his predecessors and concluded with the Russian Government an understanding or agreement of which the present miseries of Persia are the direct result, and which has brought about a situation equally dangerous to British interests and discreditable to British honour, this fair reputation

---

1   This first section of the Introduction was originally written in October, 1912, which is now published with a few modifications of the original text.

of ours has been grievously injured and, unless strong and united efforts be made, will soon be lost beyond recall.

Persia is one of the oldest Kingdoms in the world which have never lost their political identity. Her history, apart from legends, goes back nearly 2500 years, to the time of Cyrus, the Lord's Anointed, and the Persians of to-day are the direct descendants of those ancient Persians, while their language is a direct descendant of the language spoken by Cyrus and Darius. Though weakened by many national misfortunes and disheartened by prolonged misgovernment, they remain a talented people, who have perhaps contributed more than any other nation except the Greeks to the thought and art of the world; and, as I can testify from personal knowledge, even as many others have testified, a people with many virtues and many admirable and amiable qualities. One would think that such a people might have been spared, especially at the moment when, after centuries of oppression and stagnation, they had at last awoken to their miserable condition, and had set themselves with the utmost determination to remedy it. One would think that, even if England could not actively help them in their struggle after better things, she would at least sympathize with them; and that in any case she would certainly not join with Russia, her ancient rival, the implacable foe of Freedom and destroyer of nations, the oppressor of the Poles, the Finns, the Jews, the Armenians, and a dozen other nationalities, in sacrificing another victim to Russia's lust of power and greed of land. Under the guidance of a Palmerston, a Gladstone, a Beaconsfield or a Salisbury he would not have done so; but Persia's evil fortune decreed that her struggle for Freedom should take place at a time when England's foreign policy was controlled by so cynical a statesman as Sir Edward Grey. Nobody wishes to deny Sir Edward Grey's private virtues; as Home Secretary or Secretary of State for Ireland or the Colonies he might have won golden opinions; while, as Mr. Morgan Shuster says in his great book *The Strangling of Persia* (p. 224), "he would make an excellent Foreign Minister for Switzerland or Belgium, or even for Anthony Hope's Ruritania." Unhappily he evolved, or suffered his nominal subordinates to evolve, an entirely revolutionary foreign policy, which seems to have been dictated by:

(1) An exaggerated suspicion and dislike of Germany, which made any action calculated to embarrass her seem in his eyes both justifiable and desirable.

(2) An unfounded yet unshakeable belief in Russia's good faith, and her value as a potential ally against Germany.

(3) A total lack of sympathy with and contempt for all non-European States and peoples, abundantly manifested by his dealings with the Muhammadan population of Egypt and with the Governments of Turkey, Persia and Morocco, and last, but not least, in his attitude towards China. Of the four independent Muhammadan States which existed when he came into Office he has utterly destroyed Morocco to please France and annoy Germany, though in so doing he not only damaged British commercial interests, but also exposed England to the imminent risk of war with Germany; he has almost succeeded in completing the destruction of Persia to please Russia, though here again he has damaged British commercial interests, paltered with truth, honour and justice in a way to which it would be hard to find a parallel in the history of England, and aroused the deepest indignation and mistrust in India and throughout the Muhammadan world; and he has suffered without protest, if he has not actually

encouraged or connived at, Italy's unjustifiable and brutal attack on the Turkish province of Tripoli in Africa.

As a private gentleman he would, no doubt, be genuinely distressed if he saw a dog run over; but as Foreign Minister he has no scruple in sacrificing the lives, hopes or liberties of thousands of his fellow creatures; while it is doubtful whether he would give as much credit to the Persians for the gallant struggle against over-whelming odds which they maintained for six years (December 1905–December 1911) as he would give to a "game" fish which it took him half an hour to land.

It would be impossible to describe briefly, even in the broadest outline, the way in which poor Persia, struggling after freedom and happiness, has been bullied and thwarted at every turn by Russia, supported throughout by the tacit connivance or expressed approval of Great Britain. Full details will be found in Mr. Morgan Shuster's book *The Strangling of Persia*, and in my *Brief Account of Recent Events in Persia, Persian Revolution, 1905–1909* and *Persian Crisis of December, 1911.*

"It would take volumes and weeks," wrote Mr. Shuster, in a letter dated December 6, 1911 from Tehran, "to describe all the details of the complications of the situation here…but I can assure you as a man that the spectacle now presented to us here of the strangling of the national spirit of a people who have lived for centuries under the most frightful despotism and tyranny, and only recently have begun to enjoy even the sentiment of liberty, though without many of its practical benefits, is a most sickening and melancholy one."

Ask Sir Edward Grey and the defenders of his Persian policy the following questions:

(1) Is it not a fact that a year before the conclusion of the Anglo-Russian Agreement, that is to say in August, 1906, the British Representative at Tehran encouraged and aided the Persian reformers in their demand for a Parliament and a Constitution, and suffered at least 12,000 of them to take refuge in the British Legation and to use it as a base of operations, thus convincing them that Great Britain sympathized with their demands?

(2) Is it not a fact that in the Anglo-Russian Agreement of August 31, 1907, *"The Governments of Great Britain and Russia...mutually engaged to respect the integrity and independence of Persia?"*

(3) Is it not a fact that within a week of the conclusion that Agreement, namely on September 4, 1907, Sir Cecil Spring-Rice, then British Minister at Tehran, in order to allay the extreme anxiety of the Persians as to the objects and purposes of the Agreement (about which they were never consulted) caused a letter[2] to be written in Persian to the Persian Minister for Foreign Affairs declaring in the most explicit manner that Sir Edward Grey and M. Izvolsky *"were in complete accord on two fundamental points; first neither of the Two Powers will interfere in the affairs of Persia unless injury is inflicted on the persons or property of their subjects; secondly, negotiations arising out of the Anglo-Russian Agreement must not violate the integrity and independence of Persia, that neither of the Two*

---

2   The Persian text of this Memorandum *(Yad-dasht)* was published on September 14, 1907, in the Tehran *Hablu'l-Matin* (No. 115), of which a copy was sent to me soon afterwards by the Oriental Secretary of the British Legation at Tehran, marked in the margin "British Minister's Note to F. O." I published the translation in a pamphlet entitled *A Brief Narrative of Recent Events in Persia* in January, 1909, and reprinted it on pp. 190-192 of my *Persian Revolution* in October, 1910.

Powers seeks anything from Persia" so that "she can concentrate all her energies on the settlement of her internal affairs;" that "both Ministers" (i.e., Sir E. Grey and M. Izvolsky) "are entirely in accord as to the policy of non-intervention in Persia, and have left no possible round for doubt in the matter;" that the Agreement "binds only England and Russia not to embark on any course of action in Persia calculated to injure the interests of the other, and so in the future to deliver Persia from those demands which in the past have proved so injurious to the progress of her political aspirations;" that "the object of the Two Powers in making this Agreement is not in any way to attack, but rather to assure for ever the independence of Persia;" that "not only do they not wish to have at hand any excuse for intervention, but their object in their friendly negotiations was not to allow one another to intervene on the pretext of safeguarding their interests;" and that their hope was "that in the future Persia may be for ever delivered from the fear of foreign intervention, and will thus be free to manage her own affairs in her own way?"

(4) Is it not a fact that though the translation of this document published in England in January, 1909, and was frequently quoted both in Parliament and in the Press without question of its authenticity, Mr. Acland on December 5, 1911, and Sir Edward Grey on December 14, 1911, denied all knowledge of its existence; but that two months later (on February 1, 1912), having been shown a photograph of the Persian original which had been obtained from Tehran and having made enquiries and received the original memorandum from the British Legation at Tehran, the British Foreign Office, through Mr. Acland, was compelled to admit its genuineness, adding that hitherto they had been unaware of its existence? [3]

---

3   Cf. Mr. Shuster's Strangling of Persia, pp. 240-242. I possess the original document of the correspondence which culminated

(5) Is it not a fact that whereas the ex-Sháh's bombardment of the *Majlis* and destruction of the first Persian Parliament, and slaughter or imprisonment of numerous Constitutionalists on June 23, 1908 was chiefly carried out by Colonel Liakhoff and the other Russian Officers of the ex-Sháh's Cossack Brigade, Sir Edward Grey publicly stated in Parliament on three separate occasions (July 27, November 27 and December 14, 1911) that "though those Russian officers by lifting a finger could have stopped the revolution against the Sháh and prevented his deposition," they "lifted no finger to help, and he (the ex-Sháh) was expelled." Did any British Minister ever attempt formally and publicly to deny facts so recent, so indubitable, and of such general notoriety:

(6) Is it not a fact that when in July, 1909, the Constitutionalist forces, in spite of the opposition of the troops of the ex-Sháh and the above-mentioned Russian officers of the Cossack Brigade, entered Tehran and deposed the ex-Sháh, he sought and received shelter in the Russian Legation; and that, after prolonged negotiations, a Protocol was drawn up between the Persian Government on the one hand and the Russian and British Ministers on the other regarding the terms of his abdication of which the eleventh Article ran as follows:

"Art. 11. The two representatives undertake to give
His Majesty Muhammad 'Alí Mirzá strict injunctions
to abstain in future from all political agitation against
Persia, and the Imperial Russian Government promise
on their side to take all effective steps in order to
prevent any such agitation on his part. If his Majesty
Muhammad Ali Mirza leaves Russia, and if it is proved

---

in Mr. Acland's admission.

to the satisfaction of the Two Legations that in any
country other than Russia he has carried on political
agitation against Persia, the Persian Government shall
have the right to cease payment of his pension."

(7) Is it not a fact that when, on October 29, 1910, Husayn
Qulí Khán Nawwáb, the Persian Foreign Minister, informed
the two Legations that the Persian Government, having intercepted treasonable correspondence between the ex-Sháh
and some of the Turkman tribes on the Persian frontier east
of the Caspian, proposed, in accordance with the terms of the
Protocol cited above to suspend payment of the next installment of his pension (which had been fixed at the handsome
sum of £. 16,666 a year) pending further investigations, the
Legations not only refused to investigate the matter, but subjected Husayn Qulí Khán, the Foreign Minister (one of the
ablest and most upright men in Persia), to the insult of being
"shadowed" everywhere and at all times by servants of the
two Legations until the installment was paid?

(8) Is it not a fact that hardly was this payment made
when it transpired that the ex-Sháh had (unknown, as was
pretended, to the Russian Government) left Odessa, his place
of banishment, and started on a journey of intrigue through
Europe, in the course of which he visited Vienna, Brussels,
Berlin, Rome, Meran, Nice and Paris, and, in consultation
with the exiled reactionaries resident in those places, arranged his plans for invading Persia in the following year?

(9) Is it not a fact that early in 1911, Sani' u'd-Dawla, Minister of Finance, was assassinated and the life of the
Governor of Isfahan was attempted by persons who, either
claiming Russian nationality or placing themselves under
Russian protection, were removed by the Russians from

Persian jurisdiction, and of whose adequate punishment no evidence has ever been produced?[4]

(10) Is it not a fact that, although no objection was raised at the time by Russia or England to the appointment as Treasurer-General of Persia of Mr. Morgan Shuster, the American, financial expert, as soon as it became clear that he intended to work simply and solely in the interests of Persia, and that he was in a fair way to build up her finances and render her solvent, Russia set herself to thwart him in every way, until finally, actually prompted by Sir Edward Grey,[5] on November 29, 1911, she sent Persia an ultimatum threatening to bring more troops into Persia unless Mr. Shuster was dismissed; and that in spite of the fact that he was dismissed, notwithstanding the opposition of the Persian Parliament, and that a previous ultimatum of a most unjust and humiliating character presented on November 2 had also been accepted under pressure of similar threats, Russian troops were none the less poured into Persia to the number of some 25,000, and deeds of horrible ferocity and barbarity, of which something will be said directly, were committed by them at Tabriz, Anzalí, Rasht and Mashhad?

---

4   One of them at least, the Georgian Ivan (of whose villainous countenance a portrait can be seen at p. 46 of Mr. Morgan Shuster's *Strangling of Persia,* was at large in Rostoff or Kharkoff in the summer of 1912.

5   The suggestion that Mr. Morgan Shuster should be got rid of actually emanated in the first instance from Sir Edward Grey, who, on November 17, 1911, telegraphed to Sir George Buchanan, the British Ambassador at St.Petersburg, "that any demand on Russia's part for Shuster's dismissal will be met with no objections by His Majesty's Government." (Blue Book Persia, No. 4, 1912 (Cd.. 6105), No. 127, p. 52.)

(11) Is it not a fact that when, in complete disregard of his own undertakings and the terms of the Protocol cited above, the ex-Sháh, accompanied by some of his followers, and provided with arms and ammunition purchased in Europe, returned to Persia in the summer of 1911 through Russia; crossed the Caspian Sea with his brother, *Shu'á'u's-Saltana*, in the Russian steamer *Christophoros*, accompanied, as it is believed, by six Russian naval officers; and embarked on that raid which, had it not been defeated by the energy and courage of the Persian Government troops, would have replaced him on the throne from which his people had so justly driven him. Russia and England, entirely ignoring the undertakings given by their representative, in the Protocol, refused to respond in any way to the remonstrance of the Persian government, declaring that the matter concerned Persia only; and that after the definite defeat of the ex-Sháh and death of his General Arshadu'd-Dawla, they obliged the Persian Government, to restore some considerable portion of the pension which, even by their own admission, he had justly forfeited?

These are only a few of the questions to which Sir Edward Grey and his supporters may be invited to give answers. They are constantly inviting their opponents to "face the facts." Let them face these facts and explain them, if they can, in such a manner as to satisfy the world that England's honour has remained untarnished in their hands.

Of course Sir Edward Grey has said much in defense of his policy, but little which will bear the test of a careful scrutiny.

He says that, bad as things may be in Persia, they would have been worse if there had been no Anglo-Rassian Agreement.

This is like the story of the Persian doctor whose patient died immediately after being bled, and who defended himself by asserting that worse would have happened if he had not bled him, because he would have lived on and been a burden on his family!

He talks (or did talk, until the end of the year 1911) of the "loyalty" with which Russia has observed the Agreement. But black does not become white by so calling it.

He complained of American bad faith in respect to the Panama Canal, but apparently failed to see that he has himself set an example of bad faith which other nations will certainly copy. Sir Edward Grey did not keep faith with Persia because she was weak and he had nothing to fear from her; and he cannot be surprised if other nations which do not fear England break their faith with him. *"Can men gather figs from thorns or grapes from thistles?"*

He has told us that we must either go to war with Russia for the sake of Persia (which, he says, is absurd) or "work with Russia" by letting her do as she likes and looking on with sycophantic applause or hypocritical approval. It would be as reasonable to say that, if you know a man to be a murderer and a robber, you must either condone, applaud or even assist him in his misdeed and sedulously cultivate his friendship, or else fight him. Surely there is a middle course both here and in the case we are considering. From the time of the Crimean War until Sir Edward Grey came into Office the English money-market was practically closed to the Russian Government. He opened it. He found Russia weakened by the war with Japan and distracted by internal troubles, and he set himself—with only too great a success—to build up her strength, restore her financial credit and prestige, and enable her to crush all Liberal movement first at home, and then abroad. He is largely responsible for her restored strength, and should have known from her history how that strength was certain to be applied. On England and France Russia depends for the loans which are necessary for her strength, and, so far at least as England is concerned, the closure of the English money-market to Russia would be a most effective argument to induce her to retrace her steps in Persia and fulfill her clear and explicit promises to evacuate that unhappy country and cease to paralyse its Government and persecute its people. Sir Edward Grey says that the British Foreign Office cannot control and does not give hints to the British money-market; but the history of the Birch Crisp Chinese loan is too fresh in men's minds to make this contention easily credible, neither does it stand alone, as Messrs. Seligmann, whose loan to Persia was stopped by him on the very eve of its completion in November 1910, can testify.

Whether any good thing can come out of the Russian *entente* will be more doubted by all who know how she broke her promises in Persia, and with what bloody work at Tabriz, Anzalí, Rasht and Mashhad she concluded a long course of brutal bullying and flagrant violations of good faith.

II. Summary of Events Culminating in the Crisis of December 1911 [6]

The Persian crisis of December, 1911, by far the most serious which had yet occurred, was directly due to a series of aggressive and provocative acts on the part of the Russian Government, or at any rate of its agents in Persia, which, continued since the early days of the establishment of Constitutional Government several years ago, had become very much more open and violent during the second half of the year 1911.

Until the deposition of Muhammad 'Alí, the Ex-Sháh, in July, 1909, there was a constant struggle between him and his people. Although on his accession in January, 1907, and on several subsequent occasions, he swore fidelity to the Constitution granted by his father, Muzaffaru'd-Dín, in the previous autumn, he persistently strove to recover the autocratic powers enjoyed by his ancestors. Within a year of his accession, in December, 1907, he attempted by a *coup d'etat* to destroy the *Majlis* or Parliament, while in the following June (1908) he succeeded, aided by his Cossacks and their Russian officers (of whom Colonel Liakhoff attained the chief notoriety), in bombarding and destroying the Parliament, killing or imprisoning a number of the leading reformers, and re-establishing autocratic government. The city of Tabriz, however, withstood this attempt to restore the old *régime,* and sustained a siege of nine months. By April,

---

6   This second section of the Introduction was originally privately printed and issued on New Year's Day, 1912, under the title of *The Persian Crisis of December, 1911; how it arose and whither it may lead us.* It is now reprinted with a few summary modifications and the omission of the last three pages and a half.

1909, the city was reduced to the verge of starvation, and finally, with the approval of the British Foreign Office, a Russian force, commanded by General Znarsky, marched to Tabriz, raised the siege, and re-opened the roads. Although as has been often pointed out, the effect of this step was unquestionably to avert what threatened to be a terrible catastrophe and to put an end to much suffering, it cannot be forgotten that consideration for the safety of the inhabitants was avowedly not the motive which prompted the sending of the expedition. "It seems to me", wrote Sir Arthur Nicholson (at the time British Ambassador at St. Petersburg, now Permanent Under-Secretary at the Foreign Office), "that it would be the Nationalists who would profit by the arrival of the Russian force, but I submit that the chief object to be kept in view is the safety of the Consuls, even at the risk of the measures which circumstances have rendered necessary proving of benefit to the popular movement at Tabriz" (White Book (Cd. 4733), No. 208). In spite of numerous and solemn promises that these troops would be withdrawn as soon as normal conditions were restored, this withdrawal never took place, and their presence had in many ways and on many occasions put great difficulties in the way of the Persian government and before long it culminated in the horrors which will shortly be described.

Meanwhile, encouraged by the protracted resistance offered by Tabriz to Muhammad 'Alí, two separate movements for the restoration of the Constitutional Government arose and gathered force. Of one of these the centre was Rasht, near the Caspian Sea, while the other involved the Bakhtiyari tribesmen who dwell to the south-west of Isfahan. Two armies bent on marching on Tehran and compelling Muhammad 'Alí to restore the Constitution, were thus formed, and early in May, 1909, began a simultaneous advance on the capital, in spite of warnings from the Russian and British Legations, and threats that, in case of their persisting in their advance, a large number of Russian troops might be brought in to the country "to guard the Tehran-Caspian road." Both Colonel Liakhoff, commander of the Sháh's Persian Cossacks, and the *Times* correspondent were very confident at this time "that the (Cossack) Brigade alone was sufficient to deal with any attack by Revolutionaries or Bakhtiyaris, singly or combined," and the *Times* Correspondent added that though the Russian officers in command of the Brigade were no longer on the active list of the Russian army, they were nevertheless *"completely under the control of the Russian Government, owing to the fact that their pensions and their prospect of future re-instatement depend on their acting in accordance with the wishes of St. Petersburg."* It must therefore be assumed that the active part taken by those Russian officers (Blazenoff, Zapolski and Peribonozoff) in the fight at Bádámak on July 11 and 12, and in Tehran on July13-17 by Colonel Liakhoff was "in accordance with the wishes of St. Petersburg," and though Liakhoff was removed from Persia three weeks later (on August 4) it was not because he had fought but because he had failed to make good his boasts as to his ability to defeat the Nationalists. The astonishing thing is that, owing to some extraordinary lapse of memory, Sir Edward Grey should have publicly stated on three separate occasions (July 27, November 27 and December 14, 1911) that "if those Russian officers (of the Cossack Brigade) had interfered or lifted a finger, and used their influence in Tehran, the Sháh would never have been expelled." Any reference to the contemporary accounts published in the Press, especially in the

Times, would have shown him that they exerted themselves to the utmost to defeat the Nationalists, and failed.

The victorious Nationalists used their success with a moderation which excited the admiration even of the then *Times* correspondent. "Their behaviour," he telegraphed on July 14, 1909, "has been irreproachable. Order has been maintained in those parts of the town which they occupy, they have shewn mercy to their prisoners, and altogether they evince a laudable desire to carry out their plans in a civilized manner." Similarly the *Daily Telegraph* correspondent declared that "the behaviour of the Revolutionaries was absolutely correct," that "they were perfectly capable of maintaining order," and that "all were full of praise for their wisdom in preventing complications." The casualties on both sides amounted to about 500, according to the most authentic accounts, and it was worth noting that only one European was injured by a stray bullet during the five days of street fighting.

The deposition of Muhammad "Alí (who, seeing his cause to be hopeless, had taken refuge at the Russian Legation) next followed, but the negotiations as to his disposal and pension were protracted until Sept.7, 1909, when the Protocol concerning his abdication was finally signed. The yearly allowance which the Persian Government was to pay him was fixed at 100,000 *tumáns* (£16,666) a year; and the representatives of Russia and Great Britain on their part gave the following guarantee (Article 11 of the Protocol, *Blue Book* (Cd. 5120), pp. 130-191, Enclosure in No. 232):

"Art. 11. The two representatives undertake to give his Majesty Muhammad 'Alí Mirzá strict injunctions to abstain in future from all political agitation against Persia, and the Imperial Russian Government promise on their side to take all effective steps in order to prevent any such agitation on his part. If His Majesty Muhammad 'Alí Mirzá leaves Russia, and if it is proved to the satisfaction of the two Legations that in any country other than Russia he has carried on political agitation against Persia, the Persian Government shall have the right to cease payment of his pension."

"During the Nationalist advance on Tehran, Russia had conveyed some 3000 more troops (on July 8) to Rasht and Qazwin, and on July 13, 1909, Sir E. Grey admitted, in reply to a question by Mr. Flynn, that there were some 4000 troops at Tabriz, 1700 between Rasht and Qazwin, and 600 more in other places, adding that they would be withdrawn as soon as they were no longer required "for the protection of foreign lives and property from the possibility of danger.""

During the two years which intervened between the deposition of Muhammad 'Alí and the first stages of the present crisis it might be supposed that the Persians, rid of their incubus, were free to devote themselves to the task of reforming the government of their country, and especially the finances. They were, however, hampered from the first by a series of troubles for most of which agents and partisans of the ex-Sháh, aided and abetted in many cases by Russian officials, were responsible.

Thus in August, 1909, Rahím Khán, the notorious brigand who had played so conspicuous a part in the siege of Tabriz, revolted against the new *régime*. On August 29 he was captured by the Russians, but was released by them on

September 18 on payment of £20,000 Turkish and 180 camels. A month later he attacked Ardabíl, thus affording a pretext to Russian for sending fresh troops into the country and for postponing the withdrawal of the troops already at Qazwin, and on November 9 he was threatening to march on Tehran, overturn the Constitutional Government, and restore the ex-Sháh. By this time the Persian Government had already been compelled to spend £25,000 in the equipment of an army to take the field against him. On December 31, 1909, this army, led by Yeprem Khán, obtained a signal success against him, and on January 24, 1910, they had so far surrounded him that his only way of escape laid across the Russian frontier. The Persian Government called the attention of the Russian Government to this fact, and to the Article XIV of the Treaty of Turkmáncháy, in which it is provided that "His Majesty the Emperor of all the Russia also promises on his part not to permit Persian refugees to establish themselves or take up their abode in the Khánates of Qárabágh, Nakchawán, or that part of Khánate of Eriván situated on the right bank of the River Araxes," and begged them not to allow Rahím Khán to escape across their frontier, but nevertheless he was permitted to do so, and remained in Russian territory until January 1911, when he returned to Tabriz.

The case of Dáráb Mirzá, a Persian Prince naturalized as a Russian subject and holding a commission in the Labinsky Cossack régiment, which formed part of the Russian army of occupation at Qazwin, was even more flagrant. At the end of May, 1910, he obtained leave of absence, went to Zanján, and endeavored to overthrow the Constitutional Government there. In spite of the protests of the Persian Government, which wished to deal with the matter themselves,

Russian Cossacks were sent to arrest him. While returning with him to Qazwin they fell in with the Persian force sent to subdue him, fired upon them, and killed 'Alí Khán, the Persian officer in command. The Russian authorities denied all complicity in Dáráb Mirzá's attempt to provoke civil war, but unfortunately for these denials a *dossier* of original documents has reached this country containing incontestable evidence of the complicity of the Russian Colonel Rakuza, who supplied numerous disaffected Persians associated with Dáráb Mirzá in his enterprise with safe conducts, written in Persian, but signed and sealed in Russian, and threatening the direct penalties to any Persian official who should interfere with them or their families and followers. Some of the most active of Dáráb Mirzá supporters were supplied with such safe conducts signed by Colonel Rakuza.

Mention should also be made of the massacre of villagers at Varmúní near Astárá by Russian troops in February, 1911, in which some 60 persons, including women and children, were slain; and of the case of Rashídu'l-Mulk, ex-Governor of Ardabíl, who was imprisoned at Tabriz on a charge of treachery, but was forcibly released by the Russian Consul-General on July 28, 1911.

These were some of the endless series of troubles which continued, from the restoration of the Constitution in July, 1909, until the present time to embarrass, harass, weaken and impoverish the Persian Government, which was never for a moment left free to devote its energies to the restoration of order in the more distant parts of Persia, especially the South. A fresh series of embarrassments was created by the obstacles placed by Russia and England in the way of Persia's attempt to obtain a loan, save a joint Anglo-Russian loan involving on Persia's part the acceptance of terms of tutelage incompatible with the national independence which she desired above all things to maintain. On December 13, 1909, Persia enquired of the two Governments on what terms such a loan (of £500,000) would be granted to her; but on April 10, 1910, two days after the expiry of Russia's Railway Concession, she rejected the proposed conditions as inconsistent with her national safety. Two months later she entered into negotiations with a private firm in London (Seligmann's) for a loan, and this was on the point of being concluded on terms satisfactory to both parties when, in October, 1910, the negotiations were frustrated by the action of the British acting in harmony with the Russian government, which latter at the same time prevented Persia from realizing money on the Crown Jewels, said to have been valued by a French expert at £750,000. On August 25, 1910, Russia had also endeavored to extort fresh concessions as the price of withdrawing her troops; a tacit admission on her part that their presence was no longer necessary for the protection of European residents which drew forth a remonstrance even from the *Times*.

About this time also occurred certain important changes in the diplomatic and consular services of Russia and England which corresponded with harsher and more vigorous attitude of the two Powers towards Persia, and with a marked unfriendliness on the part of France (followed by England) towards Turkey which led immediately to a *rapprochement* between that country and Germany.

These changes began with the departure of Lord Hardinge of Penshurst (formerly Sir Charles Hardinge) from the British Foreign Office to take up the position of Viceroy of India, and the advent in his place of Sir Arthur Nicholson, hitherto British Ambassador at St. Petersburg;

an appointment warmly applauded by the organs of the Russian Government. About the same time (end of September, 1910) M. Izvolsky, the chief upholder in Russia of the Anglo-Russian Agreement, was removed from the position of Foreign Minister which, he had hitherto held and sent as Ambassador to Paris, his place being taken at the Russian Foreign Office by M. Sazonoff. Last, but not least, M. Pokhitanoff, whose violent and high-handed behavior when Consul-General at Tabriz was notorious, and who, with his colleague M. Petroff, was directly responsible for the two Ultimatums of November, 1911, which have produced the crisis now under discussion was sent as Russian Consul to Tehran in October, 1910. Almost simultaneously (October 16) was dispatched the British note to Persia on the state of the Southern Roads which was at first described as an "Ultimatum," though later attempts were made to invest it with a milder character. Represented in Vienna as "the *début* of Sir Arthur Nicholson, an energetic and unscrupulous politician," it caused the greatest excitement and alarm not only in Persia but in Turkey, where, at a great protest meeting held at Constantinople on October 23, 1910, violent speeches were made denouncing the action of England and Russia towards Persia, and an appeal was telegraphed to the German Emperor as the only European animated by friendly feeling towards Islam. This appeal, which apparently evoked no reply, did not benefit Islam, but it probably greatly strengthened the German Emperor's position in dealing with the Tsar at Potsdam on November 5, 1910, and in formulating the terms of the celebrated Potsdam Agreement which came as such a disagreeable surprise to England and France when its terms became known. From this point onwards Russia, assured of Germany's recognition (on certain terms) of her "sphere of influence" in Persia, appears to have had the whip-hand over England, and to have been able (probably by threats, expressed or implied, of a closer *rapprochement* with Germany) to compel her partner to acquiesce with ever diminishing resistance in the abandonment of that respect for the "independence and integrity" of Persia which both Powers had repeatedly and solemnly declared to be the underlying principle on which the Anglo-Russian Agreement of August 31, 1907, was based.

To return to events in Persia, on October 29, 1910, Husayn Qulí Khán, the Persian Foreign Minister, a man of unusual capacity and integrity, informed the two Legations that the Persian Government, having intercepted treasonable correspondence between the ex-Shah and some of the Turkmán tribes on the Persian frontier east of the Caspian, proposed, in accordance with the terms of the Protocol of August 25, 1909, to stop the payment of the next installment of his allowance pending further investigations. In response to this communication not only did the two Legations refuse to consider the allegation against the ex-Sháh, and insist on the immediate payment of the allowance but, they subjected Husayn Qulí Khán to the insult of sending two Legation servants (ghuláms) to follow him about everywhere, even into his house, until the money was paid. Strong protests were made by the Persian Government at the humiliation thus inflicted upon them, which, though represented by Sir E. Gray in Parliament as "the custom of the country," was in fact an unprecedented and unparalleled outrage. The Russian Legation was, however, bent on getting rid of Husayn Qulí Khán, whom they disliked both on account of his fearlessness and uprightness and his English education and alleged Anglophile tendencies; and on November 16, 1910, the Russian Minister demanded an apology from him for an alleged insult to the Russian Consular Agent in Káshán, a Persian of bad repute named Ághá Hasan, to whose appointment the Persian Government had consistently objected. Finally Husayn Qulí Khán was driven to resign on December 27, 1910.

Hardly had the ex-Sháh's pension been paid as a result of the pressure described above, when it transpired that he had left Odessa (unknown, as was pretended, to the Russian Government) and started on a journey of intrigue through Europe, in the course of which he visited Vienna, Brussels, Berlin, Rome, Meran, Nice, Paris and other places where his old adherents were living in exile, and made his plans for the attempt to regain his throne which occurred last summer.

Early in the year 1911 two assassinations occurred which produced a very bad effect in Persia, because in both cases the assassins were claimed by Russia as her subjects, and were removed from Persian jurisdiction. The first case occurred on February 1 at Isfahán, when a certain 'Abbás, an ex-chief of police, shot at and wounded the Governor, Mu'tamad-i-Kháqán, and killed his cousin, and then took refuge in the Russian Consulate. The second case occurred at Tehran five days later, when the Minister of Finance, Saní 'u 'd-Dawla, a reputed Germanophile who appears to have been engaged in trying to negotiate a loan for Persia, was shot by two Georgians, who succeeded in wounding four of the police before they were arrested. Two days later the new Regent Násiru'l-Mulk, who had been elected to this responsible position on the death of 'Azadu'l-Mulk in the previous autumn, finally returned to Tehran. His advent aroused fresh hopes, especially as (in compliment, it was said, to him, and to add prestige to his assumption to the Regency) the bulk of the Russian garrison (except 80 Cossacks) were withdrawn from Qazwín on March 13, a month after his arrival.

The next four months were probably, in spite of continued intrigues directed against the Government, the most hopeful which Persia experienced during these stormy years. May witnessed the arrival of Mr. Morgan Shuster and the other American financial experts whom Persia had engaged to organize her revenue and expenditure. To enforce the payment of legal taxes by means of a carefully selected Treasury Gendarmerie was soon recognized as the first necessity. This organization was beginning to take shape in July, and the command of the new force was offered by Mr. Shuster to Captain C. B. Stokes of the Indian Army, whose period of service as Military Attaché to the British Legation had just come to an end. At first the British Government raised no objection, and Captain Stokes was given to understand that his resignation would be accepted; but within ten days Russia had protested against this appointment, on the ground that it involved the employment of a British officer in the so-called "Russian Sphere," and was therefore "contrary to the spirit of the Anglo-Russian Agreement." Prolonged negotiations ensued, and for a time there seemed some hope that Russia would waive her objection on learning that the appointment had no political significance, but had been determined on simply because no other available officer possessed Captain Stokes 's exceptional qualifications for the post. The *Novoe Vremya*, however, and other reactionary organs of the Russian Press violently denounced his appointment and the situation was suddenly further complicated by the reappearance of the ex-Sháh on Persian territory with a considerable following of Turkmáns, accompanied by his brother *Shu'á'u's-Saltana*. He had returned through Russia, crossed the Caspian in a

Russian steamer, the *Christophoros*, and was said to be accompanied by six Russian Naval Officers, while the Russian cargo-boat *Djabbar* lay at hand on the Caspian to enable him to retrace his steps if his adventure should fail. His second brother, *Sáláru'd-Dawla*, meanwhile entered Persian territory on the Western side, across the Turkish frontier, and, collecting an army of Lurs, attacked Kirmánsháh.

Confronted by this double invasion and further harassed by the Russian objections to Captain Stokes's appointment and the vigorous campaign they had now instituted against the able and honest American Treasurer-General, Mr. Morgan Shuster, the Persian Government in vain protested to Russia and Great Britain against the violation of Article II of the Protocol of August 25, 1909, involved in the ex-Sháh's return. The two Powers, while admitting that the ex-Sháh had certainly forfeited his pension, declined to take any further steps in the matter, which, they said, now concerned only the Persian Government. Every effort was therefore made by the Persians to put an end to this fresh and most serious menace, and, after some indecisive engagements and many wild reports, the ex-Sháh's most capable general Arshadu'd-Dawla was defeated and shot on September 5. The victory of the Government troops was complete, and a few days later the ex-Sháh re-embarked on the Russian boat and fled back to Russia. Three weeks later his brother *Sáláru'd-Dawla* suffered an equally decisive defeat in the West at Sáwa and Nawbarán, and fled to Europe on October 4, while Hamadán, which he had occupied, was retaken by the Government troops two days later.

Now at last it seemed that, freed from these dangers, which it had overcome by its own energy, and from the burden of the ex-Sháh's large allowance, the Persian Government might hope for a little breathing space. But no sooner was it evident that the ex-Sháh had hopelessly failed in his attempt when fresh difficulties were raised by both Russia and England. England, making no allowance for the serious preoccupations which had rendered it impossible for the Persian Government to send troops to restore order in the South, announced her intention of sending a number of Indian troops to Fárs; while though, according to the *Times*, the Persian Government behaved in the most conciliatory manner towards Russia, a Russo-Persian conflict was provoked on October 9, by the overbearing conduct of Messrs. Pokhitanoff and Petroff. The property of the ex-Sháh's brother *Shu'á'u's-Saltana*, who had taken part in the recent rebellion, was declared confiscated by the Persian Government, and Treasury Gendarmes were placed in charge of his estates of Mansúriyya, Dawlatábád and Mansúrábád. The notorious M. Pokhitanoff, the Russian Consul-General, regardless of the fact that *Shu'áu's-Saltana* had placed himself under Turkish, not Russian, protection, and that, according to his own will, he not only owed nothing to the Russian Bank, but had a credit there of 18,000 *tumáns* (£3600), took upon himself to interfere. Two members of the Russian Consulate in uniform, accompanied by ten Russian Cossacks, entered the house and threatened to fire on the five Treasury Gendarmes unless they at once retired, which they did. Next day a strong body of Treasury Gendarmes returned, and, finding only a small guard of Persian Cossacks, evicted them. "All these proceedings," said the *Times* correspondent in his telegram of October 10, "appear to have been due to the initiative of M. Pokhitanoff, the Russian Consul-General. The Russian Minister appears to have rectified the matter, and the incident now seems to be closed, except that the

Persian Government is now addressing a protest against the action of the Consul-General."

Unfortunately, so far from the incident being closed, it led directly to a much more serious crisis. After the confiscation had been effected by the Treasury Gendarmes, two officials of the Russian Consulate, Petroff and another returned to the house and began to revile and abuse the Persian gendarmes on duty there. Being unable to provoke an incident of any kind (for the men had been strictly enjoined not to allow themselves to be drawn into any altercation), they departed to the Russian Consulate and declared that they had been insulted and threatened.

A few days after this (on October 17) Russia definitely refused to withdraw her objection to the appointment of Captain Stokes to command the Treasury Gendarmerie, and though the *Times* had stated on August 4 that "neither the British nor the Indian Government had any power to prevent Captain Stokes from accepting the appointment," means were found to meet Russian's wishes and to prohibit him from taking up the post to his acceptance of which no objection had originally been made.

Next day the *Times* published a leader criticizing Mr. Shuster's actions, and especially his protest against Anglo-Russian policy in Persia, which he described as essentially "hostile to the regeneration of Persia," and Mr. Shuster at once announced his intention of justifying his criticisms by a statement of facts which had come under his observation. His indictment duly appeared in the *Times* of November 9 and 10, and was feebly criticized in a leading article of conspicuous weakness on November 11.

Meanwhile Russia, encouraged by her success in pre-venting the employment of Captain Stokes, and finding the indulgence of the British Foreign Office practically unlimited, raised, on October 22, a fresh objection to the appointment of twenty additional Swedish officers who had been asked for by the Persian Government, and apparently obliged the Swedish Government to yield on this point on November 7. On October 27 the first detachment of Indian troops landed at Bushire, and on the same day it was an-nounced that 200 more Russian troops had landed at Anzalí, that they would be followed by 1700 more, and that 1900 more would advance from Julfá to Tabriz. That the sending of these Indian troops to the south would at once be fol-lowed by the sending of a much larger number of Russian troops to the north was exactly what had been feared by those who deprecated any partition of Persia, and the result in this case fully justified their apprehensions.

On November 2 there was a sudden recrudescence of the *Shu'á'u's-Saltana* incident. The Russian Minister, M. Poklevski Koziell, who was supposed to have dissociated himself entirely from the conduct of the Consul-General, M. Pokhitanoff, presented a verbal Ultimatum to the Persian Government demanding: (1) that the Treasury Gendarmes should be at once removed from the *Shu'á'u's-Saltana* prop-erties; and (2) that the Persian Foreign Minister should apologize for the alleged insult offered to the Russian Con-sular Officers. He also returned the Persian note of protest, although he had previously acknowledged and answered it, and demanded an immediate reply to his Ultimatum. The Persian Government at first refused to apologize for an offence never committed, but expressed their com-plete readiness to submit the whole question to impartial investigation, and to apologize if it could be shown that they or their officials had been guilty of any discourtesy, but finally, having received on November 11 a written Ultimatum in the same sense, and being advised by the British Legation, whose advice they sought, to yield to *force majeure*, they gave way, and the required apology was tendered on November 26 by the Persian Foreign Minister.

Any hope that this undeserved humiliation would appease the Russian Government was dispelled by the presentation of a second yet more unendurable Ultimatum on November 29, in which Russia put forward three fresh demands, viz.—(1) that the Persian Government should dismiss Mr. Shuster and Mr. Lecoffre; (2) that they should undertake to appoint in future no foreigners in the Government Service without first consulting the Russian and British Ministers; (3) that they should pay an indemnity for the expenses involved in the dispatch of the Russian expedition, which the compliance of the Persians with the first Ultimatum had not stopped [them from sending it]. Compliance with the terms of the second Ultimatum was also demanded within 48 hours.

The acceptance of this Ultimatum evidently involved on the one hand a complete renunciation of Persia's position as an independent State and the final abandonment of the hopeful reforms so energetically pushed forward by Mr. Shuster, and on the other hand offered no sure hope of a final settlement. It was a case of the Wolf and the Lamb, and the Lamb at last turned at bay. On November 30 the *Majlis* "unanimously refused compliance with the Russian Ultimatum," and on December 1, Mr. Morgan Shuster published a still stronger defense of his action, ending with the following words:

> I was early offered the plain choice between serving
> the Persian people and only appearing to do so, while
> actually serving foreign interests bent on Persia's
> national destruction. I have no apologies to offer for
> my course.

The events of December, 1911, are within the memory of all. There were delays and pauses which aroused transient hopes that the Russian advance might be stayed, and that Sir Edward Grey, while publicly defending every step taken by Russia, might in secret be endeavoring to restrain her cupidity, which evidently deemed the moment opportune for the satisfaction of her secular ambitions in Persia. But the advance of the Russian troops continued, and on Christmas Day arrived sinister rumours of frightful bloodshed both at Tabriz and Rasht, with open threats on the part of the Russian Government of field courts martial and wholesale executions on the model of those employed with such terrible ferocity in the Baltic provinces some years ago. The details of these events were not fully known for some time, and telegraphic communication with Tabriz, Rasht and even Tehran was interrupted, wholly or partly, down to the end of 1911, but there was from the first every reason to fear that, as the *Times* correspondent said, "When the veil is lifted, it will reveal desolation."

III. The Russian Reign of Terror in North Persia

All the humiliations swallowed by the unfortunate Persians in November to December 1911, their acceptance of the two ultimatums of November 2nd and November 29th, 1911, the *coup d'etat* by which the Cabinet dissolved the more sturdy and patriotic *Majlis*, the pitiful attempts to secure England's good offices to avert bloodshed, the strenuous efforts to prevent a popular outburst of indignation by controlling the transmission of news to and from the provinces, proved vain, and failed to save four of the chief cities of North Persia from the horrors of Russian invasion and martial law.

In three of those cities, Tabriz, Rasht and Anzalí, fighting broke out almost simultaneously on December 20 and 21, 1911. How it actually began in each case is not yet known in full detail. The Persians assert that the Russians provoked it at Tabriz by entering private houses and mounting on their roofs (a thing repugnant to all Muhammadans on account of the seclusion in which their women live) on the pretext of laying telephone-wires, by molesting inoffensive citizens, both men, women and children, and by disarming or attempting to disarm the National Volunteers (or *mujáhídín*) who, since the preceding August, had been compelled to defend the city against *Shujá'u'd-Dawla*, the ex-Sháh's notorious partisan, and now, under the Russian aegis, the tyrant of Tabriz. There is some evidence in support of this view, for:

(1) N. Tardof, the Russian correspondent of the Moscow Paper *Russkaya Slovo*, described in full detail similar provocative acts committed by the Russians soon after they first entered Tabriz in April, 1909 (see my *Persian Revolution*, pp. 283-291, and compare pp. 274-282).

(2) As Mr. Morgan Shuster says at p. 203 of his *Strangling of Persia*, "One significant fact: at the same time that the fighting broke out at Tabriz the Russian troops at Rasht and Anzalí, hundreds of miles away, shot down the Persian police and many inhabitants without warning of any kind. And the

date happened to be just after the Persian Cabinet had definitely informed the Russian Legation that all the demands of Russia's ultimatum were accepted, a condition which the British Government had publicly assured the Persians would be followed by the withdrawal of the Russian invading forces, and which the Russian Government had officially confirmed *unless fresh incidents should arise in the meantime to make the retention of the troops advisable.* In the light of these events, is it probable that it was the comparatively helpless and foredoomed Persians who at Tabriz, Rasht and Anzalí started simultaneous attacks upon vastly superior bodies of Russian soldiers?"

(3) According to a letter contributed to the *Manchester Guardian* of Sept. 6, 1912, by Mr. G. D. Turner, who obtained his information in Tabriz about a month earlier, "the Russians withdrew from the mills the grain supplies for their troops the day before (the fighting began), and 700 soldiers were forced-marched from Ardabíl through winter weather." All this points to an anticipation of a conflict by the Russians on December 20, the day on which it actually broke out.

(4) Although the Russians subsequently alleged that they were "treacherously attacked" by the Persians, the original statement of the Russian Consul at Tabriz (Blue Book (Cd. 6105) No. 319) is simply that "a party of Russian soldiers were engaged in repairing a telephone last night (i.e., on the night of December 20) when a member of a police patrol attacked one of them. *The Russian fired and killed two of the patrol.*" Hence, even on the Russian showing, the first blood was shed by Russians. As regards Rasht and Anzalí, the same Blue Book (No. 322) merely states that "shots were exchanged", "firing started suddenly and at once became general", "the escort of the Russian Consul *started firing* on

the Sabze Maydán", "the immediate cause of the commotion is unascertainable", "three Cossacks and at least eight Persians were killed", and that there was "an affray at Anzalí on the 21st of December in which one Russian officer was wounded and ten Persians killed." The Persian accounts are all explicit that in each case the Russians were the aggressors.

The fighting was most severe at Tabriz. It lasted all through the day of December 21, 1911, from an hour after sunrise until an hour after sunset. The losses were heavy on both sides, and, according to independent European testimony, the Persian National Volunteers had the best of it, and, had they been properly led, might have annihilated the Russian force then in Tabriz. As it was, they had no leader and no common plan of action, but fought in groups without definite system or objective. There was, as Mr. Shipley, the British Consul at Tabriz, telegraphed on December 22 (Blue Book [Cd.6105] No. 320), "no general disorder," "the Persian population remained perfectly quiet and no European had been molested." Indeed while the Russians occupied many important buildings and looted the offices of the Provincial Council and the Law Court, as well as many private houses and bazaars, besides killing several non-combatant Persians, the Persians set a guard over the European Banks and merchants' offices to protect them from harm.

On the following day (Friday, December 22, 1911) fighting was renewed, and continued until about two hours before sunset, when an armistice was concluded, and on December 24 and 25 Mr. Shipley, H.B. M.'s Consul at Tabriz reported (White Book [Cd. 6264] No. 19) that "the local authorities were endeavouring, in co-operation with the Russian Consul, to stop fighting and no firing took place on December 25." He added that at this time "communication between the Russian Consulate and the commander of the Russian troops had been cut off, as the troops, having failed to make any headway, had been compelled to concentrate in their camp." In other words, the Persians at this juncture had much the best of it, but were anxious to restore peace with their adversaries. Poor people! They did not know (telegraphic communication with Tabriz having been interrupted) that already 5000 fresh Russian troops were on their way from Julfa, and that already on December 23 "the Viceroy of the Caucasus had been instructed to order military commanders, in consultation with Russian Consuls, to proceed to severest punitive measures" (White Book, No. 15), while the *Novoe Vremya* was demanding "merciless retribution" and "extermination of the *fidá'ís*" (National Volunteers), and declaring that "true humanity required cruelty". As Mr. Shuster says (*op. cit.* p. 202);- "experience has amply demonstrated that the Russian Government, having the power, never does *less than it promises in cases of this kind. It is safe to say that the horrors of Tabriz will never become fully known. The Russians saw well to that.*" *In the same strain the Times correspondent telegraphed from Tehran on December 28 that save for a brief interval on December 27, telegraphic communication was entirely interrupted, but that it was to be feared that "when the veil was lifted, desolation would be revealed."*

A corner of the veil—only a small corner—has now been lifted; and the series of photographs published in October, 1912,[7] and now appended to this book (some of which first

---

7   They were published by Messrs. Taylor, Garnett, Evans and Co., Ltd., Blackfriars Street, Manchester in a pamphlet entitled *The Reign of Terror in Tabriz: England's Responsibility with photograph and a Brief Narrative of the events of December, 1911, and January, 1912*, price six pence.

appeared in the *Sphere*, the *Graphic*, the *Anglo-Russian*, *Free Russia* and *Egypt*) have conveyed to the people of this country some idea of what the unhappy city of Tabriz—one of the largest, fairest, most beautiful and once most prosperous cities in Persia, and the chief centre of the Constitutional movement for which it stood out so valiantly in the siege which lasted from June, 1908, until April, 1909—has endured and is still enduring at the hands of the Russians and their chosen tool *Shujá'u'd-Dawla*.

Twelve of these photographs (marked A to L) reached this country, through a channel which cannot be indicated, about July, 1912, and are believed to have been taken by a Russian officer who allowed copies of the original negatives to pass into other hands.[8] A second set of the same twelve photographs was bought in a shop in Tabriz early in August, 1912, by Mr. G. D. Turner, and brought by him to this country. Both sets were inscribed on the back with the names of the victims, of whom 23 in all are shewn in the twelve photographs, and, save in two or three cases of the more obscure victims, the independent inscriptions exactly tallied.[9] In the following series of letters, ranging in date from January 6 to September 29, 1912 and embodying the depositions of fugitives who had escaped from Tabriz,

---

8 In an article entitled *Russia in Persia, by an Armenian*, which appeared in the American *New Age Magazine* of August, 1913 (pp. 99-109), it is stated that the photographs, some of which are reproduced here, "were taken by a native Persian on the spot," who "risked his life to secure them." I mention this statement for what it is worth, but incline to the opinion expressed in the text.

9 Some apparent discrepancies in nomenclature are explained in the Enclosure in Letter No. 20 *infra*, which gives detailed particulars of all the victims represented in the photographs.

full and detailed descriptions are given of the deaths of the 23 victims represented in these photographs, and of many others; and it will be noted that most of them were either learned ecclesiastics, like the *Thiqatu'l-Islám*, Shaykh Salím, and *Ziyá'u'l-'Ulamá*; young men of talent and promise like *Sádiqu'l-Mulk*; founders of schools and philanthropists like Hájjí 'Alí Dawá-furúsh ("the Druggist"); writers like Mirzá Ahmad Suhaylí, his fellow sufferer; or National Volunteers who had specially distinguished themselves by their bravery and energy in the defense of Tabriz, such as Yúsuf of Huk-mábád, Mashhadí Hájjí Khán, Hájjí Samad the tailor, 'Abbás 'Alí the grocer, and Mírza Áqá Bálá-Khiyábání; or relatives of such, like the two lads Hasan and Qadír (aged 18 and 12 respectively) whose brothers, conspicuous amongst the Na-tional Volunteers, succeeded in escaping; or notable orators, like Mirzá 'Alí of Wayjúya.

A second series of seven photographs (lettered N to S), taken by European residents in Tabriz, was also brought to this country by Mr. G. D. Turner.

These frightful photographs, though they do not rep-resent the worst horrors perpetrated in Tabriz since New Year's Day, 1912, on which the Russian executions began, are calculated to bring home to the people of this country, in a way that nothing else can do, the results of that sub-servience to Russia which is the outstanding feature of Sir Edward Grey's foreign policy, and the terrible responsibility which we as a nation have incurred. This responsibility, as

will immediately be shown, far exceeds mere passive connivance on our part, since our Government joined the Russian
Government in urging the reluctant Persian Cabinet to recognize *Shujá'u'd-Dawla*, the author of the worst barbarities,
as Governor of Tabriz. [10]

It is necessary to distinguish between the immediate actions of the Russians and those yet more barbarous actions
committed by their tool, their protégé and their nominee
(who also was our nominee) the infamous *Shujá'u'd-Dawla*.
The Russians erected gibbets, gaily decorated with the Russian colors, on which they hanged in batches men whose
only crime was daring to defend their own homes against a
foreign invader. Many of those hanged were not even accused
of having taken any part in the fighting. When the British
Government ventured some remonstrance and pointed out
how Muhammadan feeling throughout the world would be
outraged and stirred by the execution of so great an ecclesiastic and so learned, virtuous and generally respected a man
as the venerable *Thiqatu'l-Islám* on the most solemn day of
the Muhammadan year, the 'Ashúrá or 10th of Muharram,
which is comparable to the Good Friday of the Christians
(White Book [Cd. 6264]. No. 52 & 70), they merely replied
(*Ibid,* No. 75) that "he was a thoroughly bad character" (i.e.,

---

10 The gradual weakening of the British Government's opposition
to the recognition of *Shujá'u'd-Dawla*, and the corresponding
strengthening of the Russian Government's demand for his
retention as Governor of Azarbáyján are very clearly apparent
in the White Book *Persia,* No. 5, 1912 [Cd. 6264]. Thus on
January 5, 1912, Sir George Barclay told Mr. Shipley not
to receive a call from *Shujá'u'd-Dawla* "as he is in rebellion
against the Persian Government and is not even *de facto*
Governor of Tabriz"; while on February 25, Sir E. Grey enjoined
of Sir George Barclay "if there was any prospect of obtaining his
appointment as Governor-General?"

in Russian official parlance, a Liberal), had acted "as head of the *fidá'ís*", and "was not an orthodox Persian, but the chief of a dissenting sect."

These hangings were carried out in the most barbarous manner; the victims were neither pinioned nor blind-folded, and had to watch the sufferings of their fellow-sufferers while awaiting their own turn. In many cases they continued to struggle for ten minutes or more after they were hanged, and in several cases the rope broke. Thus in the case of Bedros Andreassian, a highly respected Armenian citizen who was hanged by the Russians on the Armenian New Year's Day, the rope broke twice, and a young Russian officer who protested against the unfortunate man's being hanged a third time was reprimanded and punished for his humane attempt at intervention. The *Thiqatu'l-Islám* (as clearly appears in the photograph) was hanged below his seven fellow-sufferers as a further indignity, and the bodies were left hanging during the whole day (January 2, 1912) succeeding their execution.

Mr. Shipley, H.B.M.'s Consul at Tabriz, while admitting (White Book, No. 20) looting by Cossacks, one case of killing of non-combatants without provocation, and the possibility that some women and children were killed during the bombardment, "did not believe that there was any justification for the accusation of general inhumanity on the part of Russian troops." The Persians, on the other hand, assert that many innocent men, women and children were shot down, and in particular declare that Hájjí 'Alí Khatá'í, a quiet, peaceable merchant who had kept entirely aloof from politics and occupied a beautiful house near the Bágh-i-Shimál, where the Russian camp is, was killed with eight members of his family (his wife, one of his daughters, his son, his son's newly-wedded wife, his servant, a child six years of age, and his cousin). The only survivor of the family was a girl whose leg was so severely wounded that it had to be amputated. The house was looted and occupied by the Russians. Hájjí Muhammad 'Alí Khán, another merchant of Qárabágh, was also killed with his wife and family, and many women were killed in the Ahráb and Márálán quarters. Mr. G. D. Turner, in his letter in the *Manchester Guardian* of September 12, 1912, confirms the fact that many women and children were killed, especially on December 27, and non-official European residents at Tabriz, though they dare not write freely for fear of the Russian censorship, speak with evident horror of the events of those days.

The worst atrocities, however, were committed by *Shujá 'u'd-Dawla*, the notorious partisan of the ex-Sháh, who, having vainly besieged Tabriz since August, 1911, and created a great scarcity and dearness of food, entered the town on January 2, 1912, when the resistance of the National Volunteers had been completely broken down by the Russians, and, under the Russian aegis, established himself as Governor, and proceeded to indulge in a carnival of extortion and cruelty of which some of the photographs here published give a faint idea, but which cannot be described in detail in this place. He imprisoned, tortured, hanged, strangled, and stabbed; he cut men in two like sheep (as is shown in one of the photographs) and hung their bodies up in the bazaar; he sewed up the mouths of those suspected of a love for the Constitution; he nailed horse-shoes on to their feet and drove them through the streets; he cut out their tongues and plucked out their eyes. One of his favourite punishments is to throw the victim into a large tank round which are stationed men armed with sticks, who strike at the sufferer's head whenever it shows itself above the water, until he dies either from drowning or from loss of blood.

This is the monster who, in spite of the protests of the Persian Government, has been placed in absolute control of the unhappy city of Tabriz by Russia, actively aided by Great Britain. That Great Britain, too, is directly responsible for his deed is clearly demonstrated by the last White Book (Cd. 6264), as the following passages show.

(No. 32). On December 29 Mr. Shipley telegraphed from Tabriz that *Shujá'u'd-Dawla* would come to Tabriz in four or five days, and that Miller (the Russian Consul) said that "as the Russians could not themselves undertake the administration of the town, in view of the *unanimous expression of popular opinion* (!) he would be unable to oppose his coming, and would consider him as Governor *de facto*." "The feeling in the town is, so far as I can tell," adds Mr. Shipley "as Miller states, and the opinion of such Europeans as I have been able to consult coincides with my own, namely, that there would be no opposition to Shuja's appointment provided the difficulties of his connection with the ex-Sháh can be overcome and *if his appointment is sanctioned by the Central Government*."

(No.55). The Persian Minister for Foreign Affairs on January 3, 1912 urged the Russian and British Ministers to induce the Russian Government to assist them, amongst other ways, in expelling *Shujá'u'd-Dawla* from Tabriz.

(No.59). The British Minister at Tehran telegraphed on January 5 to Mr. Shipley, the British Consul at Tabriz, instructing him to receive no call from *Shujá'u'd-Dawla*, "as he is in rebellion against the Persian Government, and is not even *de facto* Governer of Tabriz."

(Nos. 63 and 64). Sir Edward Grey telegraphed to the British Minister at Tehran on January 6 that Mr. Shipley reported that *Shujá'u'd-Dawla* "was not ill-received by the inhabitants of Tabriz," and that "he did not think he would be a bad governor." Next day (January 7), accordingly, the British Minister telegraphed to Mr. Shipley that he "might receive and return *Shujá'u'd-Dawla's* call, as he appears to be *de facto* governor," but that his "relations with him could not be official until the Persian Government recognized him as Governor."

(No. 116) On January 23 the British Minister at Tehran telegraphed to Sir Edward Grey that the Persian Cabinet were "in great anxiety in consequence of information which they have received that the forces of *Shujá'u'd-Dawla and other agents of the ex-Sháh* at Ardabíl and other places in Azarbayjan were contemplating a combined movement on Tehran."

(No. 200) On February 14 M. Sazonoff informed the British Ambassador at St. Petersburg that "the Russian Government had agreed that the Sipahdár should replace *Shujá'u'd-Dawla* at Tabriz, and that the latter should be given another post." Two days later, however (No. 208), M. Sazonoff said that though "the Russian Government *would not absolutely insist on Shujá'u'd-Dawla being retained at Tabriz*", "*the post was one that required a strong man*", and that "he was not sure that the Sipahdár possessed the necessary qualifications for it."

(No. 224) On February 23, M. Sazonoff communicated to the British Ambassador at St. Petersburg a telegram from Mr. Miller the Russian Consul at Tabriz, "stating that the acting British Consul (at Tabriz, i.e., Mr. Stevens, the Consul,

Mr. Shipley, having left on February 9) had telegraphed to Sir G. Barclay (the British Minister at Tehran) that *it was in every way desirable to recognize Shujá'u'd-Dawla, who was popular and possessed influence amongst nomads, as Governor General*", and that he (Mr. Stevens) "was opposed to the appointment of the Sipahdár, who was surrounded by *fidá'is* and Armenians, and whose arrival might give rise to fresh disorders."

(No.232). On February 25 Sir Edward Grey enquired of the British Minister at Tehran "whether there was any prospect, in view of our combined action concerning the ex-Sháh, of obtaining the consent of the Persian Government to the appointment of *Shujá'u'd-Dawla* to the post of Governor-General; and, if so, what confidence they could place in his loyalty to them?" "Mr. Shipley," he added, "is inclined to agree that it might be desirable that the appointment should be given to Shujá."

(No. 234) On February 26 the British Minister at Tehran telegraphed to Sir E. Grey the text of Mr. Stevens' telegram of February 16 advocating the appointment of *Shujá'u'd-Dawla*, on the ground that "he was the only man able to maintain order in Azarbayjan, and was greatly feared by the numerous lawless tribes", though his subordinates *Rashídu'l-Mulk* and *Rafí'u'd-Dawla* were "the curse of the Town and province" and "exacted money from rich and poor". At the same time the British Minister declared that "*the opposition of the Persian Government to the appointment of Shujá'u'd-Dawla as Governor was as strong as ever*"; and that a telegram just received from Tabriz, again from Mr. Stevens, describing *Shujá'u'd-Dawla's* "programme in favour of the ex-Sháh," and the likelihood of "trouble very soon unless steps are taken *by the Persian*

Government to thwart such intrigues", confirmed his own "strong doubts whether he (Shujá') could be trusted to remain loyal to the Persian Government."

How completely *Shujá'u'd-Dawla* was obedient to Russian commands is well shown by Nos. 263, 270 and 273. From the first it appears that on March 5 meetings advocating the return of the ex-Sháh were held at Tabriz; that the elders of the quarter were *compelled to attend them*: and that flags inscribed with the words "Long live Muhammad 'Alí Sháh" were displayed over the shops. From the second we learn that on March 6, the Russian Minister at Tehran sent instructions to the Russian Consul at Tabriz to warn *Shujá'u'd-Dawla* against those proceedings; and from the third, dated March 7, that "the demonstrations in favour of His Majesty (sic!) have eased." *If then there had existed any desire on the part of the Russian and British government to put a stop to the horrible atrocities committed by Shujá'u'd-Dawla, is there any reason to doubt that this could easily have been done by means of a similar protest?* But there is not a single word in the White Book about these atrocities, which have now become matters of notoriety, and of which the photographs accompanying this text will serve to convey some faint idea. For those atrocities the British Government have a direct responsibility, since they have joined the Russian Government in maintaining their perpetrator, *Shujá'u'd-Dawla* in the position of absolute authority which enables him to commit them, and that in spite of the sustained opposition of the Persian Government. Shall such vile deeds, then, only move us when, as in the case of the Putamayu atrocities, our Government has no direct responsibility?

For the maintenance of this monster *Shujá'u'd-Dawla* in authority Russia, supported by Great Britain, is directly responsible. On February 23, 1912, M. Sazonoff told the British Minister at St. Petersburg that, "*although he had no desire to force the Persian Government to appoint Shujá'u'd-Dawla, it would in his opinion be very much wiser to keep him on as Governor-General—at any rate for the time being; for he could not answer as to what effect might be produced on Russian policy if disorders were to break out at Tabriz again*" (White Book, 224).

It is in order that the British representatives and the British people may clearly realize for what crimes against humanity our foreign policy has made us responsible that the following *Letters from Tabriz* with the photographs which serve as part of the evidence for the truth of their statements are now published.

In comparison with the horrors perpetrated at Tabriz, the hangings, shootings and destruction of buildings and especially printing-presses at Rasht and Anzalí sink into insignificance. [Furthermore] they were followed by the establishment as irresponsible tyrant of a monster like *Shujá'u'd-Dawla*. The wanton bombardment by the Russians of the sacred Shrine of Mashhad in April, 1912 (this is on the pretext of dispersing those who were agitating in favour of the ex-Sháh) was, however, an act of barbarous sacrilege and vandalism calculated to outrage the religious feeling of all Muhammadans as much as the circumstances attending the execution of the *Thiqatu'l-Islám* at Tabriz. It can hardly be supposed that such outrages to Muhammadan sentiment were not deliberate on the part of the Russians, as is indeed suggested in the White Book (Cd. 6264), No. 52, p. 18, and it must be assumed that the object was either to bring about armed risings of the Persians which might afford an excuse for further and fuller military occupation of the country, or so to violate their religious feelings as well as their patriotic aspirations as utterly to cow them and break their spirit.

For such broken spirit and shattered hopes, as for the "anarchy" now existing in Persia, Russia and Great Britain are directly responsible, and, if there be a Reckoning, will one day be held to account.

Mirzá 'Alí *Thiqatu'l-Islám,*
Tabriz's learned philosopher and lover of liberty.

TRANSLATION OF
THE LETTERS

PREFACE

The motives which have prompted me to translate and publish the following *Letters from Tabriz* are three in number.

First, the conviction that to seek out and make known the truth in any matters of general and public interest is especially incumbent on those who have access to sources of information not available to the majority of their fellows; and that this obligation holds good in a still higher degree where, through ignorance, interest or malice, the truth has been more or less distorted or concealed; even as the Arabs say:

اذا ظَهرتِ البِدعةُ فليظِر العالِمُ علمهُ

"When evil innovations appear, then let him who knoweth declare his knowledge."

Secondly, the firm belief that the whole policy underlying the Anglo-Russian entente (of which the bitter fruits, visible in so many regions of the country, are especially evident in Persia, and above all in the lamentable events described in these letters) is equally immoral and unwise; that out of this evil innovation no good can come; and that every effort should be made by all who hold this belief to oppose its continuance and to remedy, so far as is possible, the manifold evils which have already resulted from it. [1]

Thirdly, and chiefly, the desire to make the only reparation now possible to the victims of Russian cruelty and oppression, who perished on the scaffold or in the dungeons and torture-chamber in the winter of 1911-1912 at Tabriz and elsewhere, by showing that in the first great majority of cases they were innocent of any crime save patriotism, and, proved the sincerity of their patriotism by faithful service to their country during their lives and admirable fortitude in their death.

---

1   In this connection mention should be made of a most terrible indictment of the policy here denounced entitled *The Fruits of our Russian Alliance*, by H. N. Brailsford, published by the Anglo-Russian Committee, 56. Lincoln's Inc. Fields, and sold for one penny.

No. 1

Translation of Telegrams from Tabriz transmitted to England by the *Anjuman-i-Sa'adat* of Constantinople on December 26, 1911, 7:41 a.m.

"On December 21, the Russian troops made an attack, seized the Government (administration) and trampled school children under foot, killing and despoiling innocent men and women and looting shops. The inhabitants, after extraordinary forbearance, began to defend themselves and forced the Russians to evacuate the Government buildings.

December 22. The Russians bombarded the city from the Bagh-i Shimal (North Garden) until sunset. Consternation and excitement are increasing hourly.

December 23. In consequence of orders from the Central Government to cease fighting, the inhabitants took no steps to defend themselves, but the Russians again renewed the bombardment, firing from the environs of their Consulate and the Garden at women and other innocent persons, wounding and taking captive many of the wives and children of respectable citizens, and setting fire to numerous buildings and mosques.

December 25. The inhabitants being still quiet, the ferocity of the Russians greatly increased; they killed many women and children and set fire to numerous buildings. If tomorrow they do not desist from their savage attack, the inhabitants will be compelled to defend themselves. We beg you to communicate this telegram to the chief newspapers and influential centres of Europe."

(Signed Anjuman-i-Ayalati (Provincial Assembly of Tabriz)

"Publish the above Tabriz telegram, protest against the barbarous actions of the Russians, and take all possible steps immediately.

(Signed) Anjuman-i- Sá'adat (Persian Society of Constantinople).

No. 2

Translation of a Communication from the Anjuman-i-Sa'adat of Constantinople, dated Muharram 12 A.H. 1330 (January 3, 1912), and containing the following "purport of an official telegram received from Tehran."

"According to a telegram which has been received from Tabriz, on the 8th of Muharram (A.H. 1330 December 30, 1911) the Russian general reached Tabriz, and on the 9th instant arrested a number of Constitutionalists. On the 'Ashura (10th of Muharram, A.H. 1330 = January 1, 1912) they hanged eight persons, amongst whom was the *Thiqatu'l-Islam*, the great *mujtahid*, a man who enjoyed the confidence of the *'ulama* throughout the Kingdom and who was resorted to by all the people, together with *Sadiqu'l- Mulk*, Shaykh Salím and several other respected citizens.

The Persian Cabinet, having regard to the advice of the Ottoman Government, accepted the Russian Ultimatum simply in order to avoid giving any pretext for further bloodshed, in the hope that the Russians might refrain from bloodshed and other violent actions. Unhappily, besides the earlier slaughter of innocent people which they made in those earlier days, by inflicting martyrdom in the worst form on so sacred a day on this eminent ecclesiastic and on sundry Sayyids and others who enjoyed the respect of the nation, they have assuredly established in the hearts of all Muslims an eternal enmity by those epoch-making deeds of cruelty. The diffusion of these tidings and the effects of such conduct will render it impossible for the Cabinet to survive or to succeed in silence popular ebullition. This evil dealing and bloodshed on the part of the Russians is an offence not merely to the World of Islam but to Humanity.

According to what is heard they intend to establish in Tabriz a Russian administration and Russian courts of justice, and to appoint on their part Russian controllers of the police and the finances; while, notwithstanding the fact that all the National Volunteers who took part in the defense of the city have either been killed, or taken captive, or are in hiding, they have nevertheless brought in to the city *Shuja' ud-Dawla* and the other Reactionaries."

(Signed) Anjuman-i-Sa'adat

We entreat you to publish and make plain in the sight of the civilized world, in whatever way you consider most expedient and proper, these blood-thirsty atrocities of the Russians, and, to communicate them to the (Persia) Committee."

Eight persons were killed in the first hanging by the Russians in Tabriz. The *Thiqatu'l-Islam* hangs in the center (no. 5 from the right).

No. 3

Translation of a letter written from Constantinople on January 6, 1912, by a well-known citizen of Tabriz.

"I reached Constantinople some days ago, and was intending to offer my devotion and sincere friendship when very terrible reports arriving in constant succession from Persia, and especially from Tabriz, deprived me of all calm and collectedness, so that the distraction of my senses left me no opportunity for the discharge of this duty. The Great Tragedy and Supreme Catastrophe of Tabriz – that unfortunate city which of all the cities on earth has been the most sorely afflicted of Heaven, and which for the last five years has been trampled under foot by the cruelty of domestic and. foreign tyrants – has entirely consumed as with a fire the hearts of the Persians.

For the last month the Russians have been continually at work to bring about some disturbance in Tabriz, and have striven, so far as lay in their power, to goad the inhabitants to anger. The people, however, who were aware of their designs, bore all patiently, until finally the Russians, not ceasing their endeavours, began to provoke riots in the streets and markets; and at length, having fixed a quarrel on a policeman, they killed two of the police, and thence arose the beginning of the fighting.

After a great number of the people, including women and children, had been killed in this fighting, and many houses had been destroyed, and part of the bazaar had been looted by the Russians, they took possession of the Government House, the Citadel, and the various offices of the State. For a few days there seemed comparative tranquility: the fresh Russian troops arrived at Tabriz from Julfá, and these, on their arrival, proceeded to direct their fire upon a large portion of the city and to bombard it. Then they began to arrest many innocent persons, and on the *'Ashura,* or 10th of Muharram (New Year's Day, 1912), which is the great day of solemn mourning in Persia, they publicly hanged on the gallows a number of persons, including great ecclesiastics and *mujtahids*, members of the Provincial Council, merchants and high officers. Amongst these victims were the chief *mujtahid* of Azarbayjan, *Thiqatu'l-Islám,* who enjoyed great fame throughout all Persia; Shaykh Salím, one of the *'ulama* of Tabriz, a member of the Provincial Council of Azarbayjan, and one of their most famous speakers, who from the beginning of the Persian Constitution until now was constantly active, and played an important part in all the affairs of the Revolution, who had worked hard for six years, and was one of the first persons who at the end of Rajab, A.H. 1324 (September 19, 1906) took refuge at the British Consulate in Tabriz in order to demand the Constitution; and *Sadiqu'l-Mulk,* one of the most influential members of the Provincial Council and one of the most promising military graduates of Persia, who had completed his military studies in the Turkish Military Colleges and afterwards in Europe, and was one of the most intelligent, determined, accomplished and zealous of Persian patriots, in whom great hopes were *centred* and who was of most use to the nation, men like him being very rarer especially amongst those versed in military science, which is that whereof Persia most stands in need. He was for some time *Kárguzár* of Kirman, and was afterwards appointed as member of the Turco-Persian Boundary Commission for the delimitation of the frontiers, and resided for nearly three years at Urmiya. Last year he came to Tabriz, and was elected to the Provincial Council.

"Well, on the day of the *'Ashura* the Russians hanged a number of the citizens of Tabriz amongst whom were those three. The names of the others I do not yet know, but apparently they were all men of consequence and notable patriots. *Thiqatu'l-Islám* and *Sadiqu'l-Mulk*, had taken absolutely no part in the fighting with the Russians, and as regards the former especially there is no doubt that he was the last person to take part in such action; nay, there is not a probability of one in a thousand that he either participated, approved or acquiesced in it, for he was a very peaceable and moderate man. Indeed, there is no doubt that the dissemination of the news of his martyrdom will be reflected throughout the Shi'a world, and will affect it deeply, and indeed the Constantinople newspapers today report disturbances at Baku in the Caucasus, so that the Russians have been obliged to reinforce their troops there as a measure of precaution. I hear today that Shaykh 'Abdu'llah of Mazandaran and Aqá-yi-Shari'at of Isfahan, who are the great *mujtahids* of Najaf, have set out for Persia from that place, accompanied by fifty of the *'ulama* of Najaf and Karbala, to preach a *jihad;* and that M. Charikof, the Russian Ambassador here, has gone to the Sublime Porte and requested the Ottoman Government to prevent them from entering Persia. What will be the end of it?

Today I read in the newspapers here that Sir Edward Grey's position is shaken, and that he will shortly fall. I do not know whether there is any truth in this or not, but (even if there is) I fear that the fall of Persia will precede his, and that the antidote may arrive only after the patient's death; nor do I know what policy his successors would adopt, or what they could do, finding themselves face-to-face with a *fait accompli*:

At all events, I am personally deeply affected by these last events, nor do I know when the Lord of Truth and Justice will take vengeance on the oppressors, or whether a day will come when Justice will manifest itself in the world, and the weak ones will be left in peace in their nests."

No. 4

Translation of another letter from the same, dated Constantinople, January 16, 1912.

"The latest news from Tabriz is equally pitiful and critical. The Russians are continuing to put to death the last children of our fatherland and those young men of talent and perception who constituted the hope of Persia's future, and seek to extirpate and destroy the very fiber and root of the tree of Patriotism, and utterly to extinguish the Light. Thus they have put to death the editors and writers of the newspaper *Shafaq* (the Afterglow) the most important of the newspapers of Azarbayjan, who were for the most part young men who had first attained maturity and who were in the flower of their youth. Amongst these was Mirzá Aqá Riza-Zada, editor of the *Shafaq*,[2] who was only twenty years of age, and who this very year completed his higher studies in the American College to qualify himself for a diploma. He was a very sensible, well-conducted, zealous and intelligent young man. Another of the victims was Hájjí Alí *Dawá-furúsh* (the Druggist) who has worked for the last ten years in the way of progress and civilization, who for the last six years until today was one of the chief intellectual guides of the people and founders of the Constitutional Revolution, and who at the very first was one of the leading men who in A.H. 1324 (A.D. 1906) took refuge at the British Consulate at Tabriz in order to demand a Constitution, during the time when

---

2   It afterwards transpired, as will appear in later letters, that the editor of the *Shafaq* was fortunately not amongst the victims, and that the poet Mirza Ahmad Suhaylí was the only person connected with this paper who was hanged by the Russians.

Muhammad 'Alí Mirzá (then Crown Prince) was governor of Azarbayjan. From this day until now this man, now taken into God's Mercy, has not rested for a single moment, and has always been one of the chief protagonists of the Constitution in Azarbayjan. During the Tabriz Revolution and the resistance to Autocracy three years ago he superintended the barricades in person, was wounded in the arm, and was in hospital for three months. He also showed especial zeal in promoting education, and the College in Tabriz known as *Madrasa-i-Sa'adat,* which counts nearly three hundred students, was founded by his exertions. Of worldly wealth and ties he had none, save a house and two motherless children, eight years of age, a girl and a boy. The Russians blew up his house with dynamite.

Russians put to death many other persons, the names of some ten of whom are known to me. Besides these they cut the throats of seventy-five persons living in Húkmabád quarter of Tabriz (one of the remoter quarters of the city), whose inhabitants are chiefly agricultural laborers, and hanged them on gibbets.

Such is the news which, bit by bit, is arriving here, though I still have no detailed information. The later details I have obtained from an official source. In these days the newspapers speak of the sending of English soldiers to the South of Persia, and I fear that Sir Edward Grey's policy may have brought near the doom of Persia."

No. 5

Translation of an article which appeared in the Turkish newspaper *Yéni Iqdám* (the New Progress), No. 667, dated the 7th of Safar, A.H. 1330 (January 27th, 1912): "Cruelties of the Russians in Tabriz."

"The deeds and performances of the Russians in Tabriz cannot be connected with the world of civilization and humanity.

The *Novoe Vremya* does not cease, by means of sophistical articles and prejudiced statements, to lay the guilt on the Persians.

In consequence of the atrocities recently perpetrated in Persia generally and in Tabriz particularly, a great meeting was held in London: and speeches and addresses were delivered by many honourable, fair-minded and liberal persons with the object of enlightening European public opinion.[3] This appears to have displeased the above-mentioned newspaper, which immediately published an article in which it exerted itself to impugn and contradict these English statements.

---

3   This alludes to the great meeting at the Opera-house on January 1912. Browne's note. On the 15th January 1912 the Persia Committee organized a mass meeting of protest to the Anglo-Russian agreement on dividing Iran into two spheres of influence at the (Hammerstein) Opera House, London, where some 3,000 people gathered. Browne was one of the speakers. See Mansour Bonakdarian, *Britain and the Iranian Constitutional Revolution of 1906-1911*, Syracuse University Press, 2006, pp. 306-307.[Ed.]

The blood-thirsty deeds which Russia has chosen to commit in Persia, and especially at Tabriz, are of so tragic a character that they make the hair stand on end, and overwhelm with sorrow and grief not only the Persians but all mankind, without distinction of race or creed.

The most truthful and impartial English newspapers cannot refrain from discussing and enumerating the Russian cruelties. The *Daily News*, *Spectator*, *Manchester Guardian*, *Evening Times*, *Egyptian Gazette* and *Review of Reviews* criticize the detestable deeds and abominable actions of the Russians in Persia, and in the name of humanity demand that England should intervene.

The Egyptian newspapers, generally with *al-Mu'ayyad* at their head, expose with proofs and evidences the inhuman deeds of Russia, and make the deliberate intention and purpose of the Russians to do evil to the Persians the subject-matter of successive articles.

In order to attain its objects, the Russian Government has been seeking pretexts on every side, and, as soon as an opportunity arose, it did not recoil from the most cruel action, but did all in its power to deliver the *coup de grace*. Those whom the Russians hanged and slew in Tabriz were not men of little importance and merit. That each of these poor unfortunates was a zealous patriot possessed of many virtues and distinctive merits has been certainly proved. These poor victims strove both materially and spiritually for the elevation and advancement of their country, did not hesitate to sacrifice their personal advantages for the public good, and exerted themselves day and night with prolonged efforts to benefit and humanize their compatriots.

In the first batch of victims who fell into the snare of Russian tyranny and became the objects of Russian deceit was so learned a man and so great a philosopher as the *Thiqatu'l-Islám*. The manner of his execution was so strange that it is impossible not to be astonished thereat. The Russians brought him in a fine and elaborately-furnished carriage to their consulate in Tabriz, and, after showing him the utmost respect, required him to give them a paper, written in his own hand and sealed, with his own seal, declaring that he was well content with them, and had himself invited them to Tabriz to effect certain reforms. When, however, the *Thiqatu'l-Islám* excused himself from listening to these requests, they sent him to the gallows. These barbarous acts of the Russians took place on the 10th of Muharram.[4] The fame of the learning and virtue of this venerable man was reflected not only throughout all Persia, but in all Muhammadan and Eastern lands. The daily paper *al-Mu'ayyad* published in Cairo devotes to him a whole leading article, entitled 'The ink of divines and the blood of martyrs' and expresses its sorrow and regret at his loss.

In order to confirm for readers of the *Iqdam* our impartial statements about Persia, which are based on facts and proofs, the following extracts from the article in *al-Mu'ayyad* are here appended.

If the highest honour belongs to him who fights alike with his ink and his blood, then how manifest are the robes of honour wherewith is invested that learned thinker and holy martyr the Imam *Thiqatu'l-lslám*, Mirzá 'Alí b. Musá of

---

4   This, the *'Ashura,* is the most solemn day of mourning in Persia and in Shi'a communities, being the anniversary of the slaughter of the Third Imam, Husayn the son of 'Alí, at Karbala by the myrmidoms of the Umayyad Caliph Yazid.

Tabriz, of the destruction of whose pure life at the hands of the Russians, on account of his advocacy of the defense of his country and the protection of his fatherland, news hath reached us!

If such of the Russians as shed his blood were possessed of any sense of justice, they would know that to one of their own race who acted as he acted a monument would be erected in the most famous square in their cities; that his memory would be immortalized in the pages of their history; and that the defense of one's native land is the finest quality whose effects vibrate throughout a living soul which learning hath purified and the search for truth hath cleansed. The *Thiqatu 'l-Islam* wrought no wrong in what he did, but was wronged in what he suffered, and is lamented by all who knew the depth of his learning, the eminence of his power in searching out the Truth, the validity of his claim, the lawfulness of his acts, the high degree in which he had acquired all attributes of purity, and what materials of honour and exalted position had accrued to him both in the hither and further worlds.[5]

Not content with this, the Russians have turned Tabriz into a vast shambles, and are slaughtering wholesale the foremost patriots, thinkers, writers, and zealous and energetic reformers of the country. By so doing they hope to leave in Tabriz not a single soul capable of opposing or withstanding them in the future. They imagine that the glorious Persian land which produced these men cannot again give birth to others like or even superior to them. How vain a fancy! How false a belief! How do they know that Persia,

---

5   I.e., "both in this and the next." A Turkish paraphrase of the above quotation follows, which is here omitted.

which nourished in her kindly bosom such great monarchs as Jamshid, Darius, Artaxerxes, Shapur "of the Shoulders," Nushirwan, Sháh Abbas and Nader Sháh, such poets and writers as Firdawsi, Sa'di, Háfiz, Anwari and Rudaki, Badi'u'z-Zaman of Hamadan, Firuzabadi and the like, may not bring to life and raise up in the future men yet greater that the *Thiqatu 'l-Islam*? Nay, there is no doubt that talented and patriotic men will arise in hundreds from every drop of the blood of these victims sacrificed to Russian tyranny and treachery!

An English friend of mine resident in Tabriz wrote me a letter in which he thus describes the detestable conduct of the Russians: --"The character and quality of the persons executed by the Russians were far above the ordinary, and each one of them had rendered great services to his country. The persons executed during this week were as follows. Mirzá Mahmúd of Salmas, who after acquiring the theological sciences and new arts at Najaf, returned to Tabriz immediately after the proclamation of the Constitution in order to enlighten the minds of his fellow-citizens; *Ziya' u'l-Ulama,* who was also acquainted alike with modern Western sciences and arts and with numerous foreign languages, and his uncle --men of learning like these were sent to the gallows. The chemist Hájjí 'Alí *Dawa-furush,* who had devoted his zeal and expanded his energies on founding in Tabriz a preparatory college, the *Madrasa-i-Sa'adat*, equal in organization and progressive tendencies to a foreign college, was also hanged, and immediately after his execution this *Sa'adat* College which he had founded was closed by the Russians.

In the course of this same ill-starred week the youthful editor of the *Shafaq* (Dawn), the most independent, liberal and patriotic of the Tabriz newspapers, was also executed. In consequence of the destruction of these poor men, who were accounted alike the most honourable and the most zealous of the progressives of Tabriz, all the people are weeping tears of blood. Neither my pen nor my tongue is able to indicate or describe the vehement grief and affliction of the populace, of the degree of this detestation and enmity towards the Russians which they entertain in their hearts.

I never imagined that the Russians were so cruel in heart, or that the Persians could show themselves so fearlessly and carelessly patriotic; but what I have seen with my own eyes and heard with my own ears compel me to state this fact. All my life long I shall never be able to forget this tragedy which I have witnessed, and the words which I have heard from the mouths of those who were hanged, even on the gallows.

The Russians also arrested and hanged the two young sons of a certain Karbalá'i Aqá 'Alí. When these young brothers, who were not yet twenty years of age, were brought to the gallows, they kissed the ropes which were being adjusted round their necks and in the Azerbaijani Turkish raised a cry to heaven, 'Long live Persia! Long live the Constitution!' whereat the eyes of the spectators were drowned in tears, and the freedom-loving citizens, heedless of such Russian cruelties, sobbed aloud.

God knows that I, though an Englishman and a partisan of neither side, was unable to restrain myself from tears. These young victims of the gallows had committed no crime personally or actually, but because their elder brother was amongst the number of the National Volunteers who had withstood the Russians, and because the latter had been unable to capture him, they sought to gratify their vengeance by hanging these poor young brothers.

As regards other actions of the Russians, I am ashamed to write them down or declare them. Only this much will I say in brief, that the Russians have cleared out the schools in Tabriz and expelled the pupils; and have converted all the Government Departments and methods of administration into forms compatible only with the most despotic form of government. Against the will of the inhabitants they have appointed Governor of Tabriz a man who, during the days of autocracy, when Mohammad 'Alí was Crown Prince acted as his secretary, and who bears the title of *Shuja u'd-Dawla*[6] and to him they have given the title of *Beyler-beyi*. There is no evil which this tyrannical wretch has omitted to inflict on the liberals and on the unfortunate townsfolk. Those who have not obtained the permission of this man are unable either to enter or leave the town. He inspects and takes note of all who enter the city. The Russian soldiers go in empty carriages to the houses of the Liberals, and, after seizing and confiscating their goods, burn down their houses. In the present condition of things, no one, except the partisans of Russia, dares utter a sound. There is no one who is not deeply and painfully affected by these proceedings of the Russians.

I am so disgusted that I am ever ashamed of being a European, for, seeing the perpetrators of these cruelties to be Europeans it is impossible not to feel detestation of them. Knowing that I shall distress you also by these words of mine, I still do not refrain from writing you a true account of these matters. My dear friend be assured that both the Russians

---

6 The text of the original has *Rafi'u'd-Dawla*, but it is clear that the person meant is that notorious ruffian Samad Khan *Shuja' u-Dawla* of Maragha, the chosen protégé of Russia.

and other Europeans desire that those cruelties should remain hidden and concealed; but since I cannot thus trample my conscience under foot, I see no harm in speaking the truth. Although you are permitted to publish these words of mine, you must not at present mention my name, though you may make it known when you are compelled to do so."

Here end my friend's statements. It will be seen what things the Russians have done, and who knows what they will yet do! God knows that the deeds of the Russians in Tabriz surpass even the deeds of the Italians in Tripoli. They show no mercy either to truth and right, or to humanity. Everything in this world has its limit, but it is impossible to fix a limit to these cruelties of the Russians. Whereas with all nations and creeds it is held necessary to respect learned Divines and spiritual leaders, the Russians slay and hang them without scruple and hesitation.

The generality of Muhammedans, besides all the Persians, are profoundly affected by the cruel deeds perpetrated in Tabriz by the Russians, and there is no doubt that very bitter sense of hatred against them has been awakened in the hearts of the Persians and of the Muslims. It is impossible to read without indignation and astonishment the telegram addressed through the instrumentality of the *Iqdam*, and published in our issue of the day before yesterday, by the Ottoman Kurds who have taken refuge in the Turkish Consulate at Urmiya to the Chamber of Deputies. This telegram has doubtless been duly considered by the Sublime Porte and the Foreign Office. An effort on the part of the Sublime Porte to safeguard the rights of its subjects whom it is bound to protect, and at the same time, in the name of Islam and humanity, to put and end to these actions of the Russians,

would be both proper and welcome. No one could prevent the Ottoman Government from exercising this right. In
this matter the English, the Egyptians and the Indians have
participated and continue to participate in the views of the
Ottoman Government..."

(Signed) S.M.T.

Ziya' u'l-Ulama, a scholar, linguist, and President
of the Courts of Appeal

No. 6

Translation of a third letter, dated January 28, 1912, from the writer of Nos. 3 and 4.

You expressed your concern at the happenings of Tabriz, and the tragedies which have taken place there; and indeed as fresh news gradually comes in the matter appears ever the more awful. One of the fugitives who, with many dangers and difficulties, and almost intolerable hardships, the account of which is like some romance, succeeded in escaping, arrived here two days ago, and relates deeds of horror of which the mere recital makes the hearer's hair stand on end. The Russians set fire to many houses in the Márálán quarter, in which women and children also were burned to death, while many innocent non-combatants were slain. Thus they slew about ten of the household and children in the house of the Khata'is, which is situated near the *Bágh-i-Shimál*, or the Northern Garden, and looted three of the bazaars, viz. those of Mihád-mahin, Khiyábán and Darb-i Bágh-i-Misha, besides many of the shops. The soldiers stripped many of the inhabitants in the streets, blew up many of the houses with dynamite, and destroyed in the same manner the Castle of 'Alí -Sháh (built by the Minister of the Mongols so named, who was a contemporary of the historian and vizier Rashidu'd-Din Fazlu'lláh). As for the patriots whom they slew, speak of them without fearing to incur the guilt of exaggeration; men so full of zeal that my pen is unable to describe their perfections or their virtuous qualities. And in how heart-breaking and savage a manner did they put to death the late *Thiqatu'l-Islám*, from whom, according to what is related, they first demanded with threats in the Russian Consulate that he should sign a document approving the doings of the Russians, which thing he refused to do so they beat him savagely, then put a rope round his neck and dragged him along the ground to the *Maydan-i-Mashq*, or Drill Square. There he sought permission to perform his prayer, and, having made the ablution and performed a prayer of two prostrations, he made a speech in which he recalled the greatness of the Martyrs of the Holy Day, that is to say the *'Ashura*, or 10th of Muharram, and expressed his faith in the future life of Persia, and the immortal quality of the Persian spirit; after which they hanged him on the gallows. Many of the reactionaries of the town were there to see.

Now they compassed the death of these poor people in the most savage manner in the world; for while those who claim to be civilized do not slaughter even sheep in sight of one another, they kept these poor victims standing in a row while they put them to death one by one in succession with slow deliberation, in the presence and before the eyes of their fellow-sufferers. When it came to the turn of Shaykh Salím the Orator, who was also a Member of the Provincial Council, although, according to letters received from Tabriz, he had already been so severely beaten that he was at death's door and would assuredly have died if they had not killed him, and although he was scarcely able to speak, yet, according to the correspondent of the Russian newspaper *Novoe Vremya*, who was present at the execution, he desired to make a dying speech; but he had only uttered the words, "Say from me to the *Anjuman* (Provincial Council)" when the hangman suddenly stopped his mouth and would not suffer him to proceed.

But the most extraordinary courage and unexampled bearing was shown by two lads, the two younger sons of

Karbalá'i 'Alí, known as "Monsieur", who was the chief of the National Volunteers, and who had four sons, of whom these two were the youngest. Their names were Hasan (aged 18) and Qadir (aged 12). The courage shown by these filled all men with amazement, and exalted the name of Persian self-devotion. After the flight of their two elder brothers with a party of the National Volunteers, who fled to Salmas and thence passed into Ottoman Territory, and are now wandering on the frontier and are continually telegraphing to Constantinople asking for instruction from Tehran, to which the Government at Tehran replies that since they are in rebellion against the Russians they cannot intervene, so that many of them are left hungry and exposed to the cold, and in may cases ill; after this, I say these two lads were left wandering about, and wherever they went, none dared give them shelter, until at last they went to a certain merchant, who was a Russian subject, and who was a connection of theirs. This man hid them for three days in his office, but afterwards thrust them forth, and they seeing no hope anywhere, went straight to the Russian Consulate, saying "We are Constitutionalists who love our country; we have no place whither we may flee; do with us as you will." The Consul thereupon handed them over to the court-martial, who condemned them to be hanged. When they came to the gallows, the younger boy, after reviling the Russians and the Tsar, etc., cried in a loud voice in the Turkish language, "Long live Persia! Long live the Constitution!" Then, closing his eyes, he adjusted the rope round his neck with the utmost intrepidity, and exclaimed "Kill me quickly!"

At all events continually until now tidings successively arrive of executions, slaughtering and hangings. Amongst the most notable of the victims are the following:

(1) *Thiqatu'l-Islám.*

(2) Shaykh Salím, the orator, a Mullá, and member of the Provincial Council.

(3) *Ziya'u'l-'Ulama,* one of the 'ulama, a man well skilled in the modern sciences and in the French, Russian and English languages, as well as in many arts, and the author of several printed books and translations, and President of the Courts of Appeal.

Four constitutionalists hanged by the Russians. The names from right to left are as follows: Mirzá 'Alí "Natik" ("The Orator"), Hájji Samad "Khayyát" ("The Tailor"), Mashhadí Hájji Khan, and Mashhadí Shukúr Kharazzi. Three Russian soldiers and a Persian attendant are seen in the foreground.

(4) Mohammad-qulí Khán, maternal uncle of the above.

(5) Mirza Mahmúd of Salmas, one of the *mujtahids,* who was elected in the first degree to represent Urmiya in the National Assembly.

(6) The *Shaykhu'l-Islam* Hájjí Mirzá Abdu'l Amir, one of the *'ulama* and a Tabataba'i Sayyid, of the family of the old *Shaykhu'l-Islam* of Azarbayjan, who lived a hundred years ago.

(7) Mirzá 'Alí of Wayjuya, the first orator and preacher of the Constitutionalists, and a leader of the Democrats.

(8) Mirzá Hájji Áqá Rizá-záda, editor of the newspaper *Shafaq* (Dawn), concerning whom I have already written in detail, pointing out that this man was, without exception, the greatest of all the victims, and the chief hope of the country's future. I am, indeed, more grieved on his account than for any other, for he and the Mirzá 'Alí mentioned immediately above are an irreplaceable loss to Persia.

(9) Hájjí 'Alí *Dawá-furush* (the Apothecary), one of the chief Constitutionalists of Ázarbayján.

(10) *Sádiqu'l-Mulk*, a member of the Provincial Council and a full-qualified military officer.

(11) Mirzá Ahmad Suhaylí, one of the Constitutional merchants.

(12) Mashhadí Ibráhím, one of the very best of the Constitutional merchants.

(13) Mirzá Ahmad Khán-i-Binábí.

(14) Mashhadí Hájji, captain of the National Volunteers.

(15) Shukúr, father-in-law of the above.

(16) Hájji Samad the tailor.

(17) Yúsuf of Hukmábád, whom they barbarously cleft in two and slew with torments.

(18) Ná'ib Ahad.

(19) and (20) two national Volunteers names unknown.

These are they whose names have come to hand from one source and another. Yesterday the telegraph brought news of the execution of eighteen more. The executions go on continually, and they desire to leave no one, and to extirpate the very root and fiber of patriotism. So far as is known some four hundred heroes are under arrest, whom they are gradually sending before the Court-martial.

In Qazwin also the Russians have demanded that the Government shall arrest fourteen Democrats, whom, failing this, they will themselves arrest. In Tehran also Reaction rules supreme, the Government is altogether inclined towards the Russians, and is entirely at their disposal, and is dealing very harshly with the Liberals. Indeed I have even seen it stated in a letter from a well-informed correspondent that deliberations are now in progress between the Russians and those who now direct the affairs of Persia as to the arrest, imprisonment, or exile by the Government of a number of persons, of whose names the Russians will furnish a list, the estimate of the number of these varying from 36 to 250. I myself have received information that in Qazwin the Russians have called upon the Government to arrest 14 persons, failing which the Russians themselves will arrest and punish them. In Tehran they have actually arrested several of the Democrats. Everywhere, in short, patriots, and especially Democrats, are suffering."

No. 7

Translation of a fourth letter, dated February 1, 1912, from the writer of Nos. 3, 4 and 6.

Some time ago, after my arrival in Constantinople, I sent you a letter, intending to follow up the correspondence, but certain events, besides the mental agitation whereof you know, did not suffer me to do so. Meanwhile I read your letters in the newspapers, and your effective speech at the London Meeting,[7] for which sincere efforts on your part neither I nor my compatriots are able adequately to express our gratitude. I have also received and read the pamphlet entitled *The Persian Crisis of December, 1911*, which you published on the occasion of the New Year, and of which you were good enough to send me a copy. It is excellent, both succinct and comprehensive; but certain points struck me on which I deem it necessary to make some remarks.

On page 4, at the end, you say that Rahim Khán *again revolted* against the Persian Government, whereas in fact he *continued in revolt* from the beginning, i.e., from the time of the siege of Tabriz. After the arrival of the Russian troops at Tabriz and the proclamation of the Constitution by Mohammad 'Alí Mirzá, he removed his forces and three guns from the Julfa-Tabriz road where they had been stationed to Ahar, which is the chief centre of Qaraja-Dagh, taking with him a number of prisoners of the people of Tabriz who were in his camp, and there remained, seizing and governing the province of Qaraja-Dagh, and disregarding the orders of

---

7   I.e., the Opera House meeting of January, 1912.

the Persian Government, even the numerous and stringent orders sent to him by the Cabinet of *Sa'du'd-Dawla* and by Mohammad 'Alí Mirzá himself, that he should release these captives. (Rahim Khán's army was one of the three armies charged with the siege of Tabriz and the holding of the roads approaching it on different sides. Básminch on the East or Tehran side was occupied by *'Aynu'd-Dawla* and his forces; the Southern and South-Western sides, on the way to Gugan and Maragha, were held by Samad Khan *Shuja'u'Dawla* of Maragha; while the roads to the North and the North-West leading to Julfa, Khuy and Qaraja-Dagh, were held by Rahim Khán Chalabiyanlu.) When Mohammad 'Alí was deposed, Rahim Khán increased his rebelliousness. After the (Russian) troops had gone to Qaraja-Dagh, and taken from him money and camels, and returned to Tabriz, he had a seizure which resulted in the paralysis of half his body. Thereupon the Russian Consul at Tabriz sent the Russian doctor attached to the Consulate to treat him, and within a week of the arrival of this Russian doctor at Ahar, Rahim Khán suddenly recovered, mounted his horse, assembled his troops, made peace with his enemies the Sháh-sevens, formed an alliance with their chiefs who were in Khalkhal, concluded a treaty with the *Amir-i Asha'ir*, whom all the Sháh-seven tribes had chosen as their chief in their revolt and rebellions, and attacked Ardabil. (In this campaign Rahim Khán was at the head of all the tribes of Qaraja-Dagh, to wit, the Qara-Khánlu, Husaynkalu, Hájjí 'Alílu and Chalabiyanlu, which was his own tribe; while Buyuk Khán, the *Amir-i-'Asha'ir* of Khalkhal, chief of the Shatiranlu tribe of the Sháh-sevens, was in command of all the 36 tribes of the Sháh-sevens, such as the Fuladi, Yurdachi, etc., so that these two persons, to wit, Rahim Khán Chalabiyanlu, entitled *Sardár-i-Nusrat*, and Buyuk Khán, *Amir-i-Asha'ir*, Shatiranlu, were in joint control of the army of confederate tribes bent on attacking Tehran and restoring the ex-Shâh.)

On page 5 in the middle, you say that the Persian Government had previously requested that the Russian Government not to allow Rahim Khán to escape into Russian territory if he should endeavor to do so; but the following point has been overlooked, viz. that the Russian Minister at Tehran accepted this demand on the part of the Persian Government, and promised that this should not be allowed. Moreover, the Persian Government, through the Russian Legation at Tehran, requested that a special watch might be kept on the Russian frontier at the point where it was possible that Rahim Khán might seek to escape across it, (viz. near the Bridge of Khuda-afarin over the river Araxes), in order to prevent him from doing so. But the Russians on the contrary set mounted men on the bank of the Araxes, and even a few in the middle of the stream, to watch, so that if Rahim Khán should arrive, they might swiftly come to his help. When Rahim Khán escaped into Russian territory, and news of this reached the Persian Government, and it complained to the Russian Government, the Russian Minister in Tehran and the Russian Minister for Foreign Affairs in St. Petersburg officially denied that Rahim Khán had crossed over into Russian Territory until finally news of Rahim Khán the brigand came from the Government House in the town of Ekaterinodar. Thereupon the Persian Government, through its Minister at St. Petersburg, demanded in the most urgent terms that he should be surrendered to them in accordance with the Treaty (of Turkman-chay), seeing that he had carried off much property of many people, including several thousand sheep, and had with him nearly two hundred of his followers and kinsmen. The Russian Government, however, refused to surrender those notorious thieves, brigands and highway-robbers, on the point that they were merely political offenders!

On page 6, in the middle, you speak of *Rashídu'l-Mulk*, the former Governor of Ardabíl, and his possible rescue from his prison in the Government House (at Tabriz) by Russian regular troops; but it may not be out of place to add that, having removed him from prison, they took him to the Russian Consulate where, two or three days later, he left the city and joined the army of Samad Khán *Shujá'u'd-Dawla* of Maragha at Básminch, situated at a distance of two parsangs from the city, whom he aided in making war on the Persian Government and people. He was commissioned by Samad Khán (who called himself "Governor-General of Azarbayjan on behalf of Muhammad 'Alí Sháh") to seize Sawujbulagh, Miyan-du-ab, etc., (which had remained loyal to the Persian Government) with a force placed at his disposal for this purpose, and he further endeavoured to check the forces of Hájjí IlKháni and *Nizamu'l-Mamalik*, two Kurdish chiefs of Sawujbulagh who, by command of the Constitutional Government, were attacking Maragha. Over and above all this, after he had been appointed by Samad Khán, Governor of Ardabil (where, until lately he governed in the name of Muhammad 'Alí Sháh), he was lately sent with an army by Samad Khan to attack Gilan, Rasht and Anzalí by way of Astara. After the aggressions of the Russians at Anzalí and Rasht and the expulsion or execution of the patriots of those places at the end of December, 1911, *Rashídu'l-Mulk* reached Anzalí unopposed: that same *Rashid'l-Mulk* when the Russian Consul at Tabriz, aided by three hundred Russian soldiers, delivered from the first reprisals of the Persian Government, and so permitted to undertake fresh measures against that Government. (Precisely similar was the case of Muhammad 'Alí Mirzá's chief huntsman, or *Mir-Shikar*, Ahmad Khán, who took refuge with his master in the Russian Legation two and a half years ago (i.e., in the late summer of 1909), and who was allowed to escape by night from the Russian Legation to Zanjan, where he joined himself to Mullá Qurban-'Alí and other Reactionaries. After Mullá Qurban-'Alí had been conquered and Zanjan taken by Yeprem Khán, the above mentioned Ahmad Khán again betook himself to Qazwin, where he spent some time in the Russian Consulate in that town. Finally, by the instrumentality of the Russian Legation, he obtained from the government letters of protection, whereupon he went with Dáráb Mirzá to the village of Chargar, near Zanjan, which was his own property, and with the help of his men, whom he assembled there, greatly promoted that disturbance also.)

On page 9, at the beginning, you speak of the Russian Legation's demand for satisfaction from the Nawwáb Husayn Qulí Khán on the Kashan incident, but you have not mentioned this point, that Husayn Qulí Khán was finally compelled to give such satisfaction, and, with the utmost unwillingness, to go to the Russian Legation and apologize.

On page 11 top, you state that *Sáláru'd-Dawla* collected a force of Lurs, the truth being that it was Kurds, not Lurs, whom he enlisted.

About the middle of the same page, in speaking of Muhammad 'Alí Mirzá and *Sáláru'd-Dawla* you say that, after their defeat, the former fled to Russia and the latter to Europe, the fact being that neither of them fled. Muhammad 'Alí Mirzá embarked on a Russian ship and remained at sea until he again disembarked (on Persian soil), while *Sáláru'd-Dawla* retired to Pusht-i-Kuh to his father-in-law, who was governor of that district, whence he returned again to Kirmansháh.

On page 12, about the middle, you state that *Shu'a'u'l-Saltana* was under Turkish protection, the truth being that he had become naturalized as a Turkish subject.

On the same page, some lines lower, you state that two officials of the Russian Consulate, accompanied by ten Russian Cossacks, went to the house of *Shu'a'u'l-Saltana*, whence they expelled the Persian gendarmes with threats; but you omit the fact that immediately afterwards these same Russians proceeded to Dawlatabad, where they arrested and made prisoner the Treasury gendarmes, brought them to the Russian Consulate, and there imprisoned them, until, after remonstrances on the part of the (Persian) Government, they released them, after depriving them of their arms, three hours after sundown.

These matters which I have submitted are the points that strike me. As regards the present state of affairs in Persia, it is, as you know, much worse. The present government at Tehran is completely terrorized by the Russians, and it appears probable that the Persian Government may gradually take the shape which the Russians desire. I read in a number of the *Manchester Guardian* certain matters connected with Persian affairs reported by a well-informed correspondent who spoke in terms of praise of Sir George Barclay…, and I think that the prophecies contained in that article are highly probable and a close approximation to the truth. And although the Russians are ostensibly engaged in deliberation with the British Government and concluding a secret agreement, they are on the other hand assuredly endeavouring inwardly to promote the interests of the ex-Sháh, and are pursuing a course incompatible with sincerity towards the English, whom they are deceiving. They are continually sending him arms and munitions of war and volunteers from the Caucasus, and recently a Russian war-ship named, *Gyük-tepé* on the Caspian Sea has brought a great quantity of arms for the ex-Sháh to Astarábád. They have also sent a large number–more than three hundred – of the Chechens, one of the tribes of Daghistan and a subdivision of the Lezgis of Vladikafkáz, to him, and they are now fighting for the ex-Sháh. Some Russian officers are also engaged in drilling and organizing Mohammad 'Alí's troops and Turkman followers, and there are also amongst the above-mentioned Chechens some who have served in the Russian army and acquired military science. To them is attached a certain Georgian, a Russian subject, named Amir Hajibi, who is in command of the Caucasian volunteers.

On the other hand the Russian troops in Astarábád have been ordered to arrest and punish Yeprem Khán if he should march against the ex-Sháh, by which means they prevent Yeprem from fighting for the (Persian) Government, so that now he intends coming to Constantinople in order to proceed, with a number of other Armenians, to Tripoli in Africa to take part, under Enver Bey at Benghazi, in the Holy War against the Italians.

The Russian Consuls and soldiers, especially at Tabriz and Rasht, are encouraging and inciting the Reactionaries to attack Tehran while Samad Khán *Shujá'u'd-Dawla*, the actual ruler of Azerbaijan, enjoys the support of the Russians, and at Tabriz omits nothing in the way of slaughterings, plunderings, executions, imprisonments, fines and every other kind of tyranny, carried to the extreme limits. He is now collecting troops at Miyana, situated at a distance of twenty parsangs from Tabriz on the road to Tehran, has established a camp there, and is appointing governors throughout the province of Ázarbayján. One of these is a certain *Qudratu'l-Mulk*, whom he has sent to Khuy, and who has celebrated the day of accession of Muhammad 'Alí as a festival and illuminated the town. Samad Khán himself, when he reached Tabriz on Muharram 11 (A.H. 1330 = December 31, 1911), went officially to the Russian Consulate, obtained a Russian flag, and, entering with that flag, proceeded to the Government House. His *farrashes*, moreover, wear Russian arms on the sleeves of their coats in order that the Russians soldiers may be able to distinguish them from the rest of the inhabitants and may regard them as official.

As for the cruelties perpetrated by the Russians and Samad Khán (at their instigation and under their protection) in Tabriz, the pen fails to describe them. Mirzá Mahmúd of Salmas, one of the *'ulama*, and one of those elected in the first degree to the National Assembly, was killed with every kind of villainy in the house occupied by Samad Khán, (i.e., the garden of Hájjí Nizámu'd-Dawla). While he was still alive they plucked out his eyes and cut out his tongue (for he was an eloquent speaker), and then killed him. Samad Khán demanded of him four hundred *tumáns* (about £. 80) to let him go, but this sum he did not possess and could not obtain. He is arresting a great many people from each of whom he demands a ransom of from one hundred to two or three thousand *tumáns*, in default of which he kills him. He cut the throat of Ná'ib Yúsuf of Húkmabád, and afterwards cut his body in two halves like a sheep and hung up each half separately on each side of the bazaar. Such are the deeds of cruelty committed by him and the Russians and other Reactionaries in Tabriz, and their strange and savage acts, which should I write them down, would make a book. How many houses in which were women, children, household and families did they set on fire and burn down, and how many quarters did they lay level with the ground! One of the leading Constitutionalists who is now in hiding sent a letter from Tabriz by means fraught with difficulty to one of his friends in Constantinople, and in this letter he compares the state of Tabriz to that of Nishapur after the devastations brought by Chingiz Khán:

In truth today the state of Tabriz and all parts of Azarbayjan is very lamentable. The Russians and Reactionaries oppress the people grievously. They have closed all the schools, and are entirely extinguishing and eradicating the light of Knowledge, Patriotism, Constitutionalism and Progress, and so completely destroying and extirpating these qualities that no trace of them may remain, even as the Mongols did in the time of their invasion. Henceforth no peace or comfort is to be hoped for in the world.

"The pitch remains in the ring when the stone falls out"[8]

But these men (i.e. the Russians) have even destroyed the monuments of the Mongols. The "civilized"(!) Russian Government has broken down the Citadel (Arg) of 'Alí Sháh, one of the most splendid buildings in Persia erected by 'Alí Sháh,[9] the well-known Minister of the Mongols, and has completely destroyed its towers and walls. According to

---

8 This is the second line of a Persian poem:
بعد از این آسایش از دنیا نباید چشم داشت   قیر در انگشتری ماند چو بر خیزد نگین
After this one should not expect comfort in the world [Ed.].

9 Taj al-Din 'Alísháh Jilani was the vizier of the Ilkhan Abu Sa'id (d. 1330 A.D.) and he built the Arq or citadel of Tabriz originally as a mosque. [Ed.]

current reports the Russian soldiers rob people in the streets, and the people are greatly excited and angered. I cannot write all the particulars, else my letter would be over-filled with details, but perhaps if God wills, I will set them forth more fully in another letter.

There is another point which has been brought to my notice here through a certain channel, and which I think is necessary to lay before you, namely that the Russians (whether with the connivance of the British Government or in spite of them I know not) are busy contriving and devising some mischief in the South of Persia, especially in Fars. It appears that they are inciting the *Zillu'l-Sultán*, who is now at Nice, to make his appearance with a number of Reactionaries in the South (like Muhammad 'Alí in the North), and are spending money freely; and that the Qashqha'is are acting in concert with him and are making preparations, as also *Sardár-i-Arfa'*, Shaykh Khaz'al Khán, the Shaykh of Muhammara, and other tribes of the South; and Aqá Najafí and other land-owners and persons of influence in Isfahan; and they wish to create a great disturbance, so as either to compel the intervention of English troops, so that the position of the Russians in the North may be assured; or to oblige the Russians and British Governments to divide Persia into two zones, a Northern and a Southern, under the rule of Muhammad 'Alí Mirzá and the *Zillu'l-Sultán* respectively. God knows best whether this is so.

Latterly, moreover, reports and rumours are arriving to the effect that the Russian Government is making great efforts to win over the Bakhtiyaris, hoping, apparently, thereby to induce them on certain conditions to bring back Muhammad 'Alí to Tehran. The Bakhtiyaris, moreover, incline towards the Russians, and are now more closely attached to them than to the English, for since these last events the influence and prestige of the latter have greatly declined in their eyes. And so forth, and so forth..! But to what extent these rumours are true or false, I know not, though I hope that there still remain amongst them (i.e., the Bakhtiyaris) some patriots.

I greatly desire to know something as to the effects proposed by the London and Manchester meetings, the speech of Mr. Morgan Shuster, and your other efforts on behalf of Persia, and whether public opinion has been sufficiently stirred, and whether any result may be hoped for in the near future? I should like to hear something as to the course of events, were it only once a month.

(Signed) S.M.T.

P.S. I have lately learned that *Rashídu'l-Mulk* is in command of Samad Khán's army at Miyana, and that he who went to Anzalí and Rasht is entitled *Rashídu's-Saltana*, and is a different person.

No. 8

Translation of an article on Persian Affairs which appeared in the Turkish newspaper *Terjuman-i Haqiqat* of Sunday, February 4, 1912.

"We have received the following letter from Urumiyya:

In spite of the assurances given by European politicians, we here are crushed in pieces by the burden of Russian oppression and tyranny. Since the day when the Russian soldiers set their feet here, they are working to destroy our country and our people. One wonders when this torrent of "civilized" oppressions will cease. Perhaps the most masterful tyrants, most terrible autocrats, who have left a name in history, were sometimes overcome by a sense of pity and humanity, and did not venture to perpetrate such violent wrongs and cruelties in the countries which they brought under their tyrannical heels. When these men (the Russians) strip our houses, shops and stores, destroy them, and lay them level with the dust, a blaze of cruelty and savagery shine in their countenances. In them is never a trace of mercy, or of that thing called a sense of humanity. They break us in pieces just as a soulless, senseless, cold machine crushes a man and reduces his bones to powder. I wonder what the public opinion of Europe, which, with a feverish activity, flies straight towards the centre of civilization, thinks about these heart-breaking spectacles? Nothing! Nothing at all! I wonder if the Socialists, who, when a working man, while engaged in carrying out some frightful work of destruction, is handed over to the clutches of Justice and receives punishment, qualify the government with such terms as "criminal", "treacherous", "merciless", and "violent", will deign to turn a glance of pity beyond the limited circle in which they live? No, and again No!

"I wonder what Power it is which sanctions such contemptuous treatment, such cruelty and oppression, in regard to the Mother of the East who nourished the suckling child of Western Civilization, who nursed it with such care and tenderness until it grew up? Where and who is the source and promoter of this Power? Europe! Politics! The politicians! Oh, if it be so, perish the tyrants who strive to obliterate and destroy our sovereignty, our country, our people, our nation, our independence, which have endured for sixty ages! Broken be the hands which point their weapons against us unrightfully, merely in order to ensure their own political and economic advantages! May the feet which trample on Persia be smitten with the palsy! May the thoughts which scheme to bring us under their administration be blinded! Curses, a thousand curses, on this "civilization"! Blasted be the Western politicians who strive to steal away the freedom of others! Bravo, a hundred thousand plaudits on you who strive to preserve the rights of men!

In what state are we today? We sit on the ashes and fragments of a ruined Persia, weeping over our black fortune and cursing those who have brought us to this condition. Those treacherous hands which have poured over our heads soldiers, guns and muskets will assuredly, yes, assuredly one day themselves meet with the crushing thunderbolt of a hitherto unsuspected Power.

Some of our spiritless, treacherous officials, who twitter in the Russian consulate and open their eyes like omen-stones[10] at the clink of money are, of course, the slave of the Consul's commands and projects. These ignoble wretches, while outwardly professing patriotism and encouraging us to resist and defend our country, secretly inscribe our names in the Register of the Condemned in the Russian Consulate. These will one day receive from the Russians great rewards and bejewelled decorations. Vain thought! Behold, one of those vile creatures, who incarnate in themselves such baseness and spiritlessness in all pollution and vehemence in the wretched Governor of our city. In the middle of December the Russian Consul published a manifesto addressed to all Russian subjects, recommending them to prepare a reception for the Russian troops, which would shortly enter the city. To this invitation only a few Tartar and Armenian merchants responded. On the 20th of December (A.S.= January 2, 1912), when the Russian soldiers passed through the town, no one remained in the streets. In order not to expose themselves to a sudden attack, the Russian officers proceeded in the most cautious manner, so that they even disarmed the members of the (Persian) police force whom they met in the street.

On the 25th of January a most sinister and tragic crime was perpetrated here. Mirzá Mahmúd Khán Ashraf-záda, editor of the [Turkish][11] newspaper *Farwardin*, had published

---

10 The omen-stones were small stones or pebbles used in fortune telling. "To open one's eyes like omen-stones" is an expression in Turkish which means to open one's eyes out of surprise." Barbier de Meynard, *Dictionaire Turk-Francais.*[Ed.]

11 This newspaper was not in Turkish but in Persian and had only a satirical section in Azerbaijani (see *Press and Poetry of Modern Persia*, p. 121.) The word "Turkish" is not in the original letter and Browne , perhaps because of the Azerbaijani section, has called it "Turkish."[Ed.]

an article against the Tsar Nicholas. The Consul, as soon as he received information about this publication, at once sent several Russian soldiers to the office of that newspaper, and forcibly conveyed Mirzá Mahmúd Khán to the Consulate, where a most tragic spectacle presented itself.

"Russian Consul (addressing the Editor): -

"Do you confess that this action of yours was a very mean action? Answer quickly, or else I will now inflict the punishment which you deserve!"

Mirzá Mahmúd Khán, with manly resolution and patriotic firmness, answered: "No. I do not admit its meanness. I wrote the truth, and I claim to have been justified writing as I did."

"Thereupon the Consul blazed out in fury, and, addressing the Russian soldiers, bade them drive Mirzá Mahmúd Khán to the open space in front of the Consulate. The soldiers thereupon drove the unfortunate editor before them to this place. On arriving there, the Consul again addressed him as follows:

"Answer me quickly. Do you admit that what you have done is a vile act?"

Mirzá Mahmúd Khán, again with exactly the same manly resolution and decision as before: -

"No, no! I am the slave of love for my country! If you should destroy me here for this charge of villainy, assuredly the pen of some other patriot will again repeat the charge; and even should a pen sufficiently pure and strong not be found in my country, the pen of Destiny will so charge you! Fear the curse and the accusation of that pen! Long live liberty! Long live our Country! Long live the Constitution!"

"Thereupon, at the officer's command, five Russian soldiers hurled themselves upon Mirzá Mahmúd, gagged his mouth to prevent him from repeating his words, then hurled him to the ground, and began to beat him in the most merciless manner. After he had received some fifty or sixty lashes, they again set him on his feet and brought him before the Consul, who again repeated his previous question:

"Do you admit that what you have done is a vile act?" Mirzá Mahmúd Khán answered: -

"No; on the contrary my action was designed to set forth the truth!"

Thereupon the soldiers again hurled him to the ground, and began to beat him again with increased severity, so that blood spurted from poor Mahmúd Khán's body and he fainted away.

Alas! When the poor man in a half-dead condition, and unable to speak, was again brought to the Consul, and the latter, striking his feet and loins, again demanded an answer to his question, the editor at length, having altogether lost control of his reason, and not knowing what he was saying, involuntarily answered, "Yes!" Then the Consul let him go, and after he had remained for half an hour in this state, his relatives came and carried him away to his house.

Another tragic event similar to this also took place. Some Russian soldiers, while walking through the bazaar, came across a fruiterer's shop. They entered it, and began to eat what fruit they pleased. Naturally the shop-keeper complained of this unjustifiable procedure. Thereupon, the Russian soldiers, crying out that he had insulted them and their nation, first beat the poor man mercilessly with the butts of their rifles, and then took him to the Russian Consulate. On the way thither the shop-keeper escaped from the soldiers and took refuge in a mosque, but, by order of the Consul, the soldiers entered the mosque, forcibly ejected him, and brought him to the Consulate, where they macerated the poor man's body under the lashes of their whips.

A few days ago the officer in command of the Russian detachments published a manifesto addressed to the people, inviting them to surrender their arms within five days. On the one hand the aggressions of the Russian soldiers, on the other hand the extreme severity of the winter, have yet further increased the misery of the unfortunate people. Today throughout the whole province of Azerbaijan dire famine and scarcity prevails.

The gallows; the knout, plundering; hunger; misery! God help us!

No. 9

Translation of a fifth letter, dated February 14, 1912, from the writer of Nos. 3, 4, 6 & 7.

First of all, before everything else, I deem it necessary to withdraw and declare untrue one or two pieces of information which I gave you in my last letter, and which have since proved to be incorrect.

One of these refers to some of those who were executed at Tabriz, concerning whom some incorrect information has reached us here. First, it was stated in the newspapers the editors of the paper *Shafaq* ("the After-glow") had been executed. I knew of no one on the staff of that paper more celebrated than Mirzá Hájjí Aqá Rizá-zada, the proprietor and editor in chief, who was also particularly obnoxious to the Russians, nor can the term "editor of the *Shafaq*" (by which term he was spoken of in the newspapers) be properly taken as applying to anyone except him. Yet notwithstanding this I still hesitated and did not feel convinced that he had really been executed, until, two or three days later, one of the newspapers, quoting from a German newspaper, specifically announced his execution in the words "they have executed Rizá-záda." Then only did I write to you those details of his biography. Recently, however, Praise be to God, I have learned that he is still safe, and by the expression "the editor of the *Shafaq*" in the telegrams Mirzá Ahmad Suhaylí, who contributed to this paper, was intended.

So again, as regards the reported execution of the *Shaykhu'l Islam* Hájjí Mirzá 'Abdu'l-Amir, this also according to later enquiries, proves to be incorrect. All the other names given were, however, correct, and up to the present moment I know the names of twenty-five of the sufferers, amongst whom were several most worthy people. Amongst those who have suffered recently are the following: -

Aqá Mír Karím, the well-known orator.

Mashhadí Muhammad Usku'i, known as '*Amu-oghlu,* who was the last of the pure, uncorrupt and patriotic National Volunteers of Tabriz.

Mashhadí 'Abbas 'Alí , the grocer, of the Khiyábán quarter, one of the leaders of the Constitutionalists of that quarter.

Mirzá Aqá Bálá, one of the defenders of the *Bagh-i-Mishah* quarter and the stockades on the Eastern side of the city. During the siege he was opposed to '*Aynu'd-Dawla's* entrenchments.

What fresh news arrives is entirely bad and conducive to cold despair. For the moment two powers, like two sovereignties, rule and govern in Azarbayjan; on the one had, the Russians, and on the other Samad Khán *Shujá'u'd-Dawla,* who had previously besieged Tabriz for six months, and claimed to control and administer Azarbayjan in the name of Muhammad 'Alí Mirzá (the ex-Sháh), and, who, after the Russians had crushed the patriots and Constitutionalists, entered Tabriz and set to work on his deed of blood, proclaiming himself governor on behalf of Muhammad 'Alí Mirzá. The strangest thing is this, that each of these two powers, acting separately on its own part and independently, bases itself with slaying, plundering, imprisoning, fining and punishing, while each gratifies its revenge and executes its victims without any interference from the other, killing whomever it will. Each one now holds prisoner hundreds of Constitutionalists. Then the Russians interrogate one by one before their court martial, and either kill them or let them go. In fact they investigate by external agencies the extent of the patriotic sentiments, love of liberty, learning and virtue of each, and if these have been exercised they kill the accused, but if not they let him go. On the other hand, Samad Khán kills some, while from others he extorts money and then lets them go. But since he demands large sums of money, which neither the person arrested nor his kinsman and friends are able to provide, he generally kills him in the end. For example, as the fine for holding Constitutional principles he demands, according to differences in the circumstances, from 500 to 2000 or 3000 *tumáns* (£.100 to £. 600). Thus from the well-known Hájjí Muhammad Bálá, who was one of the truest patriots in Persia, he extorted 1500 *tumáns* (£300), which constituted, probably, the whole of his possessions, and 800 *tumáns* more for his son- in-law 'Alí Aqá Náwbari, simply to spare their lives, and afterwards sent them as prisoners to Margha with other captives, to wit a company of some twelve persons, amongst whom was *Sayfu's-Sadat* (brother of Aqá Sayyid 'Alí Aqá, the son–in–law of the great *mujtahíd* of Najaf). The house of this same Hájjí Muhammad Bálá Nawbarí was blown up with dynamite by the Russians, together with the house of another Nawbari, who was one of the representatives of Azarbayján in the National Assembly, the only crime charged against them being love for their country. So likewise Samad Khán imprisoned Mirzá Mahmud of Salmas, one of the *'ulama*, of whom I have written fully in previous letters, and demanded of him 1000 *tumáns*, which sum being beyond the bounds of possibility he finally reduced his demand to 400 *tumáns*. Eventually, since the victim neither possessed so much money himself nor could find anyone to go bail for it, Samad Khán tore out his eyes and cut out his tongue while he was still alive and then slew him. In like manner did he deal with Yúsuf of Húkmabád, whose throat he cut, and afterwards cleft his body in two lengths-wise like a sheep, and then suspended each half on either side of the gate. And so on...

Those who have lately reached Constantinople from Tabriz relate the most appalling stories of Samad Khán's cruelties. For instance, one trustworthy fugitive from Tabriz states that the slaying and hanging of men are things which are no longer deemed of any importance, and which have altogether ceased to attract attention. Every day, Samad Khán hands over a number of his victims to be strangled, and afterwards hangs the body of each from a little ladder set up against the wall of some thoroughfare, as though it were a dead sheep. For it is the custom in Tabriz, though I know not whether it be so in other Persian cities, with certain small butchers of limited means to kill a sheep and sell its flesh not in a shop but in the street; and the butcher will kill it there in the street by cutting its throat, and after skinning it, will procure a little ladder of four rungs, which he will set up against the wall, and then, having either cut the sheep in two or not, will suspend it from the highest rung of the ladder. So thus does Samad Khán deal with the bodies of men! He is also amassing vast sums of money, which may amount to hundreds of thousands of *tumans*, and is equipping troops, whom he is sending towards Tehran, and who are concentrating at Miyána under the command of *Rashíd'u'l-Mulk*, the same criminal and traitor whom the Russian soldiers forcibly released from the government prison in Tabriz last summer and conveyed to the Russian Consulate. These troops are destined to land on Tehran and attack it, and. Samad Khán reinforces them on every side.

As for Samad Khán's tyranny over the villages and outly-
ing districts in Azarbayjan, I am unable adequately to describe
them in speech or writing, wherefore I pass over them, for
the record of them would make a large book. Of the Persians resident in Constantinople some 90 per cent or more
are from these districts, and the letters which reach them every week through various channels are like the lamentations
of the Plain or Karbala, crying out for help and demanding
succour. At Shabistar the irregular cavalry of Qarája-Dágh
are quartered in the houses of all the people, especially of
such as are Constitutionalists, and demand all sorts of things,
including large sums of money. So those poor wretches who
are here, and who, abased even beyond the Jews, amidst a
thousand intolerable and unendurable misfortunes, toil out
their very souls from morning until midnight amidst the
mud and filth in order that after several years they may go
home and spend a few days in comfort with their wives and
families, must now send thither their earnings to be given to
the Qarája-Dágh officers who are quartered in their houses,
so that their families may be saved from their tyranny!

As for the Russians, their court martial or military tri-
bunal is still at work, and they are ever busy with their
executions. I do not yet know the names of those persons
whom they have recently executed, that is to say the list
of them has not yet reached me, but I have heard that one
of several persons whom they have executed at Rasht is
Hájjí Mirzá Muhammad Rizá the *mujtahid*, president of the
Provincial Assembly, and that another is Hájjí-Aqá Khalil,
brother of the *Shari'atmadár*.[12] Of the correctness of this information, however, I am not altogether sure. The survivors

---

12 A well-informed Persian resident in Paris adds the following
note. "This is an error. He is alive and well and will shortly

too, who are in hiding, are in daily peril, since, on the pretext of searching for arms, the Russians make domiciliary visits, and so the Sword of Damocles is ever suspended over their heads. I also am the prey to a vehement anxiety and my heart is greatly disquieted.

The Russians and Samad Khán also prevent people from stirring, and give no one a passport to leave the country, not even to those who dwell in the districts referred to above, who were constantly going backwards and forwards to Constantinople, but who now come no longer. Only a number of the poor Nationalist Volunteers and Constitutionalists who left Tabriz a while earlier than the arrival of the Russians troops, and so saved their lives, went to Salmas, and afterwards, when the Russian troops pursued them thither, the poor wretches, leaving their money, luggage, arms and horses, dispersed. A number of these, amongst whom were Hájjí Pish-namáz. the *mujtahid* of Salmas, Mirzá Aqá, known as *Nala-i-Millat* ("the Nation's Cry"), Hájjí Mirzá Aqá Billúrí, Mirzá Ismá'íl Nawbarí, Hájjí Isma"il of the Amir-Khiz quarter (of whom the two last mentioned were members of the Municipal Council of Tabriz), and the well-known Ibrahim Aqá of the Caucasus, with a number of other National Volunteers, took refuge at Básh-qala' in Ottoman territory, whence finally they reached Van. Some of the Armenian Volunteers, who accompanied them telegraphed to their Central Committee, that is, the Dashnaksyun at Constantinople as follows:

"We and the Muhammad Volunteers abide here hungry and in want, and their condition is even worse than ours. A number of us without food or proper clothing are stranded

---

arrive in Paris." Browne's note. The original letter has "this deceitful charlatan..." [Ed.]

here in this bitter winter's cold, and many of us are sick and ill. Do you help us and induce them to help the Muhammadan Volunteers?"

So the Armenians here came to the Persian merchants and talked with them and urged them to do something, saying, "We have immediately sent £. 150 to our own men: do you at least send a like sum to your fugitives." No result, however, was obtained by this appeal, and not a penny was subscribed, for the Persians had no organization: so these poor people are left at Van and Básh-qala', where they are continually telegraphing for help, and none answers them.

Another section of these fugitives were under the leadership of the *Amir Hishmat*, head of the troops in Azarbayjan. These made a most gallant fight with the Russians, whom they completely overcame and surrounded, but afterwards angry telegrams reached them from Tehran bidding them cease fighting and lay down their arms, so they were obliged to leave Tabriz and come to Salmas, whence, after the arrival of the Russian troops, they fled to Urumiya, in the neighborhood of this place (according to his own telegram) *Ijlálu'l-Mulk*, the Governor, by command of the Russians and Samad Khán, brought troops against him, with guns and artillery, and besieged him in a village in the district of Dúl. After they had been besieged for eight days and were near perishing of hunger, the fugitives made a last desperate attempt to break through the beleaguers, which, after sustaining some losses, they succeeded in doing to the number of about fifty men, who, without guns, money or effects, reached a military guard-house on the Turkish frontier, where they took refuge, and where they are now in the most wretched plight. Steps have been taken here to induce the Turkish authorities to accept and receive them, and these steps have not proved ineffective.

Amongst other strange things worthy of mention is the fact that all government officials at Tabriz, even the *farrashes*, by order of Samad Khán wear Russian arms on their sleeves, so that the Russian soldiers may recognize them and not molest them, for at first these used to strip everyone whom they met in the streets, even in some cases Samad Khán's own men.

The condition of Tehran is also very bad, and an active process of "pacific penetration" proceeds apace. There will no longer be struggles and outcries about great matters and momentous acts of intemperance which will re-echo through the Press of the world; but every day things are happening in Tehran concerning one of the least of which the National Assembly would have loudly protested, and about which there would have been twenty days of struggle and dispute between Russia and Persia, the noise of which would have filled the whole world, while the Russian Government would have been put to a great deal of trouble, and, in order to prove itself in the right and justify its actions, would have been obliged to issue notes and manifestoes because in the words of the *Times*, the National Assembly had created an *impasse*, and steel struck against stone. Therefore it was agreed to alter the form of government, and to constitute a kind of administration which should not, like an unmanageable mistress, raise its clamor and outcries to heaven and put men to shame in consequence of some trifling liberty taken with it, but, when matters passed from preliminaries to ultimate intentions, the desire of the *Novoe Vremya* and the *Times* might be accomplished in the seclusion of the audience chambers and the privacy of the Cabinet, without any news of what was passing leaking out at home or abroad, but only that from time to time telegrams ostensibly of not the slightest importance and couched in the most ordinary form should appear in the newspapers, such as that "in accordance with the urgent request of the Persian Government, the Russian Government has consented to increase the number of officers in the Cossack Brigade, of which the numbers will be raised to ten thousand more", that "in accordance with request of the Sultán of Morocco, French troops have occupied the village of so-and-so"; that "in accordance with urgent demands of the Persian people, Samad Khán has become Governor of Azarbayjan, and that the people of that province (for what should the Russians have to do with it!) have proclaimed him Governor"; that "in accordance with the urgent demand of the Sultán of Morocco, the French Government has agreed to reform and administer the finances of that country"; that "in response to a demand on the part of the Persian Government, the British Government, in view of the ancient friendship subsisting between the two states, which happily still endures, has undertaken that organization of the gendarmerie in the South"; that "in consequence of the urgent demands addressed by the Persian Cabinet to the Russian Legation in Tehran, the Russian Government has undertaken the rectification of the Perso-Turkish frontier"; or "has agreed to another loan of ten millions"; or "has undertaken to restore order on the Northern roads", and so on.

Well, when was the platter hotter than the *potage*? Even in Europe [there] are to be found persons who say, "You wrong Persia, and compel her by force to agree, and do not allow her to manage her own affairs. Consider how in the time of the late mad *Majlis* they refused in their folly to accept the ready money and red gold which it was attempted to thrust upon them, until they were compelled by Ultimatums and the sending of troops to lend them money!

According to the most recent news, bread is very scarce and dear in Tehran, and so also in Tabriz, where also thefts, looting and other acts of aggression abound, so that public security no longer exists. The deliberations about Persia between Russian and British Governments are not yet concluded, while on the other hand the *Zillu's-Sultán*, *Sawlatu'd-Dawla*, and others are busy with consultations in order that in the spring they may appear somewhere in the South and next year may plunge Persia into fresh troubles. The project also I suspect to be prompted by the Russians. It would be well if you could inform certain centres of publicity as to this last detail, so that perhaps this plan may fail and prove abortive. I happen by accident to have become aware of this consultation.

The special correspondent of the *Temps* in Paris[13] is also restless and is busy making mischief. He should be avoided as far as possible, though some measure of apparent co-operation with him is not amiss. Send copies of this account of events in Persia so far as possible to the necessary centres of information, and transmit them to Professor Browne as well as to the newspapers. May God make great the reward of your high endeavours; and in truth it is precisely in these days, when our country is helpless and friendless, that the more loyal service can be rendered to it, now that all men flee from it and will scarcely mention its name; for during

---

13 Some one has added a note to the letter to say that a certain Persian notable in Paris is here intended.

the period of prosperity and glory of patriotism, the motives of those who drew were unknown.

I close my letter with sincere prayers for the increase of the Divine Favour towards you, and of your happiness and honour.

Your sincere friend, who is as dust at the feet of all true patriots.

P.S. According to the latest news from Tabriz, the accursed Samad Khán is treating his prisoners in the most barbarous manner, so that for the most part they would willingly put an end to their existence. Most people, even such as have no special position or consequence, are leaving Tabriz because they cannot bear to witness what is taking place there. Indeed the state of the city and the sight of the cruel deeds done there are intolerable. Even so Amánulláh Mirzá, the Deputy-Governor of Azarbayjan, though secure in the British Consulate, was unable to bear it, and slew himself. What more can I say?

No. 10

Translation of a sixth letter, dated February 17, 1912, from the writer of Nos. 3, 4, 6, 7 & 9.

Although the position of Persia is as you know, very precarious, yet, in my humble opinion, it is still not right to despair. The efforts made by you and our friends of the Persia Committee have an important effect everywhere and are by no means fruitless. Indeed, the Paris Meeting of February 12 was a direct echo of the English efforts made in London and Manchester.

Latterly, apart from the Russians aggressions, the state of Tehran itself and the Central Government causes great anxiety and but little satisfaction, for after the Russian ultimatums and the *coup d'etat* against the Constitution, the Tehran Government, despairing of help from any quarter, and seeing itself deprived of any aid or support from any Foreign State, even the British Government, has become completely terrorized by the Russians, so that it has given up entirely, submitted to the Russian demands, cast itself into their arms, and, despairing of aid from any other quarter, has wholly surrendered to them. Hence, seemingly, latterly such a Government, such a Cabinet and such a *régime* as the Russians desire is and will be maintained, so that henceforth no important news or rumours of any struggle with the Russians will come from Tehran, and the sinister processes of "pacific penetration" will continue to operate. Nay, perhaps in these days of silence matters may be done in Tehran quietly, silently and easily, without any noise or fuss, and may be settled without any outcry or struggle, which, were the Constitution and the National Assembly still in being, and the patriots free to act, would have provoked strife and opposition over each single detail, whereof the echoes would have made themselves heard through the Press of the whole world...[14] Even so it is "in accordance with desire of the Sultán of Morocco that the French Government pushes forward its troops and undertakes similar measures. So perhaps this newly-created Persia may come to regard the British Government just as the present Morocco regards Spain."

Henceforth, indeed, every superficial observer will say: "See how the affairs of Persia have improved under the present *régime*, so that now there is no struggle or outcry, nor is there any longer some daily disturbance, riot, trouble, or closing of the bazaars. The Government has become strong and has money in hand: what further need is there for a National Assembly to which proposals for borrowing or lending money should be submitted merely for it to reject them and until it should finally become necessary to force money upon them by bringing in troops, presenting ultimatums and threatening them with clubs, and that notwithstanding all this they should still cry out and refuse the money so freely offered?..."[15]

As regards the news which I sent you formerly, one item of it unluckily, or rather luckily, proves to have been incorrect, that is to say, accounts which have arrived most recently prove it to have been an error. This is about the execution of Mirzá

---

14 Here follow several paragraphs practically identical with those occurring after a similar preface in the last preceding letter [Ed.].

15 Taqi-zada is the writer of the letter and in the part omitted by Browne says that he tries to send any news of Persia that he finds to him or to Mirzá Muhammad Khán Qazwini so that he could publish them in Paris newspapers. [Ed.]

Hájjí Aqá Riza-zada, the editor of *Shafaq* ("Afterglow"); for it now transpires that the actual victim was another of the staff of the *Shafaq* named Mirzá Ahmad Suhaylí.[16] Not only was the editor of the *Shafaq* explicitly mentioned, but some telegrams actually give his name as Rizá-záda, wherefore I wrote his biography in this sense. Fortunately, however, it subsequently appeared that he succeeded in hiding himself, and we still await the ultimate result. All the other particulars were correct, and about them there is no difference of opinion. As regards the beginning of the disturbance which led to this regrettable event, so far as can be ascertained by successive enquiries, from the first the Russian intention worked in this sense, and they strove, in whatever way might be practicable, to provoke the catastrophe, whatever conditions might be advanced. Thus for several days they strove continuously by all manner of means to stir up and provoke the people. They molested them in the streets and bazaars, treated them with contempt and cruelty, insulted and interfered with them in all sorts of ways, beat children, molested Muhammadan women, and completely exhausted the people's patience. Still the people generally, and their chief men and leaders particularly, and the late lamented *Thiqatu'l-Islám* most of all, strove strenuously to be patient and endure and to give no excuse, since they clearly perceived the intentions of the Russians. And indeed they made extraordinary efforts to support and put up with the more intolerable provocation, until finally, on the 29th of Dhu'l-Hijja (A.H. 1329 = December 21, 1911), when the Russians, in consequence of the acceptance of their ultimatum at Tehran and the slipping of any excuse (for further aggressions) from their

---

16 Mirzá Ahmad Suhaylí was a poet, and he published a collection of poems in Tabriz in 1908 along with two poetic works by Hilalí and Ahli (cf. *Danishmandan-e Azerbaijan*, Muhammad 'Alí Tarbiyyat, Tehran, 1373/1994, p. 185) [Ed.].

hands, considered it necessary to make all haste to provide a fresh excuse, and so had recourse to an effective means which they always had in hand, and which was proved a decisive instrument for creating disturbances in time of need. This consisted in laying telephone wires over the roofs and through the people's houses, in such wise that at night several hours after sundown Russian soldiers were seen on the roofs of the peoples' houses, whence they dropped into their gardens to set up poles, drive in pegs, etc., so that the women and children, being frightened and terrified, began to cry out for protection: whereupon resistance was necessarily offered; until at length, near the public station, the Russians wished to enter this building to put up their telephone wires there also. The police offered resistance, and two of them were killed by the Russian soldiers, in spite of which the police still maintained their self-control, though the people were greatly excited by the events of that night. Near morning, on the other hand, the Russians ordered their troops to occupy all quarters of the town, place patrols everywhere, and disarm the people, notwithstanding the fact that the Persian Government and people were busy defending the town against Samad Khán *Shujd'u'd-Dawla*, and so could not lay down their arms, so next morning, when the people, the National Volunteers, and the Government troops came out, they found every quarter, street and thoroughfare full of Russian soldiers, who were disarming the people. In the course of a few hours they had seized about two or three hundred guns. In some cases the owners refused to surrender them, and struggles ensued, which suddenly culminated in a general fight. The Russian soldiers, unable to overcome armed men, were worsted, whereupon they began to fire on harmless unarmed people, women and children, and persons of no influence or importance, of whom they killed many. Thus one Babayeff by name, an *employé* of the Russian Consulate, fired from the roof of his house with a Mauser pistol at everyone who presented himself or passed along the street, and killed a great many.

At all events the object (of the Russians) was to create a disturbance, which result was brought about by one unseasonable, night prowling laying of telephone wires; and, just as you wrote at pp. 283-4 of your *History of the Persian Revolution*, this same telephone laying was made a means of causing great annoyance to the people of Tabriz, because the Russians, instead of carrying the wires along the streets, carried them through men's houses, which procedure furnished an unfailing means of provoking disturbances.

In practically all places controlled by the Russians, tyranny is again in full swing, and the Reactionaries are once more in possession, for first of all the Russians have removed all power of resistance of all Constitutional elements, and have thus smoothed the way for the Reactionaries, so that in all these places, especially Azarbayjan and Gilan tyranny and terror pursue their way with the utmost savagery and horror. But most of all does Samad Khán practice unbounded cruelty and oppression in Tabriz and all other parts of Azarbayjan. He behaves in the most brutal manner towards the many persons whom he holds captive, and has compelled the people everywhere to mourn and read the *Qur'an* in their houses and in the mosques for the souls of Shaykh Fazlu'lláh, Mullá Qurban-'Alí of Zanjan, Mír Háshim and other Reactionaries who are dead. For such they must needs recite the *Fátiha*, and everywhere they are busy with such observances. The tomb of the late Sharif-záda, who was one of the pillars of the Constitution and the martyrs of Freedom, and over whose grave the Nation has raised a beautiful monument, has also been destroyed and laid waste.

Samad Khán *Shujá'u'd-Dawla* forcibly shaves men's heads, which is a crime, and is renewing other–undesirable customs. All his officers and men, that is to say the *employés* of the actual Government, wear on their sleeves the Russian arms, so that the Russian soldiers may recognize them. There is no security for the people of Tabriz. Famine and high prices prove hard upon them. Samad Khán is also collecting troops and money to go and help Muhammad 'Alí Sháh, and is sending these troops to Miyana, where he has established a camp under the control of the notorious *Rashídu'l-Mulk*. Yet withal we are assured (God save us)[17] that "the Russians are not intervening in anyway in the internal affairs of Persia", and that they "are observing the Convention of 1907 and respecting the integrity and independence of Persia!"...

Some of the cruelties of the Russians at Urumiya also were reported in the *Terjuman-i-Haqiqat*, published in Constantinople, especially in respect to Mirzá Mahmúd Khán Ashraf-záda, the chief editor of the Persian newspaper *Farvardin*, a most accomplished, admirable discerning and zealous youth. This, too I forward for your perusal. [18]

---

17   Browne translates "Máshá Alláh" as "God save us" which does not give the sarcastic meaning of it. Perhaps it can be translated in this context as "Of course." So the sentence would be: "Yet withal we are assured, of course, that .the Russians are not intervening in anyway in the internal affairs of Persia." Here Taqi-záda writes that by chance he has recently obtained a copy of Browne's "History of Persian Revolution" and he enjoyed it tremendously. "Though" he adds "there were some obvious mistakes and they should be corrected." [Ed.)

18   A translation in full of this extract will be found on pages 85-90, No. 8.

No. 11[19]

Translation of a seventh letter, dated February 26, 1912, from the writer of Nos. 3, 4, 6, 7, 9, & 10.

The news which comes from Persia and especially from Tehran is bad, and reaction and Russian influence have on the whole gained greatly in strength. Latterly it has even been rumoured that the Liberals are in danger from the government, and there is a report that Mirzá 'Abdu'l-Husayn Khán *Wahídu'l-Mulk* has been arrested and imprisoned, and the *Mustawfi'l-Mámálik* exiled. Some say that some fifty of the Liberals are in prison, but I know not whether these reports are correct or not. No news comes from Tehran, but there is no doubt that Russian influence is greatly in the ascendant. Tabriz and Rasht remain in the same miserable condition, save that at Tabriz some one is put to death every day and sometimes several. The prisons are full. Samad Khán *Shujá'u'd-Dawla* rules in the name of the Russians: Russian sentinels guard his house, and his head gaoler is a Russian. Whoever he wishes to kill he hands over to the Russians to be put to death, so that the Russian soldiers are practically his executioners and *farrashes*, while he in turn is the

---

19 This letter was originally sent to Muhammad Qazwini in Paris by Taqí-záda who sent it to Browne. A letter addressed to Taqí-záda (June 21, 1912) [*Nameh-ha-yi Paris az Muhammad Qazwini beh Seyyid Hasan Taqí-záda*, ed. Iraji Afshar, Nashr-i Qatreh, Tehran 2005, pp. 14-19] shows that Qazwini after a consultation with some Persian Society friends in Paris and omitting sentences that might identify the writer, gave a copy to the correspondent of *Le Temps* who thereupon sent it to *Hablu'l-Matin*. Taqí-záda was worried that he would be recognized as the writer and Qazwini reassured him that all the identifying sentences had been removed [Ed..]

executioner-in-chief of the Russians – a strange and insoluble enigma! It is not apparent why the Russians kill people who have done them no wrong nor fought against them, merely because Samad Khán *Shujá'u'd-Dawla* has arrested them, either by reason of some personal enmity which he bears them or because of their Constitutional tendencies, and demands from them a larger sum of money for their release, and, when he cannot obtain it, hands them over to the Russians to kill; or on what pretext they regard such proceedings as lawful. This matter surpasses my understanding, and I do not know why the representatives of Foreign States then say nothing. If the Russians were to persecute those who, whether rightly or wrongly on false evidence, were charged with defending themselves and using arms against them, there would at least be some appearance of reason in it (although 95 percent of these people were innocent, and the charge of defending themselves was in regard to most of them an absolute falsehood); but what amazes one is that Samad Khán *Shujá'u'd-Dawla* should seize merchants, artisans, and persons of no political consequence on account of their Constitutional tendencies, or merely with the view of extorting money, and, when he wishes to kill them, should hand them over to the Russians, who, though knowing nothing of the arrested person, or what he is supposed to have done, forthwith hang him. It is true that, in order to afford proof of the savagery of the Persians, the Russians purposely appoint one of Samad Khán's executioners to carry out the sentence of death, whether by hanging or cutting the throat; but the Russians soldiers participate in the arrests, the transportations, the furnishing of guards, the convoying to the gallows, etc.

In the course of the last few days a number of those who were National Volunteers from the first, and other fugitives from Tabriz, have arrived here. Amongst them is the eldest of Karbala'í 'Alí "Monsieur". From the statements of all of these, and especially several particularly deserving of credence, such as the brothers Iskandaráni and Mirzá 'Alí Khán (the Lieutenant of Petros Andressian, chief of the *Dawa'ir-i-Thalatha*,[20] who was executed by the Russians), who is proceeding to Europe and may perhaps come to see you, and others. It has been established certainly and beyond doubt that the Russian themselves brought about the conflict, exasperating the people of thousand of devices which it would take long to describe in detail, and finally firing the first volley and making the first attack themselves; after which, in the most shameless manner, they telegraphed to all the world stating that "attacks on the Russian troops had taken place at Tabriz and Rasht, and that for some time the people of Tabriz had planned their conflict, and had arranged it in consultation with the Constitutionalists of Tehran and Constantinople!" So all the world, and even I myself, being then in Paris, supposed that one fine morning the people of Tabriz suddenly attacked the *Bagh-i-Shimal* (North Garden) and the Russian camp there; whereas in fact the exact contrary was the truth, and not a single one of the inhabitants had dreamed of quarrelling with the Russians. So likewise in Rasht, which was even more wonderful.[21]

Hájjí Sayyid 'Abdu'l-Wahháb, the *mujtahid* of Rasht, a member of the Provincial Council, who was imprisoned by

---

20 The *Dawa'ir-i-Thalatha*, or "Three Circles", was the name given to the threefold tax on opium, alcohol and tobacco.
21 The original word is "a'jab" which instead of "wonderful" has to be translated as "even stranger."[Ed.]

the Russians and has lately been banished and has come to Constantinople, gives a very strange account of the Catastrophe of Rasht, so that I should very much like him to be able to go to Europe and narrate these happenings in his own words. According to his assistant, who is in my view wholly to be depended upon, the beginning of this fighting in Tabriz, Rasht and Anzalí, which broke out in all those places at the same hour of the same day, was in Gilan as follows. In Rasht and Anzalí the shops and bazaars had been shut on account of the question of a general strike and the Russian ultimatum. In Anzalí on the morning of that day Russian Cossacks entered the bazaar and urged the people to open their shops. In particular they compelled the porters, who were on strike, to embark cargo on the ships; and the people refused to submit to this coercion. At this juncture one Aziz Bey,[22] an officer in the Russian army, who, with the soldiers under his command, had been sent to open the bazaar and put an end to the strike, was heard to say to his Muhammadan secretary and interpreter who accompanied him, as he glanced at his watch, "It is still three hours short of the time, and I do not know whether to begin now, or to wait till the proper time." At all events he finally struck a porter with his whip to compel him to resume work and stop the strike, saying at the same time, "It is the Emperor's command: you must stop the strike." Thereupon the porter declined to recognize the Emperor's orders, saying, "We are not the subjects of the Emperor but of our own King." This was sufficient excuse for them, and they cried, "Thou hast spoken disrespectfully of the Emperor!" Then the officer in

---

22 "Aziz Bey", the name of the Russian army officer, in the original letter appears as "Quli Bey." [Ed.]

question struck the porter and killed him, and ordered his men to fire a volley on the people. The poor wretched porters, who had no weapons save their cords and sticks, tried to defend themselves. A number of people were killed, and the town again became tranquil. The Russian Consul in person rode out with his Cossacks, issuing his orders and making his dispositions. He compelled the bazaars to open, and himself assumed the control of the Government.

What happened at Rasht was even more extraordinary than this, on the same day as that on which happened at Anzalí the events described above, at two hours before sunset, when the Provincial Council was actually sitting, news was suddenly brought that the (Russian) Consul-General had ridden out with his Cossacks and was promenading the streets. He subsequently proceeded to the *Urwat'l-wuthqá* Press, which is the most important printing-press in Rasht, where he dismounted, and ordered the Press to be broken up, destroyed and looted, and all the printed and other papers in it to be torn up. Amongst these latter was one of which the loss is most regrettable and deplorable. Mr. Rabino, the British Consul at Rasht, has been at much pains to collect useful information and the ancient books of Persia; has striven for a long time to compile a history of the Persian Revolution and to bring together all the necessary documents and papers; has been for several years in correspondence and communication with Professor Browne to whom he has sent many useful documents and books and for whom he has found many valuable things; and has latterly published a book (a most excellent publication, which you perhaps have seen) on the history and enumeration of the Persian newspapers, in which he has compiled a list of some two hundred Persian journals, giving in each case the name, nature, date, editor, politics, etc., with all necessary statistics; of which work I have seen a printed copy in the possession of Professor Browne at Cambridge. This distinguished man had in the course of several years, with much trouble, completed a most valuable work on the events of the Revolution and the history of the province of Gilan from the beginning of the Constitution down to the present day, and had entrusted it to the aforesaid Press to be finished. The original copy, moreover, was at the Press, whence they were engaged in setting it up in type. This book, the printed sheets and the original, the savage Russian Cossacks destroyed and tore up. Subsequently when the British Consul complained, the Russian Consul merely replied, "I did not know that your book was there!"

At all events, after the destruction of the Press, when news was brought to the Provincial Council and the different Government Departments, they were astonished, and did not know what was the cause of these events; but they recommended that, whatever the Russians might do, no one should molest them, or furnish them with any excuse. Meanwhile, after destroying the Press, the Russians began to fire volleys without any reason, and killed some seventeen persons in the thoroughfares, and began to arrest others, and to disarm the police and soldiers of the Persian Government. They also attacked the caravansary where the Tálish cavalry under orders for Tehran were quartered. These men, as it happened, were for the most part out, but two of them who were there the Russians killed, and carried off their horses.

At this juncture in the neighborhood of the Police Station several shots were fired by the police in the air (not at the Russians), and at once in the course of a couple of hours everything came to a standstill. Next day the Russians on the one hand began again to arrest people and to invade their houses to search for arms, invading the houses of most of the principal citizens and looting them. On the other hand the Members of the Provincial Council and others went to the telegraph-office and communicated with Tehran, informing them of what had taken place. In this connection the most amazing and astonishing thing, which fills men's hearts with sorrow, was that from Tehran the Ministers, ʿulamá, and others, continued to send the most emphatic and peremptory telegrams, saying, "We beg you to stop fighting, we entreat you to discontinue the contest!" Whereas in fact there had been no fighting in Rasht, but only on the preceding day, shortly before sundown, as has been already mentioned. The Russians fired volleys for the space of an hour, and killed a number of innocent people. It is not an extraordinary thing that the Persian Government should believe the false reports of the wicked Consul, and should not listen to telegrams coming through its own official channels from the clergy and members of the Provincial Council and Government of the City?

At all events, the Russian soldiers and Cossacks subsequently again invaded the bazaar and streets, and began to constrain and compel the people to stop the strike, but for three days they did not succeed in opening the shops, until a proclamation was published in the city from the Russian Consulate to the effect that all the people of Gilan were "under the protection and care of His Majesty the Emperor; that all administrative affairs were referred to the Consulate": that "all ill-disposed persons who should act in opposition to the Russian Government would be punished"; and that "the people must re-open the bazaars." The people of Rasht immediately published a manifesto in answer to this

proclamation, saying, "We are the subjects of the Constitutional Monarch Sultán Ahmad Sháh, and we recognize none
other than him." No sooner was this leaflet published and
issued that the Russian Consul at once ordered the *Khayru'l-
Kalam* Printing Press, when this manifesto had been printed,
to be destroyed; and it was forthwith completely looted.

Subsequently, on the 4th of Muharram (A.H. 1330 =
December 25, 1911) the Russians besieged the Telegraph
Office, arrested Hájjí Sayyid 'Abdu'l-Wahháb, who was
there engaged in communications with Tehran, put him in
chains, and carried him off to the other prisoners, twelve in
all, amongst whom was the Chief of the Police. After one
day's detention, they cast them into the hold of a ship, with
their feet in fetters, and took them to Baku, where they
cast them into the State Prison, keeping them apart from
one another, vexing and tormenting them frequently, and
preventing them from saying their prayers. Subsequently
they also hand-cuffed them, and when they set them with
their hands and feet thus chained before the horses, when
the Cossacks were escorting them (from one place to another): then later continually struck them from behind with
the butts of their guns and cast them to the ground, crying,
"Run, run!" and again striking them. In short, the Russians
carried their savagery to the highest degree.

After keeping them thus imprisoned for about two weeks
there, they were again brought back through the people in
the same manner, placed on a ship and sent back to Rasht.
They were made to run on foot and in chains, in the most
cruel and barbarous manner, through mud and slush, thorns
and briars, from Pira-Bazar to Rasht, the object being to
parade them like captives in the streets and bazaars, and then
to take them to the Russian Consulate. They only arrived,

however, some two hours after sunset, so that this was impossible. So they were again taken to the Russian Consulate and confined there, and next day they hanged four of them, including the Chief of Police and the *Shaykhu'l-Islam* of Langarud. This Sayyid ('Abdu'l-Wahháb), however, was released, in consequence of the intercession made on his behalf by the *Ná'ibu's-Saltana* (the Regent) and the Sipahdár from Tehran, but was exiled for five years. So far as can be ascertained, it was stated from Tehran that the Sayyid was guiltless of any offence; and the question necessarily occurs to one's mind whether the Tehran Government would have saved the others, and the unfortunate Tabriz victims, or not?

At all events, after declaring a protectorate and claiming the rights of government, the Russian Consul in Rasht brought in the *Mafákhiru'l-Mulk*, a noted Reactionary, and made him deputy Governor. He also made the notorious *Sharí'at-madár* (who has become a Russian subject), and especially his son, Hájjí Mirzá Riza, his general agents, and these are now in control of all administrative affairs. The *Mufakhiru'l-Mulk* is busy all day with the affairs of government, and every afternoon he takes his report to the Russian Consul and receives instructions from him. The *Sharí'at-madár* also is practically his factotum in Rasht, and acts as Consular Agent. He is continually going backwards and forwards to the Russian Consulate, and to him all matters are referred by the Consul, whose Deputy he has practically become.

At the time when the Russian Consul was completely misleading opinion in Tehran and abroad by means of his false reports, and was engaged in publishing the exact opposite to the truth concerning all these events, a number of Constitutionalists, much distressed on this account particularly, went to the British and Turkish Consuls, and begged them to transmit a true and exact account of these events to the proper quarters, laying before them at the same time a statement of the real state of the case for their perusal, and asking them in case they should find it correct and conformable to the facts, to corroborate it with their signatures. Both Consuls fully corroborated the contents of the document, but would not sign it, such action on their part being contrary to custom and etiquette. They promised, however, to communicate the true facts of the case to their respective Legations. The Russian Consul was not at first aware of the circumstance that the other two Consuls had, contrary to his desire, reported this account of what had happened as correct; but, on hearing this fact some days later, he was greatly annoyed and vexed, and began to collect false depositions, obtained by compulsion, to refute the Consuls' statements, and in particular set his men to collect, from this quarter and that, signed and sealed declarations to the effect that the British and Turkish Consuls had taken part in these conflicts and attacks on the Russian troops, and had participated in them; and he obtained from his prisoners by forcible means declarations in this sense. Amongst other things, he sent the above-mentioned Hájjí Mírzá Riza, the son of the *Shari'at-madár*, to this same captive Sayyid (to wit, Hájjí Sayyid 'Abdu'l-Wahháb, the narrator of these particulars) to urge him to write and furnish such a declaration against Mr. Rabino, the British Consul, and Khalid Bey, the Turkish Consul. The Sayyid at first wished to refuse, but seeing that it was the Consul's order, and compulsory, he wrote and delivered it under compulsion. The son of the *Shari'at-madar*, moreover, had brought with him a form of declaration in his own writing, and had told him to write thus; and, by a fortunate coincidence, the original of this document and form of declaration, in the handwriting of the *Sharí'at-madár's* son, was overlooked by him, and remained in the Sayyid's hands. (This last fact, however, should not at present be published, until the original arrives here, else the original may perhaps be seized and destroyed in Persia).

Two or three days later the Russian Consul brought forth this Sayyid from prison, summoned him to his presence, and said: "The Persian Government has gone bail and become surety for you to the Russian Government, therefore permission will be given to you to go straight to Karbalá, so make your preparations as soon as possible and depart thither. But first you must give a document to the Consulate wherein you declare that you undertake and find yourself never in the future to oppose the Russian Government." The Sayyid thereupon took up a piece of paper and wrote something to this effect: "I undertake henceforth, as I have done heretofore, to respect all treaties and experiments between the Russian and Persian Governments." Then said the Consul, "Read what you have written". When he had read it, the Consul blazed up in anger, and said: "This is not what is required: you are still in your former ideas, and wish to throw dirt in my eyes. Do you not know how we hanged Yúsuf Khán, and so-and-so, and so-and-so, or how in Tabriz we slew the *Thiqatu'l-Islám*, Shaykh Salím, and so-and-so and so-and-so? Now this is an act of pure grace we propose to release you, you must write exactly as I dictate, afterwards you can say outside, "the Consul extorted this declaration from me by threats and compulsion, or you can say anything else that your heart desires." Then he obtained from the Sayyid this declaration of non-resistance to the Russians, yet still he did not release him, but sent him to the *Sharí'at-*

madár, in whose home all the arrangements for his journey should be made, and the son of the *Shari'at-madar* carried him off to his house.

Amongst other most barbarous deeds (committed by the Russians) are the torturing and tormenting (of their victim) by cruel tortures in order to compel them to answer in the manner desired at their interrogation concerning those under arrest. Thus, by means of a thousand tortures, punishments, coercion and threats, they constrain their prisoners to give such-and-such answers when confronted with cross-examination and judgment. Thus do they manufacture artificial and compulsory testimony to fix guilt upon various (innocent) persons... Indeed the aggressive conduct and actions of the Russians in Persia (just as in their own country) is of such a sort and degree that one fails to enumerate or detail them; but in a simple sentence one may say that they have made manifest all the signs of annexation. This being the case, there is no further need for detailing their daily actions, even as we do not think of detailing them, for example, in the case of Tiflis, or of saying (in speaking of that place), "Today the Russians did such-and-such a deed, or arrested so-and-so."[23] And today they are acting in almost the same masterful manner throughout the whole of Northern Persia, especially in Gilan, Astarabad, Khurasan, Mazandaran, Qazwin, and especially Azarbayjan...

In Tabriz matters continue the same miserable course. Reaction reigns in the full scope of its violence and terror. In the different quarters of the city they have instituted assemblies for reading the *Qur'an* and reciting prayers for the

---

23 In the original Persian the word "Teflis" does not make sense but Browne has translated it accordingly and rather elaborated the original sentence. Taqi-zada could have meant *"talkhis"* which means "making it short," [Ed.].

souls of the "Martyrs of Autocracy", or the "Ten Martyrs", as they named such persons as Mír Háshim, Shaykh Fazlulláh, Khumámí of Rasht and the others. They forcibly shave people's heads, and change their clothes. In the course of these disturbances many innocent women and children have been killed, and, according to the statement of Sa'idu'l-Mulk, who has recently escaped from prison and come to Constantinople, nearly a thousand persons perished. In particular one Bábáyeff, secretary of the Russian Consulate, killed with a Mauser pistol from the roof of his house everyone who passed though the street, mostly innocent and insignificant persons. The same Sa'idu'l-Mulk, who was the commander of the Government Army in Tabriz against Samad Khán Shujá'u'd-Dawla, and who was captured after the entry of the latter into the city, and was in his bonds for some twenty-six days, and was only released after the payment of about 4000 tumáns (£ 800) relates as follows. In Samad Khán's prison some eighty persons were bound to one chain, their necks in chains and their feet in stocks, in one small room. He also related very many of the barbarities to which these unfortunates were submitted, so that he who hears of them must needs weep. They would come and take those who were to be executed from besides their companions, to whom they would afterwards relate the details of their deaths. He also states that they only released those so confined in chains twice a day, morning and evening, to fulfill the needs of nature, and then kept them by a well, still tied together, so that the poor wretches must needs fulfill their need side by side like animals. Some, who were very punctilious as to the due performance of their prayers, must needs have recourse to the day ablution (with sand). All the new colleges have been closed, and the children (who attended them) are vagabond. The *Madrasa-i Sá'dat*, which contained five hundred pupils, and was the most distinguished college in the city, is occupied by Russian troops, who have taken up their quarters there. The Russian flag flies over all the Government buildings. The cannons belonging to the Government have been carried off to the Russian camp in the *Bagh-i-Shimal* (North Garden) and planted head downwards in the ground (like the Persian and Turkish cannons at Tiflis, which you have perhaps seen), and fastened together with chains. Another wonderful thing is that the Persian Cossacks who are in Tabriz are under the same command as the Cossack Brigade at Tehran, yet take their orders from Samad Khán *Shujá'u'd-Dawla*, and proceed at his command to the performance of their various duties, visiting in particular, by his orders, the neighboring villages, and forcibly recruiting troops and soldiers for Tabriz, whom Samad Khán may send against Tehran; notwithstanding the fact that the wages and allowances of these Cossacks are still paid mostly through the Russian Colonel at Tehran, and that they are supposed to be under his orders!

According to the accounts and to the belief of persons who have lately arrived here, and who were with the late *Thiqatu'l-Islám* during these troubles, Mr. Shipley, the British Consul, in reality caused his death and the deaths of others like him; for during the few days of the disturbances and after those were over and the National Volunteers had fled, namely from the 4th to the 8th of Muharram (A.H. 1330 = December 25-29, 1911), when the Russian reinforcements were advancing from Julfa towards Tabriz, conferences were taking place, chiefly at the British Consulate, between a number of the clergy and chief citizens under the presidency of the late *Thiqatu'l-Islám* on the one hand, and the Foreign

Consuls and particularly the Russian Consul on the other, as to the best means for putting an end to the conflict. The British Consul succeeded in so convincing and reassuring the late *Thiqatu'l-Islám* as to the cessation of hostilities that not only did he himself not think of hiding or betaking himself to flight, but also completely reassured and tranquilized others who had confidence in him (like this same *Sa'idu' l-Mulk*, who has now arrived here), telling them that he had discussed the matter with the Consuls and satisfactorily arranged the matter, in such a way that it had been agreed that the Russian reinforcements which were on their way from Julfa would not enter the city, but would fetch a circuit to the *Bagh'i-Shimal*; and that, moreover, they would not molest the people, save in the case of those who had taken an actual part in the fighting, concerning whom investigations would be made (though in fact most of them left the city). Such, indeed, was the late *Thiqatu'l-Islám*'s confidence that only two hours before he was arrested he wrote a letter to this same *Sa'idu'l-Mulk*, who had written to him in great trouble, to reassure him and bid him remain tranquilly in his own house; in which letter he quoted the following verse of poetry:

تو که فلس ماهی حیرتی چه زنی ز بحر وجود دم
بنشین چو طوطی و دم بدم بشنو خروش نهنگ لا

"How canst thou, whom art but a scale of the fish of
    amazement, venture to speak of the Ocean of Being?
Sit still like the parrot, and listen every moment to the
    roaring of the Sea-monster of 'No'!" [24]

---

24 This obscure verse is from a poem often attributed to the Bábí heroine *Qurratu'l-'Ayn*, entitled also *Janáb-i-Táhira*

Moreover the British Consul made all his reports to the Government of which he was the accredited agent in conformity with the wishes of the Russians and the Russian Consul, he being a man totally devoid of sympathy with the Persians. Take for example, all those horrors at which the hair stands on end, and savage tragedies which befell the Persians, and of which the victims were in many cases innocent children and unarmed old men of humble condition, and which did not take place during the course of fighting (for it cannot be asserted that they were slain during the progress of battle) but rather the ravening and blood-thirsty Russian Cossacks fell like mad dogs on those who happened to be passing through different quarters, and made them targets for their bullets. In the actual fighting, without any exaggeration, at no time could ten of these Cossacks stand against two of the Persian National Volunteers, while often a hundred of them, for all of their artillery and cannons, were defeated by ten, so that they even abandoned their guns in the *Darb-i-Khiyábán* and fled. In particular there was a White Cossack post situated near to the Russian Consulate to serve as a guard-house and place for sentries, in which were stationed some hundred Cossacks. And although not a single shot was fired in that neighborhood, and there was no fighting, these Cossacks sallied forth through the public thoroughfare and main highway which was adjacent to their post, and is known as the *Bázárche-i-Mihád Mahín*, fired on the great crowd and concourse of people who were passing along that important street from both sides, and killed many

---

("Her Holiness the Pure"), and a variant has چو طوطى instead of بنشین چو طاهره. By others it is ascribed to Jámí or to Suhbat of Lar. 'No' probably refers to the formula لا الله الا الله ("There is no god but God").

innocent people. At last news of this reached the National Forces, who in the course of an hour surrounded and dispersed the Cossacks.

On that day of evil omen, very early in the morning, the Russian troops had occupied all the quarters of the city and the chief thoroughfares, in order to disarm the National Troops, and were scattered in small bands throughout the different districts; and when at length a conflict resulted, and fighting broke out in every quarter, many of the Russians were killed. Afterwards, when the Russian reinforcements reached Tabriz, they began to find the bodies of those slain here and there and everywhere; and wherever such were found, without any further investigation as to whether the owner of the house had anything to do with the matter or not, they forthwith blew up the house with dynamite and hanged its owner; while His Excellency the British Consul was good enough to come and inspect these corpses of men dead for ten days in order to inform his Government of the barbarities perpetrated by the Persians! Meanwhile, the Russians photographed them and published the photographs in their papers. But when, on the other hand, the notorious incident of the barber took place, as to the senseless brutality of which no one entertained the slightest doubt, His Excellency the British Consul said not one single word.

In brief, then, the case of the above-mentioned barber was as follows. On that day, Mashhadí Muhammad Ja'far the barber was in his shop or elsewhere when, as it chanced, fighting broke out in his quarter, and the Russian soldiers poured into his house and fortified themselves therein. After they had been overpowered by the Persian National Volunteers, the poor barber, returning to his house, found there the body of one of the Russian soldiers. After tranquillity had been restored in the city, he went to the Russian Consulate and informed them, so that they might come and remove the soldier's body, and give it burial according to their own rites. So they came and took it away. Some time afterwards, when the barber was busy with his work in his shop, the Russian soldiers came and arrested and carried off him, his apprentice and another person. Since the generality of the people knew him to be completely innocent and no partisan of any party, and that from the beginning he had taken no part in the Revolution, and had not borne arms, nor was the kind of man to do so, but was a very devout, pious and God-fearing person, therefore his neighbors strove to protect him, bore witness to his absence of partisanship, and went to the Russian Consulate, and afterwards to Samad Khán *Shujá'u'd-Dawla* and Hájjí Mirzá Hasan the *mujtahid*, whom they begged to mediate on the barber's behalf. Both of them, and especially Samad Khán, made great efforts to secure his release, but were unsuccessful. Finally the Russians hanged both the barber and his apprentice, and according to one account the Russian Consul said, in reply to the intercession of Hájjí Mirzá Hasan, "The death of a hundred of the *'ulamá* (of Persia) is not as important as the death of one (Russian) soldier", thus belittling the affair. This incident greatly affected the people's feelings, even the Reactionaries more especially by reason of the execution of the apprentice also with his master.

So likewise in the case of Mashhadí Muhammad Usku'i, better known as 'Amu-oghlu ("Cousin"), of whom one may say without exaggeration that he was the best and most high-principled of the National Volunteers of Tabriz, a man of the highest moral character, and an ardent and devoted patriot. This man on that fateful day saved and protected the lives of some seven or eight helpless Russians, and stationed in his house several Russian soldiers and one officer who were fugitive, and after the danger was over took them to the Russian Consulate and handed them over to the Consul. After this he not only received assurances of protection, but the office of Superintendent (*Shaḥna*) of the bazaar was conferred upon him. Yet some days later the Russians incited *Shujá'u'd-Dawla*, Samad Khán to arrest and hang him.

For more of these cruel tragedies, and a thousand more like them, had the British Consul eyes to see, but he is loud in his lamentations over the Russians killed in Battle. He does not make any objections or enquire why Samad Khán hoists the Russian flag over his house and over the Government Buildings, or why his men wear Russian badges on their sleeves.

Let us pass on, however, from these matters, of which a full and detailed account would be interminable. What appears to my sight very important is this concealment of the truth and disguising and distortion of the real state of affairs in which the Russians are engaged. By Heaven, God is my witness that in all this killing, hanging, despoiling and plundering, nothing so consumes one's heart as these perversions of the truth (which by Allah, burn one's very vitals) which are published throughout the world, even in those few newspapers which are friendly to Persia. Everywhere they write and speak of the "attack on the Russians", whereas this statement has even less basis than the "indivisible atom". In truth, there is in the world no misfortune beyond this, that a man should in the same time suffer a thousand injustices, and should yet be represented throughout all the world as unjust and a tyrant. Therefore, I especially hope that, according to your promise, you will publish some of these facts which I have brought together in this brief statement, and the accuracy of which I am convinced...

Further, I desire to trouble you about two matters in respect to which you should exert yourself to the utmost possible extent. The first is that you should write to ...[25] and induce him to persuade [Mr. Lynch] to write to the *Sardár-i-As'ad* and urge him to convene the National Assembly once more, warning him that otherwise the public opinion of Europe may turn against him. For, according to the latest news, the hopes of the reassembling of the *Majlis* and of new elections are weakening, and there is ground for fearing that it may be postponed on various excuses and pretexts, and that the intentions of the Government and of the men in power at Tehran may not be sincere. Secondly, the most strenuous efforts should be made to prevent M. Mornard and the other Belgians remaining in control of the Treasury, for, should they remain, there is but little hope of any reforms. While the Russian influence will be greatly increased...

---

25 The names which are omitted are Mr. Browne and Mr. Lynch in the original letter [Ed.].

No. 12

Extracts from official Persian despatches.

(a)   Safar 26, A.H. 1330 = February, 15, 1912

The number of Russian troops (in Persia) is as follows:

In the city of Tabriz	5500
Khuy, Urmiya and Salmas	1700
Anzali	5000
Gilan and Qazwin	6000
Mazandaran	500
Astarabad	500
Khurasan	2300
Hamadan	200
Total	21,700

A number of the troops in Tabriz left four days ago with twenty guns. It is also announced that they will leave Qazwin in the course of the next two days. The total number of Russian troops in Persia is about twenty-one thousand.

(b) Prince *Shu'á'u's-Saltana* has sent a telegram of the following purport, dated the 1st of Rabi'i (A.H. 1330 = February 19, 1912), by means of the Russian telegraphist from Astarábád to Yúsuf Khán of Herat, the leader of the rogues and rascals of Mashhad the Holy, through the Russian Consul General of that place:

"To His Honour Muhammad Yúsuf Khán, care of His Excellency the Consul General of the Glorious Russian Government."

"Your representations have been laid at the August feet,[26] and have caused heart-felt joy. The Royal Cavalcade will set out to visit, the Holy Threshold of the Imam Riza. Convey my sincere greetings to my loyal and zealous brothers of Khurasan."

(c) It is customary on the arrival of Ambassadors at Anzalí to fire a salute of several guns. The Turkish Ambassador arrived, and the (Persian) Government wished to render the customary honours. The Russian soldiers prevented this. An appeal was made to the (Russian) Consulate at Rasht, but he would not consent. Further, they (the Russians) refuse to restore the Government supplies which they seized in the time of the Revolution.

(d) The Turkish Ambassador arrived at Anzalí and waited there, but the customary honours were not paid. The officer commanding the Russian troops, in whose possession the guns were, concealed himself in Anzalí. Finally the Ambassador disembarked at Anzalí in a most distracted and distressed state of mind, and thence proceeded, having no other recourse, to the house of the (Turkish) Consular Agent at Rasht, where he refused to accept any kind of hospitality on the part of the (Persian) Government. After the true state of the case had been made known to him from various quarters, however, and he realized that the fault was not on the part of the Persian Government officials, he went to the house of the *Sardár-i-Mu'tamad*, whence he telegraphed an

---

26 I.e., have been submitted to Muhammad 'Alí, the ex-Sháh.

account of the matter to the Sublime Porte, and asked for instructions as to whether he should proceed to Tehran or return (to Constantinople).

Samad Khán Shujá'u'd-Dawla

No. 13

From the Turkish newspaper *Terjuman-i-Haqiqat* (date uncertain; probably about March 10, 1912).

For the attentive consideration of the Civilized World.

The Russians in Tabriz.

(The following is a letter received from Baku, of which the substance has been preserved, though it has undergone some trifling changes in form.)

After the Bulgarians at Ishtip had thrown bombs into the Muhammadan Mosque, the Muslim inhabitants of the town, being greatly excited, killed several Bulgarians, whereupon Europe was loud in its outcries. Yet the Ishtip incident was nothing compared to what happened at Tabriz. At Ishtip the populace, in consequence of an act of treachery of which they were the victims, were roused to fury and so committed this fault; while here (at Tabriz), they perpetrated their crimes carefully and deliberately. It is possible, I think, to forgive the former, but impossible to condone the latter. The massacre brought by these was, perhaps, worse than that of which those were guilty.

The Tabrizis who have arrived here relate that 280 persons have been executed by the Russians and Samad Khán, while 300 persons were killed in battle. Another 300 are in prison. The remaining inhabitants, who have not yet suffered such misfortune, know not from day to day how long they will remain safe and sound. For Samad Khán, the Reactionary who, profiting by the Russian operations, has usurped the position of Governor does exactly as he pleases.

Tabriz has assumed the form of a vast prison-house. No one can leave the city. The Consulates of "Civilized" Europe receive no refugees. The unarmed and shirtless people can find no place of refuge whence they can resist the barbarities of Samad Khán. Most of those who have escaped execution or imprisonment have been plundered. Deprived of their possessions, some of them are in daily expectation of a brother's death, some of a son's, and each seems to be turned into a lifeless body. Many more sit mourning the deaths of kinsmen, but even in such mourning they cannot freely indulge. The prisons are full of heavily-fettered captives. These poor wretches, surrounded by a thousand kinds of insults and humiliations, await the hour when they, too, shall be sacrificed to "European Civilization". Many of them, without awaiting their turn, surrender their lives in heavy chains on that same prison floor. The old *farráshes* come daily, spit in the prisoners' faces, curse their faith and their principles, and revile them. Every two or three days they give the prisoners each a loaf of bread and a glass of water, and, even while doling out to them this miserable pittance, they say: "Eat, so that you may be able to walk to the gallows!" After such a reminder just think what agonies the poor prisoner suffers even while eating his bread! Every day these *farráshes* come to the prison and relate to the prisoners in an exaggerated fashion the manner of their comrades' execution with all kinds of details, and in conclusion announce to them how they, too, will be executed in a similar manner. Some yield up their souls even as they listen to so terrifying an announcement.

Let me relate you a story which may serve as a specimen of the precarious lives and vicissitudes of such patriots as have not been captured, so that you may be able to form some idea of the extent to which Tabriz has become the theatre of tyrannies. One of the Tabrizis who has arrived at Baku described it as follows:

"One night, after the entry of Samad Khán into the city, one of my companions came to me. I went with him. My companion knocked at a door. They answered him from thence. We went to another street, where again he knocked at a door. A voice came forth. Subsequently my companion prepared a white bread and cheese, and placed them in a cloth. We set out, and presently reached an old and ruined bath, of which the roof had fallen in. Thence he threw down the cloth, and afterwards descended himself. I accompanied him in his descent. We lit a candle, and passed, with extraordinary anxiety and disquietude, underground and in the fearful darkness of night, through several chambers of the bath, until we finally came to the furnace-room, entered its narrow door, and stopped. My companion called out, "O So-and-so!" No answer came. At length he uttered his own name, saying, "It is I! I have brought you bread and water." Then a weak voice was heard. We advanced, and I saw one buried up to his neck in the ashes. Helped by my companion, I succeeded in extricating the man, to whom we gave the food which we had brought. At first he was so weak that he could not eat it, but presently he ate a little, after which he again crouched down in his place of refuge amongst the ashes."

Add to all these tragedies and tyrannies the hardships of the writer!

This man who kept himself warm in the ashes of the furnace room in the interior of a ruined bath was one of the chief citizens of Tabriz, and one who had been wont to eat well and live in luxury. Besides these (who are in hiding), nearly 1800 of the inhabitants have fled from Tabriz, whose families, receiving no news of them, believe them to be dead. If you are "civilized", and in the name of "civilization" could commit such crimes upon us, let us in no wise desire such "civilization!"

Hájjí ʻAlí *Dawa-furush* (the Druggist)

No. 14

Translation of an eighth letter, dated March 13, 1912, from the writer of Nos. 3, 4, 6, 7, 9, and 11.

...In these days the things which appear most important in the affairs of Persia are three in number. First, the question of a second summoning of the National Assembly and fresh elections, for, so far as one can judge from externals, there is little intention of convening it, and the Russians are urging those at present in charge of the affairs of Persia not to convene it again. Moreover, according to statements made in the Russian papers, the Russian Government has demanded, and will continue to demand from the Persian Government, the banishment and expulsion from Persia of most of the chief Constitutionalists....

The second question which is of great importance, and which is perhaps, one of the greatest blows to the independence of Persia and the chief means of its Russification, is the invasion of the different Government departments, such as the Finance, Posts, Mint, etc. by Belgians, and especially the appointment of Mornard as Treasurer General, which is one of the worst of evils....

The third question is connected with the new schemes of the Russians for increasing the numbers of Persian Cossacks under the instruction of Russian officers, of which the harmfulness is manifest, so that one might ever say that the harm which will result from it would neutralize and balance the advantage which would result from the evacuation of Persia by the Russian troops.

The condition of Tabriz and of the whole of Azerbaijan continues as miserable as ever, and the executions and demolitions pursue their course. The patriots, in successive bands, are taking refuge in Ottoman Territory, and up to the present time some thousands have crossed over onto Turkish soil, some of whom are gradually arriving in Constantinople, including Members of the Provincial Council of Tabriz, editors of newspapers, writers, and the like. These describe the state of Tabriz and the condition of those Constitutionalists who remain there as most heart-rending. Most of them are fugitives and in hiding, and are continually in the extremity of hardship, misery and peril, for everyone who is found, or whose place of hiding becomes known, is put to death. Samad Khán *Shujá'u'd-Dawla* has caused it to be proclaimed throughout the city that if any "malignant" (by which he means "Constitutionalist") is found in any house, and if the owner of the house has not himself come to notify the fact, the house will be looted and destroyed. A letter on this subject was published in the *Terjuman-i-Haqiqat*, of which I enclose a copy. (See the last extract, No. 13.)

There are no signs of any evacuation of Tabriz by the Russian troops: on the contrary, some signs are apparent which point to the permanence of their occupation. Apart from the fact that they formerly erected certain churches and other buildings in the *Bagh-i Shimal* (Northern Garden) where their camp was situated, which sacred buildings would be difficult to torch hereafter, according to letters recently received from Tabriz, they have buried the Russian soldiers who were killed in the Government building which formerly served as the head-quarters of the Police.

The political situation of the Ottoman Empire also does not seem satisfactory, for on the one hand there is the Russo-

Austrian rapprochement, on the other the visit of the Prince of Montenegro to St. Petersburg, and again the dismissal of M. Cherikoff, the Russian Ambassador at Constantinople, whose tendencies were pacific. All these signs are bad.

The Russians are making great efforts to have the Turco-Persian frontier disputes in the neighborhood of Khuy, Urmiya, Salmas and other parts of Azarbayjan, solved and settled as quickly as possible, and are very importunate in this matter. They are also endeavoring to secure the settlement of these differences in favour of Persia, that is to say, that the Turks should evacuate such Persian territories as they have occupied around about Urmiya, etc., these places being important military and strategic positions. It is to be feared, however, that after the Turks have evacuated them, the Russian soldiers will occupy them. At present the Russians are busy in Urmiya, sided by the Russophil government of that place, in compelling and inducing the people of Urmiya, their Kháns and nobles, and especially the Chaldean Christians of that region, to sign fictitious petitions addressed to the Russian Emperor and the Parliaments of the different European states praying that the Russian troops should not depart from Urmiya or evacuate that part of the frontier. The Perso-Turkish frontier commission are assembling at Constantinople, and it is now a week since the Persian representative arrived here...

No. 15

Extract from a letter written by a Persian resident in Paris on April 17, 1912, enclosing two letters from Tabriz.

I forward to you enclosed herewith two letters from Tabriz about the recent tragedies, sent to one of my friends residing in Constantinople; who sent them to me, in order that you may place them amongst the documents and records which you possess concerning events in Persia. Although the contents of these two letters are practically identical with the accounts furnished you by ... [27], which have been sent to you by ..., yet since they contain the thoughts and express the sentiments of persons who saw these tragic events with their own eyes, and were perhaps even involved in them personally, it is probable that on this account they will not be devoid of a certain value...

Enclosure 1 in No. 15

Tabriz, 23 Safar, A.H. 1330 (February 12, 1912).

May I be the sacrifice of your fortunate presence!

---

27 The names omitted are Taqí-zada and Muhammad Qazwini respectively . Unlike the other letters that are sent to Browne mostly by Taqí-záda, these two letters along with the accompanying note are sent by Husain Kazim-zadeh Iranshahr from Paris, on April 17th 1912. Apparently this is his first correspondence with Browne. Kazim-zadeh says that until then he was studying in Belgium and recently has come to Paris and is writing to him. [Ed.]

Your auspicious letter, dated the 3rd of this present month (=January 23, 1912) arrived and was duly read. You enquired about the state of the province, the circumstances of the conflict, and sundry other matters. Although the state of the country has not left one much inclination or disposition for such effort, and one's being recoils from the task of writing down the essential facts, yet since I deem it my duty to obey your Honour's command, I therefore submit to your fortunate presence what I can recall to mind or have been able to ascertain about these events.

As regards the beginning of the conflict, on the 25th and 26th of Dhu'l-Hijja (A.H. 1329 = December 18 and 19, 1911) the Russian Government brought in a number of soldiers and Cossacks from Ardabíl, and quartered them in the caravansarays of Hasan Aqá of Ganja and the *Kalántar,* situated near to the Old Bridge and still nearer to the Government House and the Chief Police Station, which they had cleaned out for this purpose. The National Volunteers and members of the Provincial Council, being aware of their intentions, transferred to the Arg (Citadel) the cannons and ammunition which were in the head-quarters of the Provincial Government, that is to say, the *Áli Qápú,* and appointed some five hundred of the National Volunteers to remain on guard night and day in the Citadel, which, indeed, they had greatly fortified and strengthened. They had even constructed a bake-house in the Citadel for the National Volunteers, so that, in case of necessity, they should have no need to go outside; and they had transported to the Citadel all the rifles and ammunition which were stored at the Chief Headquarters of the Police. Notwithstanding all this, they continued to behave with the utmost respect and friendliness towards the Russians, until, on the evening of

Thursday the 29th of Dhu'l-Hijja (A.H. 1329 = December 21, 1911), several hours after sunset, the latter suddenly and without warning rushed upon the Chief Police Station, the Government House, and the High Court of Justice and took possession of them, besides shooting two of the Police who were on guard at the Police Station. Before dawn the Russians also poured into the *Rástá-Bázár* and stripped everyone whom they saw.

On the morning (of Friday, December 22, 1911), when the National Volunteers were informed of these events, Amir Hishmat, who was Captain of both Volunteers and Regulars, at once waited on the Deputy-Governor and the Members of the Provincial Council, and complained, declaring that their patience was at an end, and that it was a thousand times better to die than to lead so wretched a life, and that, even if permission should not be accorded them (by these authorities), they would fight. According to what I have heard, the Deputy-Governor and the Counsellors, *nolens volens*, gave permission so to do, and bade them defend themselves. Thus it was that the fighting and firing began, and that in the course of a few hours the Russians were compelled to evacuate the Government offices, the Courts of Justice, the Chief Police Station, and the bazaars and quarters (which they had occupied), and to retire in fright to the *Bágh-i-Shimál* ("North garden"). In all these several centres of conflict the Russians sustained considerable losses, while of the National Volunteers also some were killed, amongst the most notable of them Rajab Bey, the servant of Ibrahim Aqá and Ná'ib Mahmúd, the brother of Ná'ib Muhammad Aqá-yi-Khiyábáni. By noon not one single Russian soldier was to be seen in all the city outside the *Bágh-i-Shimál* on which constant artillery fire was directed from the Citadel, with great effect. The Russians on their part continued to direct their fire from the *Bágh-i-Shimál* on the Citadel and the various quarters of the town, and fired more than five hundred shots at the Citadel in the course of this one day; in spite of which not one single brick fell from the Citadel walls. Both sides fought fiercely until sundown, and it went hard with the Russians, who sustained severe losses. On the side of Márálán the National Volunteers even occupied for a while half of the *Bágh-i-Shimál*, until night intervened and put an end to the conflict.

On the following day (Saturday, December 23, 1911), ere it was yet light, firing was again begun on both sides. An attack was even made on the Russian Consulate, by which a fresh fight took place. They also fought in the *Bázarcha-i-Mahád-Mahin*, where the Cossack barracks was formerly situated, forced the Russians to evacuate this building, and, brought in some twenty horses belonging to them. The Russians, perceiving that they could not withstand men who were thus ready to die, that might set fire to those houses which adjoined the *Bagh-i-Shimal* on the side of the *Kucha-i-Sadr*, the Márálán quarter, and the street of the late *Aqá Mir Fattáh* and threw dynamite into them, so destroying all their houses, and killing in that one night more than five hundred women, children and men who had taken no part in the struggle. In the house of Hájjí Hasan-i-Khatá'í alone eighteen persons both male and female, were killed, and how many more were wounded. As for Hájjí Hasan-i-Khatá'í's house, they so utterly destroyed and laid low that fair and beautiful building that not even a trace of it remains. [Those streets still are in ruins and even in day time, out of fear, no one can pass through them. The remaining people of that quarter have gone to other quarters with their families.][28]

We are, however, straying from the matter in hand. On that day the people, seeing matters thus, perceived that should a few days more pass in this fashion, the whole town would be laid in ruins; which, in fact was the case. Ninety per cent, moreover, were ready to put an end to the Constitution and bring in Hájjí *Shujá'u'd-Dawla*, but dared not breath a word for fear of the ill-disposed. These, in search of some pretext, said, "One remedy lies in this, that we should go en masse and bring Hájjí *Shujá'u'd-Dawla* into the city". So they assembled bands of people out of the bazaars and mosques, and with lines of "O for Islam!" "O for Religion!" "O for the Holy Law!" set their faces towards Básminch. On their way thither they purposely diverted their course in front of the Provincial Council, and, their chief object being to put an end to such institutions, they made some speeches to excite the populace, and, making a sudden attack, looted the building and tore the *Anjuman's* flag in pieces, crying, "We do not want a Constitution!" Cries of "Long live Muhammad 'Alí Sháh!" were raised; and in short the building occupied by the Provincial Council, which formerly belonged to Prince *Zafaru's-Saltana*, and had recently been bought by Hájjí Muhammad Báqir Tajir-báshi (Chief of the Merchants), and was valued at 15,000 *túmáns* (about £. 3000), was in one moment so destroyed that it was as though no building had ever stood there, and its site is now a spacious desert.

After thus wrecking the *Anjuman* and accomplishing their desire, these people set out for Básminch. Hájjí *Shujá'u'd-Dawla* had said, "These are the holy days (of Muharram);

---

28 The parts in brackets are added by Browne.

please, God, I will enter the city or the 11th of Muharram (A.H. 1330 = January 2, 1912), and will make you all tranquil." And so it fell out, for on that very day he entered the city with the customary Persian pomp, and took up his abode in the Garden of Hájjí *Nizám'd-Dawla*, where he still abides, burying himself with administrative affairs.

In short on that day some of the merchants and leading citizens saw that the business was turning out ill, and might very probably yield no good result thereafter; wherein, indeed, they judged correctly. So they met together at various centres, especially in the house of the late lamented *Thiqatu'l-Islám*, to see whether some way might not be devised to put and end to the fighting. The poor *Thiqatu'l-Islám* aided by *Ziyá'u'd-Dawla*, the Deputy Governor, on that day, when bullets and cannon-balls were pouring round him like hail, went backwards and forwards ten times, alone and unattended by servants, to the British Consulate, and finally three hours after sunset, went in company with the British Consul to the Russian Consulate, where, after prolonged discussions, it was finally agreed that the National Volunteers should surrender their arms and cease fighting, and that the Russians also should refrain from molesting innocent women and children, and from burning the houses of the Musalmans. After the above-mentioned agreement had been arrived at, he went and assembled Amir Hishmat and the other National Volunteers in one place, and, having explained what had happened, told them that it was expedient that they stop fighting, and not imperil to no purpose the lives of innocent women and children, nay, even of the entire population of the city, while waiting for some definite instructions from the demoralized capital, Tehran.

Amir Hishmat and the other National Volunteers, perceiving they had now to deal with two enemies, the Russians and the very inhabitants of the city, went by night to the Citadel, which they evacuated, carrying off as large a supply of ammunition and cartridges as they could, and departed from the city towards Khuy and Salmas. Such as were ignorant of the course of events and could not depart remained in hiding in the city.

When it was morning we all knew that the National Volunteers had departed. The Russians again issued forth from the *Bagh-i-Shimál* and attacked the various government offices.

شب پره بازیگر میدان شود   مهر درخشنده چو پنهان شود

When the bright sun disappears
The moth again becomes the player on the stage.

On that day the sound of cannons and musketry was no longer heard, and the people were on the whole left in peace. But since the Russian Government is never faithful to its promises, it trampled under foot all those agreements which it had made with the poor *Thiqatu'l-Islám*, the Deputy Governor and British Consul, and on the following day (Monday December 25, 1911) they bombarded the city on all sides from dawn until dusk with mountain guns.

Indeed that day was a strange one. The poor *Thiqatu'l-Islám*, again went, accompanied by the British Consul, to the Russian Consulate, and the bombardment was stopped. God is witness what a claim the poor *Thiqatu'l-Islám* had on the gratitude of the people of this city when he departed from them. May God exalt his rank in Paradise, and raise him up with His Saints! By God's Truth and by His Chiefest Saint[29], after that (i.e. the *Thiqatu'l-Islám's* death) neither power nor sensation nor motion was left in the people of this city. Whether small or great! I have read in history that when the Afghans captured Isfahan, an Afghan made ten Isfahanis lie down side by side, and said, "Do not get up until I go to discharge a need of nature, and then come back to cut your throats"; and those ten men, on account of that one Afghan, dared not stir from their places.[30] Even thus were we, nay, even worse. When we see a Russian soldier or Cossack, it is as though the Angel of Death approached: and we humble ourselves in terror before him. Seeing the field thus clear, they began to practice all kinds of tyranny and aggression, of such sort that God alone is our refuge! One is ashamed to speak of them: may no true believer behold and no unbeliever see the like of them! In one day, on the pretext of searching for arms in the *Rásta Bázár*, they took from the people more than a hundred gold and silver watches.

At night several of them went to a house and did whatever they pleased. I do but hint briefly at what happened: whether by day or by night they did no fall short in the perpetration of whatever was possible.

On the most holy day of Muharram (the tenth = January 1, 1912), towards afternoon, a Russian officer, accompanied by twenty Cossacks, went in a carriage to the house of the late *Thiqatu'l-Islám*, and informed him that the Russian Consul General desired to see him. He, having regard to his relation with the Consul during the last few days, supposed

---

29 The First Imam, 'Alí ibn Abi Talib, is probably intended.
30 This anecdote is told by the historian Ibnu'l-Athir about the Mongol invasion of Persia in the thirteenth century.

that some fresh business had arisen, and without any apprehension entered the carriage and drove to the Consulate. As
soon as he arrived there, he was bound hand and foot and
taken to the *Bagh-i-Shimal*. Shaykh Salím and his brother
Karím had concealed themselves in the Surkhab quarter in
the house of one of their kinsmen. The Sayyids and inhabitants of Surkhab found him there and dragged him with
blows to the Russian Consulate; and so cruelly had they
beaten him that he would have died even if they had not
hanged him. They also took *Ziyá'u'l-'Ulamá* and his uncle[31]
from his house and carried them to the *Bagh-i-Shimal*; and
they likewise seized the two sons of Karbalá'i 'Alí, known as
"Monsieur", and Ibrahim Kázim-záda. These (eight) were
the first to suffer on the gallows, and that, too, on the (holy
day of the) *'Ashurá*, two hours before sunset. The *Thiqatu'l-
Islám* showed no fear, but displayed the utmost steadfastness
of soul. There in the *Maydán-i-Mashq* (Drill Square), he first
performed the ablution with sand, then offered up a prayer
of two prostrations and then walked with the utmost firmness to the gallows. May God's Mercy encompass him!

The next to suffer was Shaykh Salím. Some of these
people, worse than the men of Kufa, mocked him, saying,
"Now, Master Shaykh, eat the meat which you yourself have
cooked!" Thereupon he raised his face to heaven and said,
"O God! Thou art aware of my intent: judge between me
and these people, O most Just Judge!"

Next came the turn of the sons of Karbalá'i 'Alí "Monsieur". When the rope was placed round their necks they
cried out with a loud voice, "Long live the Constitution!"

---

31 The editor has heard from one of *Ziyá'u'l-'Ulamá*'s daughters
that the uncle was very fond of him and accompanied him to
the scaffold. When one of the victims managed to escape, the
Russians hung the uncle in his place [Ed.]

When it was the morrow, the 11th of Muharram (A.H. 1330 = January 2, 1912) His Excellency Hájjí *Shujá'u'd-Daw-la* entered the city, and again began to move more briskly. On one day they arrested and hanged in the *Bagh-i-Shimal* Hájjí 'Alí *Dawá-furush* ("the Druggist"), Mirzá Ahmad, the Broker, known as "Suhaylí," and Muhammad Khán and Karím Khán, the nephews of Sattár Khán. Another day they arrested and hanged in the same place Mirzá 'Alí Nátiq ("the Orator") of Wayjuya, Hájjí Samad, the tailor, and Mashhadí Hájjí of the Caucasus, together with his father-in-law Mah-di Shukur-i-Kharrázi. Another day they strangled Mirzá Mahmúd of Salmas, formerly of the Ministry of Justice, in the Avenue (Khiyábán) of *Majídu'l-Mulk* and hung up his body; and another day they did the same in the same place to Mirzá Aqá Bálá Khán-i Khiyábání and Mashhadí 'Ab-bas-'Alí-i-Khiyábáni, the grocer. Another day they arrested and hanged on the roof of the Citadel Aqá Mir Karím the cloth-merchant, a notable orator together with Mashhadí Muhammad Usku'i, known as 'Amu-Oghlu ("Cousin"), to-gether with six other persons of less note. What words Mir Karím uttered as he went to the gallows and what things he said are hardly to be believed: may God's Mercy enfold him! Another day they cleft in twain Ná'ib Yúsuf of Hukmábád and hung up the two pieces on the Wayjuya Gate. Another day they hanged on the roof of the Citadel Hájjí Nagi the Jeweler, on the pretext that he had cut the throat of a Rus-sian soldier, together with a Georgian who had become a Musulman and (pronounced the articles of the faith just be-fore being hanged). Another day they arrested and hanged in the same place Mashhadí Ghaffár, the brother of Sattár Khán. In short, up to the present time they have hanged more than forty Musulmans and Armenians, some of whom we do not know. Those imprisoned in the Garden of Hájjí *Nizámu'd-Dawla* and the house of the Begler-begi are innumerable and beyond computation. *Rafi'u'd-Dawla* has become Begler-begi, and all the old *Kad-khudás* (headmen) are again in office, and are busy commentating, from chapter-head to foot-note, all that they have had to put up with during the days of the Constitution. Mirzá Ismá'íl Nawbarí and Hájjí Ismá'íl Qara have gone off in company with *Amir-i-Hishmat* (the captain of the National Volunteers). As to Mir Aqá Husayni and Husayn the cartridge-seller, it is not known where they are. Hájjí Muhammad 'Alí Bádámchi is in the house of the *Agence Allemande*, and has also put up a (German) flag over his house. Mirzá Husayn the preacher is not to be found, but it is rumoured that he is in the French Consulate. The Turkish Consul has also taken under his protection some of the National Volunteers. The *Sayyidu'l-Muhaqqiqin* was for some time hidden in the city, but afterwards they found him and took him before Hájjí *Shuja'd-Dawla*, who, after many revilings and reproaches, sent him to Qum escorted by four horsemen, and it appears that news of him has been received by telegraph from Zanjan. *Sadiqu'l-Mulk*, Member of the Provincial Council, was one of those whom they hanged on the Day of the '*Ashura*. Hájjí Mahdi Aqá Kuza-Kunáni and his sons are safe, on account of the friendship which for-merly existed between them and Hájjí *Shujá'u'd-Dawla*, and no harm has befallen them. They have now started a mer-cantile company of which the head is Hájjí Mushiri-Daftar and the other members are the Aminu't-Tujjár, Hájjí Mahdi Kuza-Kunáni, Hájjí Mahdi of Salmas, Hájjí Muhammad Aqá Hariri, [and] Hájjí Ismá'íl Mudiru't-Tujjár. From Hájjí Mir Muhammad 'Alí of Isfahan they extorted some money, and then, on the intercession of Hájjí 'Alí Aqá and company, let him go. There is no one left whom they have not in some way molested, or will not molest. The brother of Mirzá Muhammad 'Alí Khán "Tarbíyat" is not to be found, nor is it known where he is. Mirzá Hájjí Aqá of the newspaper *Shafaq* (Dawn) is, it is rumoured, in the American Consulate. His father, Karbalá'i Rizá, has been arrested, but they have spared his life, and he only needs money to be given so that he may be released. Of the total *'ulamá* who left the city during the days of the Constitution, none have returned save Hájjí Mirzá Hasan the *mujtahid*. It seems that Mirzá Sádiq and Hájjí Mirzá Karím the *Imam-Jum'a*, were urged to come into the city, but declined and have not come. Hájjí Mirzá 'Alí Naqi of Ganja was here before the disturbances, but has not been seen since, nor is it known where Ja'far Aqá may be. *Ijlal'l-Mulk* is, as before, Governor of Urmiya, and has again received a robe of honour from Hájjí *Shujá'u-d-Dawla*. He also is busy in Urmiya with arrests and imprisonments. Aqá Mir Taqí Qilij was wounded in the foot during the fighting, and was afterwards arrested in his house and taken before Hájjí *Shujá'u'd-Dawla*, but after he had paid over a sum of money he was sent to Karbala. *Basiru's-Saltana*, being aware of what was impending some days before the fighting began, departed for Europe.

Then there is the question of passports, which at first was and still continues to be as follows. Anyone who wishes to leave the city must obtain a certificate (*Tasdiq-nama*) from the inhabitants and elders of his quarter and take it to the Chamber of Commerce, who must write another certificate to the Begler-begi, who must send another certificate to the Passport office, after which (formalities) the passport is granted. It is impossible to contravene these arrangements, or to obtain a passport in any other way. From this side of the Qaflán Kuh to Khuy, Salmas, Urmiya and Marágha, all Azarbayjan is under the control of Hájjí *Shujá'u'd-Dawla*. *Amir-i-Hishmat* and the Natinal Volunteers who fled from the city went towards Salmas and Urmiya, and near the latter place fell in with the horsemen of *Ijlálu'l-Mulk*. After being besieged for three days, and having killed some forty of *Ijlálu'l-Mulk's* horsemen, they succeeded in reaching Salmas, where the Turkish Consul received them in the most kindly fashion, and they are now in Turkish territory.

From Tehran we have no news at all whereby we can judge what their ideas are about Tabriz; that is to say, there is no one here who is in communication with Tehran, and hence it is that we have no information.

So far as one can guess, some four or five hundred houses have been destroyed with dynamite (by the Russians), to wit all houses which were fortified by the National Volunteers, or from which they fired, and also all houses which, during the Constitution, were used for administrative purposes. They have also removed all the doors which had been placed (by the Nationalists) in the streets and passages and in short they have left nothing in Tabriz which could even serve as a specimen of the Constitutionalist management. Now the Russians are established in the *Maydan-i-Mashq* (Drill Square), the Head-quarters of the Police, and the seat of the Provincial Council, and in the *Maydan-i-Mashq* they are even employing builders and laborers to affect such repairs and alterations as they themselves require. The Commandant of the (Russian) troops has established himself in what was formerly the head-quarters of the Provincial Government, and every day proclamations designed to frighten the inhabitants are affixed to the walls. Some days ago they issued a proclamation to say that they were going to search the houses for arms, but they have not yet begun to do so.

Karbalá'i Hasan is still at Ardabíl, but Karbalá'i 'Abbás 'Alí has come from Khuy and is living in the office of Karbalá'i 'Alí. The latter has been in hiding since the beginning of the disturbances until now, and does not come out, nor can he venture to do so soon. They have looted the furniture of Hájjí Muhammad Bálá the carpets merchant, from broom to door-mat, and have destroyed the house itself with dynamite. Hájjí Muhammad himself they imprisoned, but he was released on payment of a sum of about two thousand *tumáns*, and appears now to have left the city. Possibly he may come to Constantinople. They also arrested Aqá 'Alí the son-in-law of Hájjí Muhammad and the brother of Mirzá Ismá'íl Nawbarí, whom also they released, after they had taken money from him. They have made the houses of the *Sálár* (*-i-Milli*, i.e. Sattár Khán) and the *Sardár* like unto a barren valley. It is said that from Mir Ja'far-i-Khabbáz (the baker) they took some ten thousand *tumáns*, as a condition for making no accusation against him and his sons. They have sent some ten persons as prisoners to Marágha, amongst whom are Hájjí Sayf of Khiyábán and Mullá Ghaffár of Charandáb, which two, they say, have died there, but I know not whether this to be true or not. They have looted all the printing-presses, and though ostensibly they have not interfered with the Colleges, the poor directors of these are afraid, so that there is now no college open except the *Madrasa-i Fuyuzát*, which stands in the place of the old Provincial Assembly, and which is protected by the French Consul and flies the French flag. The *Madrasa-i-Sa'ádat* is occupied by Russian soldiers and Cossacks. The *Bázárcha-i-Khiyábán* and *Bázárcha-i-Nawbar* have been more or less looted, but not to the extent which was reached in the days of the (*Anjuman-i-*) *Islámíyya*.[32] The Deputy-Governor, *Ziyá'u'd-Dawla*, who took refuge in the British Consulate, killed himself with a revolver on the 18th of Safar (A.H. 1330 = February 7, 1912), and he had also written some letters. By command of Hájjí *Shujá'u'd-Dawla* his body was removed from the Consulate and buried in the Cemetery of Sayyid Hamza. May God have mercy upon him! The *Mirátu's-Sultán*, Chief of Police, has fled, and it is not known where he is. Perhaps he is in one of the Consulates.

Yesterday assemblies were held in the Shishkalán Mosque to read the *Qur'an* for the soul of Rahim Khán of Qara-Dágh. Zargham and Arshad have also arrived, and are serving under Hájjí *Shujá'u'd-Dawla*. *Rashídu'l-Mulk* has been made Chief of Police. I have already written about the catching fire of the magazine in the Citadel, in consequence of which, it is said, the Russians sustained heavy losses, and it appears that some hundred soldiers and a number of officers perished. The Citadel itself has been so damaged and destroyed that it would take many years to restore it. They are now sending soldiers into the surrounding country, namely towards Khuy, Salmas and Urmiya.

This suffices for the present. I conclude my letter with this one statement. So firmly have they re-established the order of despotism that even ten years ago such tyranny (as now prevails) was not to be seen.

---

32 *Islamiyya* was the centre of the Reactionaries who called the Constitutionalists "irreligious" and "anti-Islam." [Ed.]

Enclosure 2 in No. 15

Tabriz, 2, Safar, A.H. 1330 (February 12, 1912).

May I be your sacrifice!

I have written twice since this grievous catastrophe, and though these letters, made up of trivialities, told you nothing of the facts, yet I wrote those few words in order that you might see my hand-writing and not be anxious. No doubt they duly reached your fortunate presence. This letter, however, according to what is known, will be enclosed in ...'s[33] envelope, so I will now tell you a little about these grievous events, and thereby make you as sated with the brief span of life offered as by this low world which so favours the vile as I myself am; for I desire you to make this the constant and daily utterance of your tongue: "Come, Death, for Life has (already) slain us!"

Although, indeed, hearing and reading are not like seeing, nor have I such ability or literary skill as would enable me adequately and fitly to describe my evil fortune, while you, moreover, are living (safe and secure) in such a place as Constantinople, and so merely warm your hands at the fire from afar. Yes,

شب تاریک و بیم موج و گردابی چنین هایل
کجا دانند حال ما سبکباران ساحلها؟

"The dark night, the terror of the waves, and so terrible a
    whirlpool:
How should the lightly-laden dwellers on the shore
    realize our condition?"

---

33   i.e., Mir Qasim 'Alí.

Now, then, can you know that during this period of two months we have not slept in peace for one hour? Now can you know how the Russian regular soldiers invade men's houses by night, or what dishonourable deeds they do, what money they take, what men they kill? How should you know what afflictions the *farrashes*, who have hungered for six years and been hidden away in unknown corners, now that their rights are again established and they have found anew the lost laws (of which they were formerly the myrmidons), bring on the unfortunate and heaven-forsaken people of this city?

My object in sending you this letter, however, was that I wished to set down in writing some of these events, and I have strayed from the subject. But this I request of you, that only you yourself will read this letter. On no account show it to one single Musalman, else that same week they will destroy my house and arrest me and cut my throat as though I were a sheep. Know this, that every merchant and merchant's son in Constantinople are all Musalmans and sons of Musalmans, devils and sons of devils, dishonourable and sons of dishonour: on no account trust them: on no account lend an ear to their outward words: they are striped and spotted serpents; and when (may God forbid this thing) the complexion of affairs is changed, then it will become apparent who these people are, how they stand, how savage they are, and how readily they would shed our blood. Only to this I consent, that, apart from yourself, there is no harm in showing my letter to … and …,[34] but trust no one else, or he will immediately, that very day, communicate the content of my letter here, and then it will be a case of "Fetch the donkey

---

34   In the original Persian the first name is Rasul-záda, while the
     second one is left blank [Ed.].

and load up a load of trouble". Then I must take the hands of my children and stretch out my hand to beg from the people of this place, I myself and none other.

So you must never write about these matters in your letters. I have thought of arranging a cypher-code to send to you, so that thence forth we may communicate with one another by means of that cypher, but at present it is absolutely inexpedient, even to the extent of a single word.

Of course, you have heard that this last fighting between the National Volunteers and the Russian regular troops began on the 29th of Dhu'l-Hijja (A.H. 1329 = December 21, 1911). On the morning of that day I was sitting in my house, drinking my tea, which I enjoyed as much as the poison of snakes, when news was brought that the National Volunteers and the police had fallen foul of the Russians and were fighting them. As soon as I heard this news all my limbs became limp: God knows that it was as though I saw these days. It is a well-known proverb: "One fool throws a stone into a well, and afterwards a thousand men of sense cannot get it out." It seems that on the previous night the Russians had seized the Government offices and put their men there, and that in the morning they gave orders that every armed man who was seen should be disarmed. This in spite of the fact that Hájjí *Shujá'u'd-Dawla* was encamped at Básminch, and that the city was in fact besieged. Moreover, the Russians had killed three men in the Chief Police Station by night. So in the morning the Russian soldiers demanded the guns of the National Volunteers and Police, who, knowing nothing of all this, had come forth armed from their houses, and who refused and declined (to surrender their weapons) until a conflict began. In short, the reports of magazine guns and repeating rifles filled the realm of Azarbayjan. It was a veritable Day of Judgment, compared to which, indeed, that promised Day of Judgment of which we have heard and in which we believe would be but an insignificant sample.

Now I do not intend to describe the fighting day by day. This much, however, must be said, that on that day the National Volunteers fought valiantly, and the Russians were compelled to evacuate the Government buildings– and other places which they had occupied, with the exception of the *Bagh-i-Shimal*, where they concentrated. In all other parts of the city not a Russian was to be seen: all of them were assembled in the *Bágh-i Shimál*, where they began to bombard the town with artillery fire.

On the other side the most prudent man of the city, amongst them the late Prince *Ziyá'u'd-Dawla* and others, together with the Members of the Provincial Council, gave the most stringent instructions to the National Volunteers that they should continue on the defensive and refrain from attacking. Consequently, the latter made absolutely no movement against the *Bagh-i-Shimal*.

In short, before the 4th or 5th of the month of Muharram (A.H. 1330 = December 25 and 26, 1911) the more prudent leaders, that is to say, the late *Thiqatu'l-Islám* and Prince *Ziyá'u'd-Dawla*, had visited the British Consulate two or three times, and the Russian Consul-General had also gone there. Finally they agreed that the firing should cease entirely, and that the National Volunteers and Police should all leave their arms at home, and should come forth unarmed, pending a satisfactory arrangement about this matter. So the city resumed a more normal appearance.

In short, be this as it may, on the 5th of Muharram (A.H. 1330= December 26, 1911) they succeeded in persuading the National Volunteers and Police to stop bearing arms, which was strictly forbidden, and rendered anyone infringing this order liable to severe punishments. That same night some of the National Volunteers and Police who were men of some standing and substance, and able to make their some whither, went by night and carried off arms and ammunition from the Citadel, that is to say, cartridges and repeating rifles, as well as all the artillery-horses they could find, and, as would appear, fled towards Khuy.

Next morning when I came out of my house I saw an extraordinary state of things. The position of those same persons who had gone to the British Consulate, and who had done all this, was completely altered, and the people ascribed all their misfortunes to the Constitutionalists; while Hájjí Mírzá Abu'l-Hasan Angaji and some other priests and preachers (*pish-namaz-ha*) were continually inciting the people to certain courses of action. Finally the Husayniyya bands,[35] amongst whom were certain other persons, entered the bazaar, where an extraordinary clamour was raised, all of them crying, "Let us go forth in this guise to Básminch, and bring Hájjí *Shujá'u'd-Dawla* and the *mujtahid* into the city!" So off they went, until, when they reached the door of the *Anjuman* (Provincial Council), these "Chosen flowers of Husayn ibn 'Alí" ascended the roof, tore down the flag which flew over it and reversed it, and then, with cries of religious fervor, continued their way to Básminch, whither, it would seen, Hájjí Mírzá Abu'l-Hasan Aqá Angaji had gone that day.

---

35 i.e., the bands of mourners celebrating the martyrdom of the Imam Husayn, who in the month of Muharram are *en evidence* in all Persian towns.

I must not omit to add that since the National Volunteers were forbidden to attack the *Bágh-i-Shimál*, the Russians daily pumped naphtha on to the peoples' homes, and set fire to them, burning in them all the women and children, others of whom they shot down with bullets, even as you have heard what they did to the Khatá'í family. In short, they utterly consumed with fire half of the Márálán quarter, all the *Kucha-i-Sadr, Charandáb, Maqsudiyya*, and every quarter which was adjacent to the *Bágh-i-Shimál*, and the "whereon a man shall flee from his brother"[36] was seen and made manifest. For fear of their lives, men would flee, leaving in the house their fourteen-year-old daughters or their wives, and these poor unfortunates were either burned or shot down. It is said that the number of those slain in this way reached twelve hundred; but of the National Volunteers perhaps only some twenty perished.

Meanwhile the crowd of some five or six hundred persons, bare-headed and bare-footed and crying "*Ya jaddena.*[37] *Ya Mustáfá!*" continued their way to Básminch; and during the 6th and 7th of Muharram (A.H. 1330 = December 28 and 29, 1911) the Russians molested nobody. On the 8th (December 30), however, they arrested Hájjí 'Alí *Dawa-furush* (the Druggist) and several others. On the 9th (December 31, 1911) they came with a carriage and carried off the *Thiqatu'l-Islám* from his house to the *Bágh-i-Shimál*. On the *'Ashurá* (Muharram 10, A.H. 1330= January 1, 1912) they hanged eight persons in front of the barracks, whose names I shall give below. As soon as these eight were hanged, it was

36 *Koran*, 65, 34.
37 That is to say: "O our ancestor." Both of these exclamations refer to Muhammad. Apparently the crowd was made up of Sayyids who called the prophet their ancestor [Ed.].

as though the heart strings of all were pulled, and a strange terror appeared in the people. On the 11th of Muharram (January 2, 1912), while the bodies of these victims were still hanging on the gallows by the barracks, Hájjí *Shujá'u'd-Dawla* entered the city with his horsemen, while before him went some hundred of those old *farráshes*, with the old cries of "Hence quickly!" "Stop where you are!" "Close your eyes!" After these came six *shátirs* (running footmen) clad in red, just as you have often seen them (in the old despotic days). In front of them was carried a flag consisting of a single piece of red bunting with a piece of blue, just these two colors, but so old and worn as to be a disgrace, and on this flag was written "the Standard of Islam". In such wise did they enter the city, and made their head-quarters in the house of Hájjí *Nizámu'd-Dawla*, where they still are. *Rafi'u'd-Dawla*, on whom the title of *Amir-i-Firuz* has been conferred, has been appointed *Beyler-begi*. The *farráshes*, moreover, wear on their sleeves the badge of the Russian Government in three colors. *Kad-Khudás* (headmen) have also been appointed in every quarter. You can imagine for yourself what sort of *farráshes* and *Kad-Khudás* there are, who all this time have been living on whatever they could borrow, and who now, when the advantage is on their side, and they have recovered the lost "Law", and how they afflict the people!

In short, from the 12th of Muharram (=January 3, 1912) these have controlled the administration. On the one hand, the Russians are busy with their hangings; on the other, Hájjí *Shujá'u'd-Dawla* cuts people's throats, or cleaves them in two and hangs their remains on the walls, or plucks out their eyes, or cuts out their tongues. "The tire woman pulls one way at the disheveled tresses of the Friend, the comb another", that is to say, this is still the case, as the Turks say,

"What escapes the thief is carried off by the soothsayer".[38] A handful of heaven forsaken, unfortunate inhabitants, whose households have been destroyed, who have suffered siege and hunger for six months, are well-nigh crushed between the upper and the nether millstone. Today, one may safely say that on the whole globe of the earth (such is my belief now) during the last thousand years the world has not witnessed any people so oppressed as the people of Tabriz. Assuredly, I can find no word short of "oppressed" to write; for there is none to heed their appeals, neither protection, nor keeper, nor savior. The poor wretches can neither sleep by night nor be at ease by day. You do not know what is going on, or what a day of wrath is ours. So far as I can gather, they arrest a man in the street, simply because he has carried a Varandil rifle[39] for a mere livelihood (and you know well enough that most of these riflemen did not know either what a Constitution is or what Despotism is, but only carried guns to earn a livelihood and a pittance for themselves, so as to give a *grán* a day in payment), and, after many torments, they decide that he shall pay a fine of twenty-five *gráns*.[40] As the poor wretch has nothing, he finally sells his bed-clothes for twenty-five *gráns* to pay the fine; and now his poor little children shiver like aspens in this winter cold. Judge from this or other cases, for you can guess for yourself the derivative forms and can form some idea of what a state of terror exists at Tabriz. From myself so far they have exacted fifty *tumáns*: the *Beyler-begi* took thirty; and my own apprentice Mir 'Alí Akbar, who came and addressed to me you know not what words, another

---

38 The original of this proverb in Azerbaijani Turkish is:

اوغری دن قورتولانی رمّال آپاردی

39 This is the Austrian Werndl rifle, which is a rotating drum-action breech loader invented in 1867 [Ed.]

40 About 10 shillings.

fifteen; and the petty *farrashes* five; so that my expenses in fines come to a *túmán* a day. Hitherto, moreover, no general amnesty has been given. I know not what will happen, or how long the poor citizens will live in this misery and torment. God be praised, however, that for the last week at any rate no one has become arrested.

We have no news from Tehran: no one receives tidings from thence, and it is impossible for anyone to write. O my dear brother, when you walk abroad in the free air or moonlight nights, remember these poor, unlucky wretches! By God, we too are men; we too are human beings; we too are of your race; we too are your fellow-creatures! Let alone humanity, after all we are living creatures; we have wives and children: would that we had a position equal to that of beasts in Europe, for not only do they treat us like animals, but they give us no rest or peace so that at least we might sometimes bear a light load! You do not know what a day of wrath and judgment broods over us. Whoever wears a turban is as a sovereign over the people, and does whatever he pleases, though it be a murder.

بر آن مملکت زار باید گریست
که فریـاد رس را ندانند کیست

"Bitterly must one weep over that land
Where they know not where to look for a protector!"

This handful of unfortunate, heaven-forsaken people are not left in peace for one single minute or instant. Sometimes for fear of the (Russian) soldiers all take refuge on the roofs of their houses and keep crying out like night-watchmen, so that at least the Russian regulars may not approach their wives and families, yet notwithstanding this, the soldiers enter their houses without hesitation, take their money, and break or throw out and destroy all their furniture. The *far-ráshes* (of *Shujá'u'd-Dawla*) are even worse. It needs a long night and midnight oil for me to relate and inform you of all these matters, for to do so by writing is impossible. Should it be possible, please God, I hope to come to Constantinople during the day of the (New Year's) festival, and, if I be still alive, to meet you, and pour out my heart's grief. For the moment, to use your own expression, "Eat one loaf, and give away another in the way of God"; for you are in Constantinople, living in a pure and free air.

The names of those who suffered on the gallows are as follows:

(1) *Thiqatu'l-Islám.* (2) Shaykh Salím. (3) *Sádiqu'l-Mulk.* (4) Hájjí 'Alí *Dáwá-furúsh* (the Druggist). (5) Mirzá Ahmad Suhaylí *Dallál* (the Broker). (6) Mirzá 'Alí of Wayjuya. (7) Mir Karím. (8) Hájjí Qafgází. (9) Mashhadí Ibráhim Qafgáychi Kazim-záda. (10) *Ziyá'u'l-'Ulamá.* (11) Muhammad Khán, nephew of Sattár Khán. (12) The brother of Sattár Khán. (13) Háshim *Harajchi.* (14) Two or three Georgians. (15) Petros (Andressian), head of the gendarmerie of the *Dáshnáksátiyun.*

There are eighteen others whom you do not know, and indeed I myself do not rightly know them. Amongst those put to death by Hájjí *Shujá'u'd-Dawla* are the following: (1) Mirzá Aqá Bálá Khiyábáni. (2) Mashhadí Muhammad, on whose face also were signs of wounds. (3) Mashhadí 'Abbás 'Alí, *Qand-furúsh* (the Grocer). (4) Yúsuf Hukmabád. (5) Mirzá Rahim of Salmas, who sat as one of the members of the Supreme Court of Justice. (6) Ná'ib Muhammad the Carpenter, the son-in-law of Mullá Hamza. There are some others also, whom I do not rightly remember. It appears that up to now they have put to death some sixty persons, besides twelve others who were sent under escort to Marágha.

Mirzá Ismá'íl Nawbarí seems to have fled, as well as others, who are no longer in the city, and who went off with *Amir-i-Hishmat* on that night (of which I have spoken above). Besides these, twelve others have been sent to Marágha. Time passes; else there are many other matters of which I would have spoken.

Mirzá Aqá Bálá Khiyábáni, strangled and then
hanged head-downwards by Samad Khán
Shuja'u'Dawla

No. 16

Three dispatches of April, 1912, concerning the Russian aggressions in Mashhad.

A. (received on April 3, 1912)

As a sequel to their procedures in Tabriz and Rasht, the Russians have now, without any reason, brought troops into Mashhad also, and are seeking some pretext for intervention there, also. Finding none they have incited Yúsuf Khán of Herat, who was sheltering himself in the Russian Consulate, and sundry other persons, to engage in a mischievous and seditious agitation, first outside and then actually within the Holy Sanctuary, on the pretext of a loyal devotion to Muhammad 'Alí Mirzá (the ex-Sháh), and to kill, plunder and shed blood. The mischief brought by these persons became serious, and then the Russian Consul and the Commandant of the Russian troops proceeded to disarm the Government Police, on the pretext that ill-disposed persons were making mischief; and took upon themselves the maintenance of order in the city. The Governor thereupon resigned; and there is no doubt that latterly the mischievous activity of ill-disposed persons resulted in great disorder; but it is well known who brought about this state of things and who instigated the mischief-maker. The Russian Consul and troops have not only actually put the city under martial law, but from the first deliberately and openly created this state of things, in order that the occasion for such interference might be forthcoming.

News has subsequently been received that the Russians have fired upon the Holy Shrine of the Imam Riza, and have imprisoned the Chief Custodian (*Matawalli-báshí*), who is the immediate representative of the Throne, in the Russian Consulate. The Persian Government wished to dismiss *Rukn'd-Dawla*, the Governor of Khurásán, who was at heart with the Russians, but the latter would not consent.

B. (received April 6, 1912).

On Saturday the 10th of Rabi' II (A. H. 1330=March 20, 1912) the Russian troops surrounded the Sanctuary on all sides. Two hours before sunset they began to fire, and attacked on all sides, and at sunset reached the Sanctuary. They entered the building and the Sacred Enclosure, and either put to flight, killed, wounded or imprisoned everyone who was in the Sanctuary or the Sacred Precincts. They also arrested the Chief Custodian (*Matawalli-báshí*), but subsequently dismissed him. The state of the Holy Threshold is actually as follows. All the holy courts and buildings, the sacred dome and the cloisters have been destroyed by cannon-balls; all the doors of the rooms in the court-yard and Mosque are broken; the surrounding doors also are in process of being broken. Since Sunday morning (March 30, 1912) there is no news from within the Sacred Precincts. They (i.e. the Russians) have summoned the treasurer, the librarian, and the head-porter, and urge them to make a list of everything. The whole court-yard and Mosque are full of Russian soldiers and Cossacks. Their horses are tied up in the middle of the court-yard, where the cannons also are left. The chief attendant (of the Shrine) and a number of other persons are under arrest. What has happened to the rest is not yet known.

C. (received April 6, 1912).

In reference to Mashhad the Holy: Monday the
12th of Rabi' II (A.H. 1330 = March 31, 1912)

Since Sunday night until now no one has been able to enter the Holy Precincts and Shrine except Russian soldiers and Cossacks, and the Holy Sanctuary is controlled and besieged by the Russians, who have committed no detail of the variety of disrespect and discourtesy towards that holy place. This afternoon both the Russian and the British Consul-General, accompanied by their respective staffs, went together to inspect the Holy Enclosure, taking with them the Chief Custodian (*Matawalli-Báshi*), and remaining there two hours. It is said that many of the precious things preserved there have been destroyed. They have entirely violated the honour paid for thirteen centuries to a Holy Place which was especially considered by the (Persian) Government. The number of those killed in the Courtyard and Mosque, so far as it is at present known, is from forty to fifty persons, whose bodies have been found.

No. 17

Translation of a ninth letter, dated April 22, 1912, from the writer of Nos. 3, 4, 6, 7, 9, 10, 11 and 14.

In these latter days the conjectures of the pessimists about the affairs of Persia have proved correct and near the truth, and it is evident that the Russians will at no time and on no occasion relax or intermit their exactions and demands for more, even after Persia has shown every kind of conciliation and made every sort of sacrifice. Not a day passes but some calamity worse than the last and newer than the newest befalls this unhappy country. Worse, more grievous and harder to be borne than all the others is this latest calamity which they have brought in the Imam Riza's own Holy Mashhad or the Sanctuary and dome of his Shrine, the grievousness of which matter transcends the powers of my expression and the capacity of my utterance. Nor, indeed, can I find any adequate cause or reason for these deeds, unless it be that they hope to break the last strands of Persian patience and endurance, drive them out of the circle of prudence and self-restraint, and madden them beyond control, so as to supply the materials for a general war with themselves in Persia, on the pretext of which they may invade the country, and, to bring it to an end, push forward into the interior, centre and south of Persia. For if the Persians rise against the Russians, and attempt to grapple with them, it is evident that the Russians, fighting their way, will reach, for example, Qazwin. Then the people of Hamadan will attack them, and a conflict will take place, and they will push on to Qazwin to silence them and take revenge on them. Then will come the people of Qum and Iraq, with whom also they will contend, until they reach Qum. Afterwards, by the same procedure, they will push onwards to Kashan, Isfahan and Yazd, that is to say to those places where the British Government has hitherto prevented them from sending troops. But when, as they themselves say, Russian blood has been shed in any land, they will be compelled to advance their troops.

And though I am not *au courant* of these high political affairs, it appears to me that on no occasion in the affairs of Persia, or even in one single affair, has British policy been able to hold its own against Russian policy; as is clearly seen in pursuing the most recent *Blue Book* in the cases of the Stokes' affair and the deposed Sháh, in both of which the Russians finally carried their point and attained their object. So now, in the case of the *Sáláru'd-Dawla*, the Russians are playing a great role, so that both the Persian and the British Governments, from their own point of view, have yielded to many, if not all, of the Russian demands, and have shown every sort of complaisance, as, for example, in the dismissal of Shuster, the acceptance of the (Anglo-Russian) Agreement of 1907 and all the other demands of the last Note of the two Governments; while all that was done in return was apparently done merely to deceive English and Persian public opinion, to wit, the removal of the mischief of Muhammad 'Alí Mirzá (the ex-Sháh), when, after all this talk and discussion, it became apparent that the Russians had merely substituted for him the *Sáláru'd-Dawla*; that is to say, when they found Muhammad 'Alí incapable of forwarding their affairs and promoting their armies, and the *Sáláru'd-Dawla* at once more capable, more cruel, and more bloodthirsty, they came to terms with him, and, ostensibly for the sake of Persia, and in response to the urgent demands of the British Government and its insistence on the non-acceptance of

Muhammad 'Alí, brought him back with an adequate allowance so that he might await an opportunity to re-enter Persia. Moreover, since Muhammad 'Alí Mirzá was near the Russian frontier, they had no excuse for not putting a stop to his advance, but the *Sáláru'd-Dawla* has been allowed to establish himself near the Turkish frontier, so that they may excuse themselves for not interfering with him on the pretext that the sending of an expedition to Kirmánsháh and these parts would arouse fears and objections on the part of the Turks. So they will now accomplish the objects which they intended to effect through Muhammad 'Alí Mirzá by means of the infamous *Sáláru'd-Dawla*. In short, what has been is, and all these blows have befallen the independence of Persia, and no change has been effected in its internal condition or in the continuance of the former tricks and intrigues. Affairs are as they were: Persia gets all the blows, England is cheated, and Russia eats the sweets, and there is the end of the matter.

The matter which very greatly and especially grieves and distresses me is that latterly, after many years of trouble and gradual development, as a result of the efforts of many persons, Public Instruction in Persia generally and in Tabriz especially, the new schools had made great advances, and were on the point of producing great results. Thus some 25 primary and secondary schools on the new model were at work in which more than three thousand children were pursuing their studies. Notable amongst these was the *Madrasa-i-Sa'ádat*, which had made great progress in learning, and counted some 500 pupils. After the recent catastrophe at Tabriz, and the invasion of the Russians and Samad Khán, all these schools and colleges were closed and abandoned, or changed to schools of the old model in connection with the mosques (which are totally devoid of worth), and the light of knowledge was totally extinguished, while the afore mentioned *Madrasa-i-Sa'ádat*, was destroyed at the hand, of the Russian soldiers and occupied by them, so that they are still in occupation of it, and during the winter burned the school desks and forms for fuel in place of fire-wood. Besides this, after these events, the Russians, in addition to their former Government College which they had in Tabriz, and which enjoyed no sort of popularity, have established a free school entitled "the Orphans College", whereby they seek to profit by the closing of the National Schools to further propagate their language and their influence.

Latterly, when news of Muhammad 'Alí Mirzá's intention to return from Persia, and of the representations of the Russian and British Governments to him reached Tabriz, the people inwardly rejoiced, but outwardly they dared not breathe a word. Samad Khán *Shujá'u'd-Dawla*, incited by the Russians, compelled the townsfolk, the chief citizens, merchants and guilds, to assemble and sign a document stating that they desired Muhammad 'Alí Sháh, and furthermore compelled them to go to the telegraph office and enter into telegraphic communications with Mashhad and other towns on this subject, so that they might re-echo the demand for the restoration of Muhammad 'Alí to the throne. And so, behold, it appears that those very provinces which were the most important centres of Constitutionalism in Persia, such as Tabriz and Mashhad, have by the indirect methods of Russian compulsion been made to appear centres of Reaction, striving to compass the restoration of the ex-Sháh. Indeed, the truth is that one is much distressed, and seeks deliverance from the world and its cruel and hypocritical people, involuntarily reciting this quatrain of 'Umar Khayyám:

در دايـــــــرهٔ وجود ديـــــر آمده ايم   وز پايهٔ بر ترين به زير آمده ايم
چون عمر نه بر مراد ما می گذرد   ايکاش سرآمدی که سير آمده ايم

We came too late into the circle of existence,
And came down from the highest rank;
Since life passes not according to our aspirations
O would that it would come to an end,
  for we have had enough of it! [41]

Seyyed Hasan Ibn Taqi (Taqí-záda)
One of the deputies of Tabriz, in exile in Istanbul, who either
wrote or was the intermediary of the letters to Browne.

41 Here Browne has omitted Taqí-zadah's comments about the
    1907 agreement and dismissal of Shuster. He also says that
    the removal of Muhammad 'Alí Sháh was in reality a window
    dressing. He is replaced by *Salár 'u-Dawla* who is even worse
    and obeys what the Russians say.[Ed.]

No. 18[42]

Translation of a tenth letter, dated July 16, 1912, from the writer of Nos. 3, 4, 6, 7, 9, 10, 11, 14 and 17.

One of my Tabriz friends has succeeded in obtaining possession of many documents concerning the intrigues, and tricks of the Russians, and their connection with Samad Khán *Shujá'u'd-Dawla*, who is now in actual control of Tabriz, unfortunately most of these documents, which he hid when he fled from Tabriz, are not at present in his hands; but one letter of Samad Khán's, werein mention is made of the (Russian) Consul's promptings, was photographed in Tabriz. Of this photograph only one copy was in this man's possession here. This I took, and now send it enclosed to you: perhaps it may be of some use. The above-mentioned friend of mine asserts that he also possesses a copy of a letter to Samad Khán from the Russian Consul himself, from whom, during the siege of Tabriz, news was daily sent about what was happening at Tehran and elsewhere, about the state or Muhammad 'Alí Mirzá's affairs and those of his followers, and about the situation of the Central Government and the Constitutional Army, as well as the necessary instructions, to Samad Khán *Shujá'u'd-Dawla* at Básminch, where his army was encamped, and which is a village situated at a distance of two parasangs from Tabriz. In particular, a constant interchange of messages was maintained between the villages of Ni'mat-ábad, where is the summer residence of the Russian

---

42 The first paragraph of this letter is also omitted where Taqí-zadah apologizes for not being able to send the final copy of *The Press and Poetry*, which Browne already has promised to publish. [Ed.]

Consul, and Básminch, which is distant there from, only half a parasang or less; and it is said that Samad Khán collected and deposited his goods, spoils, plunder and other acquisitions at Ni'mat-ábad, which is under Russian protection.

Now as regards this letter, the photograph of which you will read, it was written last year by Samad Khán of Marágha *Shujá'u'd-Dawla*, the besieger of Tabriz to a certain Sayyid Ahmad Khán, who was the agent and secret spy of Muhammad 'Alí Mirzá in Tabriz. This man was appointed by the latter from Europe, when he returned from Europe to Astarábád, to proceed to Tabriz. He had been one of the intimate associates of the ex-Sháh, and his function in Tabriz was to be his secret representative and the intermediary between him and the Reactionaries, to work for the Reaction, and to serve as a channel of intercommunication between Samad Khán and Muhammad 'Alí. He was subsequently arrested by the Constitutionalists. Zakaríyya, the Chief of the Merchants (*Tajir-báshi*), who is mentioned in the letter, was one of the *employés* of the Russian Consul at Tabriz, whom they (the Russians) entitle "Agent", and the Persians *Tajir-báshi*; for every Foreign State has a *Tajir-báshi*, who is in the employment of the Consulate. Hájjí Faraj the Money-changer (*sarráf*) is also a well-known Russian subject, and the most important of those merchants who claim Russian nationality. He has constant and close relations with the Russian Consulate, and most of the business of the Russians in Tabriz is carried out by him.

Two or three weeks ago, in response to the requests of my friends in Paris, I wrote a biography of the late *Thiqatu'l-Islám*, so far as I was acquainted with the particulars of his life, for the *Revue du Monde Musulman*, published in Paris, with a photograph of him, was, to appear in the last number of that periodical. I do not know whether you have seen it or not.

The Russians are publishing in Tabriz, by the agency of a certain Armenian, a Persian newspaper entitled *Fikr* ("Thought"), which praises the actions of the Russians in Persia and attacks the Constitution. It is well known that they secretly contribute two hundred *túmáns* (£. 40) a month towards its expenses. If you would like copies of it, I will forward them.

Enclosure in No. 18

(Translation of undated letter from *Shujá'u'd-Dawla*

to Sayyid Ahmad Khán referred to above.)

To His Honourable Excellency Aqá Sayyid Ahmad Khán.

Your letter has arrived: also the two copies of the proclamation which you sent. But according to the accounts written by Hájjí Faraj Aqá the Money-changer, Aqá Zakaríyya *Tajir-bashi*, and the (Russian) Consul, *Sáláru'd-Dawla* has sustained a severe defeat, and has fallen back on Hamadan, while His Imperial Majesty (Muhammad 'Alí) with twelve of his followers, is staying in the Russian Consulate at Astarábád. I have written to you about this, but do not know whether my letter has reached you or not. Today, Friday, I am writing you this letter. In whatever way and by whatever means you must represent to His August Majesty that, somehow and in some manner, he must assuredly, a thousand times assuredly, convey himself to Ardabíl by way of Astará, which is in our own hands, and whose Governor is appointed by me. If

His Majesty comes, he is ready. It is quite safe, I guarantee. Telegraph in whatever way is possible: perhaps he can come to Astárá, or by way of the Bridge of Khudá-áfarin. All the Sháhsevens and...[43] the Governor of Ardabíl *Arfa'u's-Sultán*, who was at Marágha (are ready). Assuredly, a thousand times assuredly, let his Majesty come to Azarbayjan, else it will all be up; as, indeed, you yourself know very well. What more need I write that you should be informed?

---

43 In the original letter there is "Vaminan" with a question mark. It seems that the transcriber did not understand it. Browne has dropped the word. Perhaps it just means *aminan* or trusted persons, confidantes [Ed.].

No. 19

Translation of eleventh letter, dated August 29, 1912, from the writer of Nos. 3, 4, 6, 7, 9, 10, 11, 14, 17 and 18.

I was much affected by the perusal of the White Book,[44] especially by the distortion of the facts about Tabriz and the disregard of all human mercy and magnanimity revealed by it. The truth is that neither the Russian cruelties, nor the aggressions of their officers and soldiers, nor the Chingiz-like savagery of Samad Khán *Shujá'u'd-Dawla* is so painful to us as the suppressions and concealments of the truth on the part of the British Consul, and his attempts to keep hidden from the civilized world the facts of the case, and to represent as the aggressors in Tabriz the unlucky Persians.

When I read in the White Book that he denied the killing of women and children by the Russian troops in Tabriz, my heart was kindled with such fire as I cannot describe; for if our people were not poor, helpless, ignorant and lacking in power, and if they were but acquainted with the principles of literary defense in (influencing) European public opinion, they would certainly have collected and recorded the names of the women and children killed, whose numbers, without doubt, were considerable. But their spiritual sufferings exceed even their material wrongs.

Notwithstanding this, in order to prove the incorrectness of the categorical denials of Mr. Shipley, who is *plus royaliste que le roi*, I shall mention several of the women and children slain by the Russian Cossacks, and I assure you on my word

---

44   "Persia. No 5(1912)" : (Cd. 6264).

of honour that these things happened as I relate them, and that all the people of Tabriz without exception know them.

First there is the case of the family and household of Hájjí 'Alí Khatá'í, son of the late Hájjí Asadu'lláh Khatá'í, a harmless, inoffensive, quiet man, somewhat ailing in health, who had taken no part in politics, and had nothing to do with the political activities either of Constitutionalists, or Reactionaries. He was one of the most respected merchants of Tabriz, very harmless, quiet and impartial, and owned a very fine and beautiful house, proverbial in Tabriz for its beauty, so that there were perhaps not two other houses in the city equal to it. It was situated near the *Bagh-i-Shimal* (North Garden), where the Russian camp is now situated.

In the recent Catastrophe of the latter days of December, 1911 (beginning of Muharram, A.H. 1330) the savage Russian Cossacks, without any cause or reason, rushed like madmen on the houses and made a general massacre. His house was one of those attacked, and, since the unfortunate inmates could find no way of escape, the Russian soldiers made a slaughter of nine members of the household, to wit the master of the house, his wife (who was a bride, and had only been married recently), his servant, and a little child six years of age who was his cousin (and two others). They then destroyed the home and took possession of it, and all these houses, that of Hájjí Khatá'í and those of his brothers, cousins and the rest of his kinsmen, all of which were adjacent to one another are still occupied by the Cossacks, who have not evacuated them, while the survivors are fugitives and vagabonds. Of the family of Hájjí 'Alí Khatá'í himself, only one daughter survives; she was wounded in the leg, and they have now amputated her leg and replaced it by a wooden one. The tragedy of this family is a very sad one, and many details might be added, but it is necessary to write them all down. Amongst other women killed were the family, house-hold and children of the brother of Hájjí Muhammad 'Alí Khán of Qarabágh, *Tájir-báshi* (Chief of the Merchants), whom the Russians slew together with his wife and family; and there were also many women killed in houses in the Márálán, Ahráb, and other quarters.

But as for the barbarities perpetrated by Samad Khán *Shujá'u'd-Dawla* (who is the executioner of the Russians, by whom he was brought into Tabriz and made Governor, and who has hoisted the Russian flag over his house, and whose myrmidons, attendants and officers wear on their sleeves the Russian arms, namely the eagle), these are such that not one tenth of them can have come to your knowledge. Apart from such daily cruelties as the mutilation of limbs, the cutting off of ears, hands and feet, and the hanging of Liberals, which happens every few days, and of which, I imagine, no rumour any longer reaches the European Press, save when a tele-gram is sent to announce the death of some person of note. Early in the month of Rajab last (June- July, 1912), when, in consequence of the movements of the Sháhseven tribesmen against the Russians and their approach to Tabriz, there was some talk and stir amongst the townsfolk, suddenly one day Samad Khán, simply to inspire fresh terror, ordered more arrests of Constitutionalists and Liberals, of whom in one day they arrested nearly a hundred, of whom he executed and put to death nearly seventy with all sorts of torments, tortures and mutilations. Of three or four of these he caused the mouths to be sewn up with needles and thread like bags or stuff; some he hamstrung; two he "haltered", that is to say, pierced their noses, put a rope through the puncture, and gave it into the hands of his *fararashes,* who led the victims round the bazaars; of others he amputated the hands or cut off two fingers; of most he cut off the ears at the roots. One, Hájjí Ibrahim Khalil by name, a merchant, because he had ventured to say, "the Constitution will return", he bastinadoed on the feet with a thousand blows, and, when he was at the point of death, exiled him to Marágha and there imprisoned him. Then there was Taqí Khán, known as *Yúz-báshi* (Captain), who was one of the chief National Volunteers and principal defenders of Tabriz four years ago, and who, after the arrival of Samad Khán in Tabriz, took refuge in the Turkish Consulate, but latterly, having regard to the apparent return of security, came out. He also was put to death, and afterwards his belly was slit open and his body was hanged on a ladder in the street, and when his bowels protruded and hung down to the ground, they tied them up with string to his belly, so that they should not fall out. So, likewise, they recently arrested one of the chief National Volunteers named Muhammad Dá'í and hanged him. When they hanged him, the rope broke and he fell; again they hanged him, and again he fell; and so again a third time, so that it was not until the fourth time that he was strangled.

This same Samad Khán it was who, on his first arrival in Tabriz, mutilated Mirzá Mahmúd of Salmas, one of the *'ulamá* of Urmiya, in the following manner. First, he cut out his tongue; then, while he was still alive, he plucked out his eyes; then he cut off his hands and feet, and finally killed him.

Besides these casual occurrences, which are repeated every few days, Samad Khán himself has invented an extraordinary method of punishment, which is inflicted almost daily without intermission. This is as follows. Political offenders are brought before him, stripped naked, and thrown into a large tank full of water, round which are stationed *farrashes* and executioners, each holding in his hand a long stick. These begin to strike the unfortunate victim on the head, and he, to avoid the blows, ducks his head under the water. When, nearly drowned, he again raises his head, they at once strike it again with their sticks, so that now he ducks his head under the water to avoid the cruel blows, and again for fear of drowning raises it again, until the blood pours from his head, and finally he dies. This punishment is generally inflicted until the victim is at the point of death, and sometimes he is actually killed; even as Samad Khán slew in this manner the "Saint of Maragha" (*Mugaddas-i Marágha*), one of the most valiant champions of Constitutionalism in that town, in the bitter cold of the winter of A.H. 1326 (= A.D. 1908-9).

It is this same murderous ruffian whom the British Consul at Tabriz applauds and glorifies. Latterly he has forcibly assembled the people of Tabriz in the mosques and telegraph-office to oppose the coming of the *Sipahdár* to Tabriz, while his followers make speeches in the mosques against the *Sipahdár* and the Constitution and in praise of the Russians, until finally he compelled the people to petition the Russian Consul, who subsequently sent his servant to the Chief Mosque to inform them that the *Sipahdár* was coming, but that Samad Khán would remain, and that no one would suffer any trouble; whereupon the people dispersed.

This same Samad Khán has also started a newspaper entitled *Fikr* ("Thought"), which openly praises the Russians and their troops. The editor of this paper is an Armenian reactionary, and the hearts of the people of Tabriz, so many of whom have sacrificed so much for their country and their Constitution, bleed on account of what he writes, though they dare not utter a word. Of Samad Khán they entertain not a particle of fear, and, were it not for the Russians, they would turn him out in a single day, nay, in two or three hours, even if this involved the loss of several hundred lives; but they fear the Russians, who pity neither small nor great, and who, without any exaggeration, massacred more than a hundred women, children, and innocent persons last Muharram.

In its last issue this newspaper, the *Fikr*, wrote as follows: "By Divine Favour and the regards of His Holiness the Proof (i.e. the expected Imam Mahdi) (may God hasten his glad Advent!) the Emperor of the resplendent State of Russia is clement and kind in regard to us people, while his ever-victorious troops are revivifying, Islam."

Consider, now, when the Musulman inhabitants of Tabriz read these words, yet can do nothing, how deeply their sentiments are wounded, seeing how openly their faith and religion are slighted, and how their patriotic sentiments are mocked, and that such words should be printed and published in their own language, their own city, and their own country!

A number of fresh fugitives from Persia have latterly come to Constantinople, such as Mírzá Mahmúd Khán Ashraf-zada, formerly editor of the newspaper *Farwardin* at Urmiya, who was arrested by the Russian Consul and tormented with whips and scourges; a full account of which event I have already sent you from the *Terjumán-i-Haqíqat*.[45] Amongst them is also Mírzá Muhammad 'Alí Khán's brother, who for nine whole months was concealed and hidden in a dark cellar and in constant danger, and about whom

---

45 The translation of this extract from the Turkish newspaper in question will be found in No.8 *supra*.

we were very anxious. Finally, he escaped in disguise, and reached Constantinople the day before yesterday. There are now some hundred persons or more here (in Constantinople), of whom ten or a dozen were amongst the leaders (of the Constitutionalists), of the Liberals of Tabriz, Khuy, Salmas, Urmiya and Rasht ...We are afraid about Sazanoff's journey to London....

No. 20

Translation of a twelfth letter, dated September 29, 1912, from the writer of Nos. 3, 4, 6, 7, 9, 10, 11, 14, 17, 18 and 19.

You asked for an account of the circumstances and characters of the Tabriz martyrs. So far as was in my power I have written down what I could, together with a brief statement of other matters connected with Tabriz, and this I send enclosed herewith. During the months of February, March and April of this year I wrote several detailed explanatory letters about the state of affairs at Tabriz and Rasht to (Muhammad Khán of Qazwin) in Paris, and I asked him to forward copies to you; for in those letters many particulars were given in detail, especially concerning the martyrs of Tabriz, etc. If, therefore, these have reached you, it was well that you should refer to them as well as to the account which I now send, for they may perhaps contain further details. If, however, they have not reached you, I especially beg you to ask for copies of them from (Muhammad Khán) so that he may send them to you in their entirety, for they were written nearer the time, and are certainly more complete... I send you also by this post a copy of the (Turkish) monthly magazine entitled *Resmli Kitab* ("the Illustrated"), together with a copy of the *Sabilu'r-Reshád* ("the Road of Right Direction"), a religious magazine devoted to the Pan-Islamic idea; and I intend also to obtain and send to you some photographs of the martyrs which have not yet reached London.

As regards the destiny of Persia, great anxiety prevails to-day as to what the Balmoral[46] conference will yield; and as the newspapers here write nothing on the subject, this anxiety [may not] be dispelled. I therefore especially beg you, if it be possible; to be good enough to send me some cuttings from the (English) newspapers on this subject, so that we may not remain ignorant of the course of events. I hear that some man of Tabriz writing mischievous articles to the paper entitled *The Near East* under the signature of "Firuz Khán." I suspect that this person is not really Persian at all, but is either a Russian or Russian Armenian, or something of the sort. At all events, if any further mischievous things of this kind should appear in the papers there, I am ready to answer them fully, and to write such answers to the English newspapers, so that they may translate and publish them, on condition that I am enabled to see the original of the mischievous article. I have not seen "Firuz Khán's" article, but have only heard of it.

I saw in Mr. Turner's letter in the *Manchester Guardian* that he wrote "if the *fidá'ís* had a capable captain or leader, they would have captured the Russian Consulate."[47] I deem it necessary to remark that the National Volunteers never had any wish to interfere with the Consulate in question, nor did the idea of taking possession of it ever pass through their minds, else they could have taken it in the course of a few hours, since the Russian Consulate was separated from

---

46 Balmoral talks were between Sir Edward Grey and the Russian foreign secretary, Sazanov in September 1912. [Ed.]

47 This was a letter (dated September 6, 1912) by George Douglas Turner, of the Young Men's Christian Association, who had resided in India and traveled through Persia in July and August of 1912. Browne refers to him later on in the book. See Bonakdarian, p. 341.[Ed.]

the Russian camp. On the contrary, the National Volunteers protected the Russian Consulate.

Since the beginning of this year and subsequently to the catastrophe, a number of Constitutionalists have taken refuge in the Turkish Consulate, where hitherto they have remained unmolested. After the *Sipahdár* reached Tabriz, it seems to have been agreed that they should be exiled from the country.

Enclosure in the above letter.

The following biographical notices follow the photographs which I published in the pamphlet entitled "The Reign of Terror in Tabriz" in October, 1912. This pamphlet, which comprised "photographs and a brief narrative of the events of December, 1911, and January, 1912", was printed and published by Messrs. Taylor, Garnett, Evens and Co. of Manchester, and is sold by them for sixpence. The original, photographs were, for purposes of reference, lettered A, B, C, etc., and these references are here made use of by the writer of the subjoined biographies.

(A)

1.   Mirzá 'Alí Nátiq (the Orator), known as Wayjuya'í, Warjli, or Warjilú. The different readings of the last word arise from the fact that on one photograph he is described by his vocation, for he was a notable orator, and on the other by the name of the quarter of the city in which he dwelt, which was Wayjuya or Warji, one of the well-known quarters of Tabriz, situated on the western side of the town, as you may

see in the map of "Tabriz during the Revolution" published in your own book. And as the names of the different quarters in the speech of the Turkish-speaking townspeople differ from the forms employed in Persian writing, such confusion must needs arise not infrequently. Thus the *Khiyábán* quarter becomes in the speech of the townsfolk *Khiyáván*; *Hukmábád* becomes *Hukmávár*; the *Devechi* (Camel-men's) quarter sometimes appears in writing as *Shuturbán*; *Mihád-mahin* is called by the people of Tabriz *Miyár-miyár*, and only in writing is the correct form used. And the same is the case with the quarter of *Wayjuya*, which we are now discussing, which is thus written and pronounced in Persian, but is actually pronounced by the people of the city as *Warji*, while those persons who inhabit it or are concerned with it are called *Warjli* or *Warjlú* in Ázarbáyjáni Turkish, though officially in writing its name appears as *Wayjuya*. This practice of calling people after the different quarters of Tabriz (which they inhabit) is very common in Tabriz, so that even in the National Assembly some of the Tabriz deputies were so known, as, for example, "Nawbari," Aqá-yi-Khiyabani, etc.

This Mírzá 'Alí the martyr was about forty years of age, and was one of the leading speakers of Tabriz, if not unique in this capacity. He was a very honest, high-principled and self-sacrificing patriot and Constitutionalist, and enjoyed great influence and popularity amongst the people. He was the son of one of the leading *'ulamá* and *mujtahids* of Tabriz, and was himself one of the *'ulamá* of the second class and a preacher. He spent his early days and the beginning of his life in such studies as are necessary to become a *mullá*, and subsequently become a preacher. From the first appearance of the Constitution he espoused this cause, in which he made great efforts, and during these last six years he devoted himself entirely to this. Night and day he strove zealously to glorify and proclaim the Constitution, and was firm and constant alike in weal and woe, in times of tranquility and revolution. During the Second Period of the Constitution he was elected a Member of the Municipal Council. During the First Constitutional Period, in consequence of his devoted efforts, he became a special object of enmity to Reactionaries like Mír Háshim, Hájjí Mírzá Hasan, etc., who were the founders of the mischievous *Anjuman-i-Islamiyya*, and suffered many troubles at their hands. During the last two or three years he was the incomparable orator of Tabriz and the preacher of Constitutionalism. One of the Liberals of Tabriz who was his devoted friend and very intimate with him relates that on the occasion of his last meeting with him, early in that Muharram (begun on December 22, 1911), while the fighting with the Russians was actually in progress, Mirzá 'Alí said, "I have a feeling that they will certainly kill me, but this causes me no anxiety except that, as I have no worldly wealth, I am anxious as to the future of my little children." It is said that after his martyrdom his little children actually begged and asked for alms in the streets in the extreme of poverty and penury. He had three or four little children, both girls and boys, who are now orphans. Our recently arrived comrade, who was in hiding in a cellar for more than eight months, and who recently succeeded in escaping and reaching this place, was also a friend of the late Mirzá 'Alí. He says that the fugitive Liberals in hiding at Tabriz succeeded with the utmost difficulty in collecting some thirty *túmáns* (£6) in the course of six months to give to his family and children; for it was not possible to keep them openly. Mirzá 'Alí the Martyr was not a fighting man, and took absolutely no part in the war with the Russians.

His only crime was his abounding patriotism and his extraordinary enthusiasm and zeal, on account of which the Russians seized him and hanged him at *Qúm Bághí*, a great fortress to the North-West of the town, which belonged to one of the well-known *'ulamá* and sayyids. All this quarter and neighbourhood was utterly destroyed by the Russians, who seized and took possession of it. The late Mirzá 'Alí was in politics a Democrat, and a most sincere, earnest and disinterested Constitutionalist and patriot. He was also a very religious and pious man, and, as some of the other prisoners relate, used to read the *Qur'an* in Samad Khán's prison. I knew him personally, and we were friends.

2.   Hájjí Samad *Khayyát* (the Tailor). He was one of the National Volunteers of the *Wayjuya* and *Rástakúcha* quarters, and was about forty-five years of age. In the Tabriz Revolution of A.H. 1326 (= A.D. 1908-9) and the uprising of Sattár Khán, he was one of the leaders of the National Volunteers, and rendered good service; but after the restoration of the Constitution, during these last three years, he took no part in politics, nor fought, nor bore arms, nor continued to serve as a volunteer, but busied himself with his own trade, which was that of a tailor, and generally supplied uniforms to the Government. The accursed Samad Khán arrested him and handed him over to the Russians, who hanged him at *Qúm Bághí*.

3.   Mashhadí Hájjí Khán of *Wayjuya*.

The variants in his name arise from the fact that he was originally a shop-keeper and artisan, and was then known as "Mashhadí Hájjí." After the Revolution, when he entered the

Government service, he was, as is customary, entitled "Hájjí Khán," or "Mashhadí Hájjí Khán." The title of "Qafqází" (the Caucasian) is, however, incorrect, for he was of Persian origin and a native of Tabriz, but he was (for a time) in business at Baku, and returned to Persia in the early days of the Constitution. He subsequently enlisted in the National Volunteers. Hence he is sometimes known by the title of "Qafqází." And this is a general observation of some importance which it is necessary to bear in mind; namely, that during the days of the Revolution in Tabriz, in the time of Muhammad 'Alí Mirzá, a great number of the National Volunteers who were with Sattár Khán were known as "Qafqází," for the reason that they were Persians who had lived in the Caucasus, that is to say, persons who, in pursuit of their livelihood, went to and fro every year to Tiflis, Baku, and other parts of the Caucasus. And since the uniforms worn by these differed slightly from those worn by the other local volunteers of Tabriz, and resembled in style the Caucasian garb, they became commonly and popularly known by the name of "Qafqází," so as to distinguish them from the other National Volunteers. Subsequently many other persons, who had never seen the Caucasus or left Tabriz, gradually entered this regiment, were clothed in the same style and garb as the others, and became known as "the Caucasian Volunteers" collectively, and by such names as "Muhammad-i-Qafqází," "Ahmad-i-Qafqází," "Hasan-i-Qafqází," etc., individually, though in reality they were Persians, not Caucasians. In the régiment of Musulman "Caucasian" Volunteers who accompanied Sattár Khán, not one in a hundred was actually a native of the Caucasus. Indeed, I personally knew no more than two who were so; but there were some Caucasian Georgians, whose number may have reached some forty-two, of whom at the end of the

Revolution only nine survived. These, however, were not called "Caucasian Volunteers" but "Georgian Volunteers." My object (in this long digression) is (to point out) that this nomenclature is responsible for a serious and common error, which grave error has been noticed in all publications in Europe, both books and articles, etc., so that even *the Times* has on several occasions spoken of these "Caucasian" Volunteers as Russian subjects, and the correspondents of other European newspapers have also occasionally fallen into this error, hearing from the common people such expressions as "Caucasian volunteers," "So-and-so the Caucasian," and the like. In Tabriz, however, this matter is as clear as the sun, so that sometimes the word "Caucasian" is actually used in the place and sense of "Volunteer." This is also the reason why this title of "Caucasian" continued to be applied after the Revolution to the Volunteers of that regiment or division, and it is likely enough that it may give rise to an historical error on the part of future historians. At all events, the late Mashhadí Hájjí was a native of Tabriz and a Persian subject, who belonged to the "Caucasian regiment" of the National Volunteers in the Revolution of A.H. 1326 (= A.D. 1908-9), just as the other "Caucasian" Volunteers were also Persian subjects.

The late Mashhadí Hájjí was about thirty-five years of age, and was one of the leading Volunteers during the Revolution of A.H. 1326. After the Revolution he became a Commissioner of Police or *Kad-Khudá* of the quarter. Formerly he had a business in Baku, where I myself saw him in A.H. 1324 (= A.D. 1906) in the reign of Muzaffaru'd-Din Sháh, before the proclamation of the Constitution, when I was traveling to Tehran. He was then in business as a shopkeeper, and was a member of the party of "Social Democrats

Working for Persia" (*Ijtimá'iyyún-i-'ammiyún-i-mujáhid-i-Irán*) at Baku. He was a very brave and zealous man. In the recent Catastrophe, that is to say, the Russian aggressions in the early days of Muharram (A.H. 1330 – end of December, 1911) he resisted the Russians and fought with them, and it is known that while he was left alone after his comrades had been scattered or killed, he, alone and unaided, slew four of the Russian soldiers. His character cannot be wholly approved, but he was relatively good and honest. They say that after his death nothing was found in his house except a little flour and a few other trifling possessions, so that it would appear that he was poor.

4.   Mashhadí Shakúr Kharrází, uncle of the above-mentioned Mashhadí Hájjí. The variant in his name arises from the fact that in the common speech they also pronounce Shakúr as Shakur, but the name "Karbalá'i Shafi", (written on one of the original photographs) is quite incorrect, and there was no one of this name. He was about forty-five years of age, and was a harmless tradesman who took no part in politics, was no fighter and took no part in the war, and had committed no fault nor taken any part in public affairs. Neither was he in any way notable, nor much regarded or considered, and it does not appear on what ground they put him to death. He was simply a quiet, peaceable tradesman, who was a patriot, a Constitutionalist, and in politics a Democrat.

(B)

1.   Hasan, son of Karbalá'í 'Alí "Monsieur" and brother of Qadír (No.7). This lad and his brother were both the sons

of 'Alí "Monsieur". As to the variant in the name, "Mirzá 'Alí of Wayjuya" is incorrect. "Monsieur-zada" is correct as regards the sense, that is to say "the son of 'Alí "Monsieur", but they were not so called.

The late Karbalá'i 'Alí, known as "Monsieur", was one of the old Liberals and leaders of the earlier Constitutionalists. He lived for some time at Constantinople, and afterwards came to Tabriz and started a china-manufactory, for his eldest son Hájjí had learned this craft, together with two other Persian boys, in the School of China-work founded by Sultán 'Abdu'l-Hamíd at Yildiz in Constantinople. His factory flourished for a long time at Tabriz, but after the establishment of the Constitution Karbalá'i 'Alí "Monsieur" because [he was] one of the heroes of the Constitution, and during the days of the Revolution he was Chief and Elder of the National Volunteers of Tabriz, whose Director and Guide he became in spite of the fact that he never bore arms and was not a fighting man. He enjoyed a great influence amongst them, and ostensibly headed the third place after Sattár Khán and Bagir Khán in authority. He was especially obnoxious to the Russians. He was very brave and devoted, and a most capable administrator and organizer, and is to be reckoned one of the chief organizers of the Revolution in Azarbayjan. The full and detailed story of his life and doings would occupy much space. He died in A.H. 1328 (A.D. 1910) leaving four sons, of whom the eldest, named Hájjí (afterwards Hájjí Khán) was one of the leading National Volunteers and principal adjutants of Sattár Khán. He is about twenty-five or twenty-eight years of age, and was subsequently made *Kad-Khudá*, or Commissioner, of the Nawbar quarter. In this recent catastrophe he fled from Tabriz with other National Volunteers and came to Constantinople. Three or four months ago he went to Tehran, but no sooner did he arrive there than the Russians notified the Persian Government, which arrested and imprisoned him, and he is still in prison.

After his flight, his three younger brothers remained in Tabriz. One of them hid himself, and even now it is not known where he is. Of the two others one was this same Hasan, aged eighteen, and the other Qadir (No. 7 in the photograph), aged thirteen or fourteen, both of whom were left as wanderers knowing not whither to turn. They were compelled to take refuge with a certain Russian subject, who kept them for two or three days in his office, but after, being afraid, turned them out, so that they were again left homeless wanderers. Being but children, they went to the Russian Consulate and surrendered themselves, saying "We are Constitutionalists, but are guilty of no other crime but this; do what you will with us." They imagined that the Russians would let them go, but [they] condemned them to be hanged, and they were accordingly hanged in the sight of all men, beside one another, with the late *Thiqatu'l-Islám* and the other five victims of the Day of the *'Ashurá*, in the Drill Square (*Maydan-i-Mashq*) known as the *Sarbáz-Khána* (Barrack Square).

It is worthy of mentioning that these two lads, especially the younger one, Qadir, displayed the utmost courage and manhood at the scaffold. They made a speech, reviling the Russians and commemorating their country, and cried with their last breath "*Yashasin Mashruta! Yashasin Watan!*" ("Long live our Country! Long live the Constitution").

The younger brother, Qadir, with his own hands adjusted the rope round his neck, and showed the greatest heroism.

These two brothers had never borne arms or taken any part in the fighting, and were only executed (by the Russians) in order to take vengeance on their elder brother, or perhaps their father, both of whom were notable Constitutionalists. Till lately their mother believed them to be imprisoned, knowing not that they had been killed, and kept preparing and sending food for them (to the prison). According to the account given by one of my relations who had seen her, she suffered the utmost disquietude and restlessness on their account, and was constantly beating her breast and tearing her hair, crying, "How can I sit quiet or eat food while they are without food and in prison?" At last one day, being unable to bear it any longer, she suddenly lost all self-control, went to the Russian Consulate, and forced herself in, weeping and crying, "How long will you keep my children?" Then they told her that the lads had been killed on the Day of the 'Ashura.

The elder of these two brothers, Hasan, had taken part in the, earlier War of Defense against Samad Khán and the other Reactionaries, but took absolutely no part in the fighting against the Russians.

2.   *Ziyá'u'l-'Ulamá*. His name was Mirzá Abu'l-Qásim, and he was about thirty-five years of age. He belonged to a great and noble family of Azarbayjan, and was one of the *'ulamá* of Tabriz. He was the son of the former *Shamsu'l-Ulamá* and brother of the successor to this title, and was adorned with all sorts of accomplishments and virtues, characterized by admirable moral qualities, and had mastered various sciences and arts. He was deeply read in the old, Oriental and religious sciences, and was also a student of the new learning. For Persia he was a *savant* of the first order. He knew French and

Russian perfectly, and some English. He used to teach many of the modern sciences, such as geometry, geography, etc., to the theological students. He was a friend of modern ideas, a Constitutionalist, and a true patriot, accomplished, steadfast, resolute and eminent. He had translated from the French and published a book entitled "the Adventures of a Frigate; or, Travels in the East." From the early days of the Persian Constitution, he was one of the Constitutionalist leaders, and he was one of the first of those who assembled at the British Consulate at Tabriz on the 29th of Rajab, A.H. 1324 (= September 19, 1906) and demanded from Muhammad 'Alí Mirzá, then Crown Prince, the proclamation of Freedom and the signature of the Constitution. Afterwards, during these six years of the Constitution and Revolution, from the beginning to the end, he was ever active in the affairs of the Nation and patriotic services, and during the Tabriz Revolution and during the siege of A.H. 1326-7 (=A.D. 1908-9), although he was not trained to arms and was one of the chief and most respected citizens, he personally bore arms, and took part in the defense, and helped to repel the attacks of Rahím Khán and 'Aynu'd-Dawla, showing great courage in this. After the restoration of the Constitution, however, he never bore arms, and during the days of the Revolution was the Chief of the Court of Justice in Tabriz; and after the restoration of the Constitution he was confirmed by the Government as Head of all the Courts of Appeal, which position he held until his death. During the First Period of the Constitution he founded the Persian newspaper named *Islamiyya*.[48] In these later days he translated several works on Law from French into Persian, which translations he intended to publish. In person, he was dignified in demeanour and moderate in views, and

---

48 See my *Press and Poetry of Modern Persia* (Cambridge University Press, 1914), pp. 41-2, No. 46.

no one ever dreamed that he could be accused of fomenting
disturbance. During the last three years he kept very silent,
stayed aloof from party politics, and played no active rôle in
events. He took no part, even the slightest, in the last catastrophe, nor even in the last Revolution, on which account
he abode tranquilly in his house, not imagining it to be in
the least degree probable that he would be in any way molested. His wife had died a few days before this event, and
he was engaged in mourning her death when the Russians
invaded his house and arrested him. At the scaffold he shewed
great courage, and, according to general report, made fine
speeches in both Turkish and Russian. He spoke first of all to
the officer in command of the Russian troops at the Barracks
(*Sarbáz-Khána*) (where the execution took place),[49] and said,
"For what fault would you kill us? If because we are Constitutionalists, do you do this by command of Muhammad 'Alí
Sháh and on his behalf? Is Muhammad 'Alí Sháh in power,
or not?" The Russian officer replied, "Yes, he is." "Then," said
Ziyáu'l- 'Ulamá, "if it is Muhammad 'Alí Sháh, send us before
him: he knows best: let him do with us what he will." When
they would not listen to him, and he despaired and knew
that he must die, he repeated this verse as they put the rope
round his neck:

منصــوروار گـــر بکشــندم بپــای دار
مردانه جان دهم که جهان پایدار نیست

If, like Mansur, they drag me to the foot of the gallows
   (*pa-yi-dar*),
I will yield up my life manfully, for the world is not
   enduring.

---

49 See enclosure1 to No. 15.

3.   Muhammad-gulí Khán, uncle of the *Ziyá'u'l-'Ulamá*. He was about forty-five years of age, or a little over. He was an old employee of the Government, and was a very harmless, quiet man, standing apart from all factions and but little known, nor did he take any active part in public affairs, though he was a strong Constitutionalist. The manner of his death was very strange, for, as Mr. Turner has indicated in his letter to the *Manchester Guardian*, he was executed by mistake, that is to say that, on account of his great attachment to and affection for the *Ziyáu'l-'Ulamá*, who was his sister's son, he followed after him as they were leading him to the gallows and embraced him, crying, "I will not allow them to hurt or harm you, and I will bear witness that you took no part in any of these things." When they reached the gallows, Muhammad-guli Khán began to beg and pray, agitated and insistent, for his sister's son, *Ziyá'u'l-'Ulamá*, and to beg for his release; and while he was so engaged they seized him also and hanged him, though he had not been arrested, but had come thither of his own accord, and had been neither accused nor suspected by anyone. Indeed, most people hardly knew him, and were greatly astonished at his death. According to the account given by some persons, he was hanged in place of another, namely Karím Khán, the brother of Shaykh Salím, whom they had also arrested, brought to the scaffold and hanged, while Karím escaped. For when the Russian soldiers charged with the execution counted the number of the victims and found them to be eight, agreeably to the sentence, they released the survivor, who was Karím, and suffered him to depart. Subsequently it became known that they had slain Muhammad-guli Khán, who was there by chance for the sake of his nephew. Karím afterwards fled and was for a time in hiding as a fugitive,

until lately he reached Tehran, where the Government arrested and imprisoned him. This affair of Muhammad-guli Khán was indeed a strange one, for in truth he was executed by mistake.

Ziyá'u'l-'Ulamá, like his companions in misfortune, had been severely man-handled before his execution, and, according to the narrative of one who witnessed the event and heard him speak, his face was very much swollen on one side. He was the only son of his mother, and it is said that in consequence she is mad with grief and at death's door and that [she] cannot endure her loss.

4. *Sadigu'l-Mulk*. He was about thirty-seven years of age, and had completed his studies in the Military College at Constantinople, from which he held a diploma. He was a very capable officer, and on his return to Persia was employed in Tehran. When *'Ala'u'l-Mulk* was Governor of Kirman, he was for a while Government Agent (*Kar-guzár*) in that city; and he was also for a while in charge of Public Instruction at Khuy. Afterwards, in A.H. 1325-8 (= A.D. 1907-1910), he was Military Attaché and Member (*État Major*) of the Turco-Persian Boundary Commission convened at Urmiya under the presidency, on the Persian side, of *Muhtashamu's-Saltana*, and, on the Turkish side, of Táhir Páshá. After this he came to Tabriz. Being keenly interested in education, and eager to render service to this cause, he joined the "Society for the Propagation of Education in Azarbayjan" (*Jam'iyyat-i-nashr-i-Má'arif-i-Azarbáyján*) which I helped to found, and served on it for nearly two years, as a volunteer, and for the Glory of God. Last year he was elected by the people, by the large majority of 3000 or 4300 voters, a Member of the Provincial Council of Azarbáyján. He was a very sound patriot, honest and of good character, and a Constitutionalist. He was also

of a very pacific, tranquil and moderate disposition, and had never borne arms, nor did he take any part in the political revolutions or civil wars, or in the more recent disturbances. He was a very quiet, honourable, honest and peaceable man, and was only executed for the crime of being a Member of the Provincial Council. His name was Mirzá Sádiq Khán. In politics he was a Democrat.

5.   The *Thiqatu'l-Islám*. His name was Mirzá 'Alí, son of Hájjí Mirzá Musá *Thiqat'l-Islam* son of Hájjí Mirzá Shafi' *Thiqatu'l-Islám*. To give a full and detailed account of the biography of this unrivalled scholar and progressive and patriotic divine would require a large volume, and I deem it best in this matter to refer you to what I wrote in the July number of the *Revue du Monde Musulman*,[50] published in Paris, pp. 294-9, and to what another person, better informed than myself, wrote on pp. 300-301 of the same issue, for these articles contain the necessary facts in some detail.

The biography, written and sent by me, and translated and sent to that paper by [Muhammad Qazwini] comprised in the original fifteen pages. Here I shall only say a few words as to the details of his martyrdom and arrest which I have lately heard from a trustworthy source. This account goes back, through one intermediate link, to the Interpreter of the Russian Consulate, who himself interrogated the late *Thiqatu'l-Islám* at the Russian Court Martial.

After the Russians had taken him from his house and brought him to the Consulate on the *Tásu'á* Day, or 9th of Muharram (A.H., 1330 – December 31, 1911), he was

---

50 As it was explained in the footnote to letter No. 11 the article in question was published in *Revue du Monde Musulman*, vols 18-19, pp. 294-301 of June 1912 not the July issue.[Ed.]

asked, in the presence of two or three Russian officers and the Consul (which assembly they most shamelessly called a "Court of Justice"), why he had telegraphed to Tehran that the Russians were killing people in the city (i.e. Tabriz) and committing other acts of aggression, he answered, with the utmost dignity and majesty, "Do you know me?" "Yes," they replied. Then said he, "Who am I, and what is my profession?" They answered, "A *mullá*." "Yes," said he; "a *mullá*, that is to say a religious leader of the Musulmans. Now the duty of such a *mullá* – is that whenever he sees that hurt befalls the Musulmans, he should make it known, and should share their misfortunes and strive to alleviate their suffering. I have done nothing except this." "True," they answered, "but why did you telegraph against the Russians?" "It was not against the Russians," he replied; "it was a statement of the facts to our own Government, and a request for help to put matters right. But I do not seek to conceal the fact, that I am not too well pleased with the Russians, and that I regard their invasion as detestable." Thereupon the Consul, Miller, cried: "Enough! Enough! It is sufficient!"

Then they led him away, and sent him, escorted by Cossacks, to the *Bágh-i-Shimál*, where was the Russian camp. The Cossacks beat him a great deal, so that his turban was knocked off his head, and brought him on foot to the Garden, which was distant (from the Consulate), half a parasang. When he was on the scaffold there was a great swelling on his head, produced by blows.

On the *'Ashura* Day (Muharram 10, A.H. 1330 = January 1, 1912) they brought the eight victims in a tumbrel (such as is used for carting rubbish, or goods and other things), surrounded by Cossacks, from the *Bagh-í-Shimál* to the Barracks. On arriving there he showed the utmost firmness and dignity and extraordinary self-possession; and indeed he was habitually very dignified, imposing and weighty in demeanour, and in the Russian Consulate also spoke with the utmost fearlessness. On reaching the Barracks, he asked permission to perform a prayer, which, after making the ablution, he did, while the other martyrs joined his devotions. Then he asked for a cigarette, which the son of Alí "Monsieur" gave him. When he had smoked it, and the ropes had been placed round their necks in presence of one another, Shaykh Salím showed some signs of fear, whereupon the *Thiqatu'l-Islám* comforted and soothed him with dignity.

It is well-known that the *Thiqatu'l-Islám* remained in his house (until he was arrested) relying on the word of the British Consul Mr. Shipley, who had assured him that no harm should befall those who had not taken up arms. So secure did he feel himself that only two or three hours before his arrest he wrote to one of the fugitives from Tabriz who afterwards reached Constantinople, in answer to a letter asking advice as to what course of action should be adopted, assuring him that he was perfectly safe, and concluding his letter with this verse:

تو که فلس ماهی حیرتی چه زنی ز بحر وجود دم
بنشین چو طوطی و دم بدم بشنو خروش نهنگ لا

O thou who art but a scale on the fish of amazement,
    how can'st thou discourse of the Ocean of Being?
Sit still, like the parrot, and hearken each moment to the
    roaring of the Leviathan of "No"!

So the man in question was reassured, and remained in his house until he too was arrested, imprisoned for a while, then fined and exiled, until he finally reached Constantinople in a state of extreme poverty.

6.   Mashhadí Muhammad Ibrahim Qafqázchí.

By "Qafqazchi" is meant a dealer in the goods of Qafqaz, i.e. Vladikafkas, which is the principal city of the province of Terek in the European Caucasus (not Trans-Caucasia), and forms part of Daghistan. For in Persia it is customary to describe a merchant who deals in the goods of any country, or who carries on business with it and is connected with it, by adding the termination – chi to the name of that country or town. Thus they talk of "Rasht-chi", i.e. one who sells Rasht goods, and so likewise "Yazd-chi", "Islambul-chi", "Tehran-chi", and so on, which do not imply that the person in question is a Rashti (native of Rasht), Yazdi (native of Yazd), Islambuli (native of Constantinople), or Tehrani (native of Tehran) respectively. This difference must always be borne in mind. In the case of the victim in question, who was a native of Tabriz, he had business dealings with Qafqaz, that is to say Vladikafkas, for which reason only, like many other merchants, he was called "Qafqazchi."

He was about thirty-four years of age. I knew him personally, and he was my friend. He was a very honest man and zealous patriot, enthusiastic, energetic, upright and virtuous; and I can say that amongst all the martyrs there was none so disinterested, so sincere, and so pure of character. In all these respects he had no equal. He was a wealthy and highly considered merchant, and had shown much activity and energy in the Constitutional cause. He was not a fighting man, but he had a large and beautiful house near the *Arg-i-'Alí Sháhi*, which he devoted for the most part to meetings and consultations of the Constitutionalists, who were wont to assemble there. This was his only fault. In politics he was a Democrat.

It is said that he went of his own accord to the Russian Consulate in order to surrender the arms he had in his house, agreeably to the Russian proclamation; and that he was arrested there. According to another account, he was arrested in his house. He was a native of Tabriz, where his family and household still dwell, and was not a native of Baku or the Caucasus. He personally bore arms for two or three days to repel the attacks of Samad Khán and the Reactionaries in the earlier revolutions, but was not a fighting man. On the scaffold he endeavoured to make the Russians understand that he was innocent, but they would not listen. The Russians took possession of his house, which they at first proposed to blow up with dynamite, but subsequently they abandoned this idea, and seized it. It is still in their possession, and is occupied by their soldiers.

7.   Qadír, son of 'Alí "Monsieur". (His name was Qadír, not Qádir, nor 'Alí Abbas, and he was the son of 'Alí "Monsieur").A full account of this thirteen-year old lad has already been given under No. 1.

8.   Shaykh Salím. He was about fifty-years of age. I have already sent you a detailed account of him. He was one of the *'ulamá,* of Tabriz, and a well known preacher. At the beginning of the Constitution he was in the British Consulate, and was one of the principal leaders and pillars of the Persian Revolution in Tabriz. He was a fine speaker, and had a great power and influence over the people. He was a special object of hatred to Muhammad 'Alí Mirzá and the Reactionaries. A full account of his adventures would be equivalent to a history of the Constitution and the Revolution in Ázarbayján.

After the bombardment of the National Assembly in A.H. 1326 (June 23, 1908) and the temporary triumph of Despotism in Tabriz before the uprising of Sattár Khán, he succeeded, with great difficulty, in escaping in disguise and in reaching Najaf and Karbalá, where he incited the *'ulamá* to resistance. Thence he came to Constantinople, where he worked for the *Anjuman-i-Sa'adat*. After the restoration of the Constitution he returned to Tabriz, and was again elected a Member of the Provincial Council, in which he represented the people until the day of his martyrdom. He took no part in the recent catastrophe, and after it went into hiding, but a member of the Reactionary inhabitants of the *Devechi* (or *Shuturbán*) quarter seized him and handed him over (to the Russians). Before his execution he had been so severely beaten that it is said that, even if he had not been hanged, he would have died. This unfortunate man suffered more than any of the other victims at the hands of the Russians. At the last moment before his execution he only said: "Oh people, I give my life for you!" Latterly his influence had declined. It is impossible wholly to guarantee the excellence of his character.

(C)

1. Muhammad Khán *Amir-tumán*, nephew of Sattár Khán. He was a young man about twenty-eight years of age, and was the son of the well-known Ismá'íl of Qara-Dágh. He was the Lieutenant Deputy and agent in all the affairs of Sattár Khán, occupied almost the position of his son, and looked after his business and that of his followers. During the Revolution of A.H. 1326 (=A.D. 1908) in

Tabriz he was wounded by a bullet in the leg while fighting with the Reactionaries, and his leg was broken and had to be amputated and replaced by an artificial leg. This young man, together with his elder brother Karím Khán, who was about thirty-five years of age, went himself to Samad Khán *Shujá'u'd-Dawla* at Básminch (a village situated at a distance of two farasangs or eight miles to the East of Tabriz) to see him and obtain an amnesty, but Samad Khán arrested both of them, brought them to Tabriz, and handed them over to the Russians, who hanged them at *Qúm-Baghí* with Hájjí 'Alí *Dawa-furush* (the Druggist) and Mirzá Ahmad Suhaylí.

(D)

1.   Mashhadí 'Abbas 'Alí the Grocer *(Qand-furúsh)*. He was about forty-five years of age, and was the elder and leader of the Constitutionalists of the Khiyábán quarter. He had great influence with the National Volunteers and Constitutionalists. He was an honest and upright man, and worked for the Glory of God and for love of his country. He took no part in the fighting, and was in no sense a fighting man, but merely a tradesman who kept a grocer's shop. I knew him personally. Samad Khán first arrested him and handed him over to the Russians, who, after interrogating him, let him go. Some days later Samad again arrested him and put him to death, that is to say hanged him with a rope from a ladder opposite the Qárí Kurpu Bridge in the middle of the street. In this manner did Samad Khán slay all those whom he put to death, hanging them in the public thoroughfare against the street-walls from a short ladder, like sheep. The remarkable thing is that many such incidents occurred, where the

Russians ostensibly released patriotic Constitutionalists whom it was impossible outwardly to convict of any crime, but afterwards secretly incited Samad Khán to re-arrest them and put them to death.

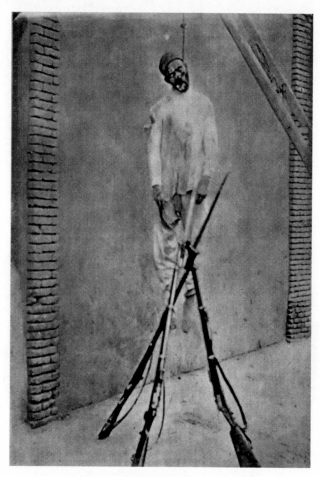

Mashhadí 'Abbas 'Alí the Grocer *(Qand-furúsh)*,
hanged by Samad Khán *Shuja'u'Dawla*.

Ghulám Khán Charandábi Muavin – the police
deputy of Charandáb – hanged by
Samad Khán *Shuja'u'Dawla*.

(E)

Ghulám Khán, Assistant-Commissioner of Police, of Charandáb. (Charandáb is the name of one of the quarters of Tabriz situated in the South-Western part of the city). He was the Deputy *Kad-Khudá*, or, in the modern phraseology, Assistant-Commissioner of Police, and was about forty years of age. He was a very brave and gallant fighter, and was one of the most renowned of the National Volunteers. From the time of the Tabriz Revolution of A.H. 1326 (= A.D. 1908) he was enrolled in the ranks of the National Volunteers and was one of the defenders of Tabriz.

(F)

Mirzá Aqá Bálá Khán of Khiyábán. (Khiyábán is a quarter of Tabriz). He was about forty-five years of age, and was one of the best-known leaders of the National Volunteers and adjutants of the celebrated Báqir Khán in the time of the Tabriz Revolution and siege. He kept guard over one side of the city, that is to say he was the captain of a section of the barricades on the North Eastern side of the town called *Bágh-i-Mishá* and *Qúlla*, whence he repelled the attacks of *'Ayn'u'd-Dawla*'s army. I knew him personally. He was originally a *mullá*, and kept a school, but afterwards, in the days of the Constitution, became a National Volunteer, and subsequently rose to be a leader of them. After going with Bágir Khán to Tehran, he returned to Tabriz two years ago, and was appointed by the *Mukhbiru's-Saltana*, the Governor of Tabriz, an officer of the Gendarmerie, in command of twenty men. Two or three months before the recent catastrophe, the

Russians seized him and a number of other gendarmes by the Aji Bridge, which they were defending against the Reactionary followers of Samad Khán, disarmed the gendarmes, and imprisoned him in the Russian camp. (This event was mentioned in the European newspapers at the time). After a while, only a few days before the recent catastrophe, they released him. He took no part in fighting the Russians in the recent conflict. Samad Khán arrested him and hanged him from a ladder at the Qárí Kurpu ("Black Bridge")[51] . He was one of the best of the National Volunteers.

(G)

Muhammad Aqá Khán, Commissioner of the Police of *Bágh-i-Mísha*. (*Bagh-i-Misha* is one of the North-Eastern quarters of Tabriz). He was formerly a carpenter, but after the proclamation of the Constitution entered into politics and became a National Volunteer. There were three brothers, all of whom died martyrs to the National Cause. One was killed during the Tabriz Revolution while fighting; against the troops of Muhammad 'Alí Sháh. Another named Mahmúd was killed in the recent fighting with the Russians. This man was one of the leaders of the National Volunteers, and was originally Commissioner of the Devechi (Shuturbán) quarter, and afterwards became Commissioner (Chief of Police or *Kad-Khúdá*) of the *Bágh-i-Misha* quarter. He took part in the final fighting (against the Russians). He was put to death by Samad Khán.

---

51 Browne has mistaken "Qári" (Old Woman) for "Qára" (Black). Hence the translation must be "The Old Woman's Bridge." [Ed.]

(H)

Taqí-off. He was about thirty-eight years of age. He was named Taqí, as was also his grandfather, and was a native of the Khiyábán quarter of Tabriz. As he had formerly been to Baku and carried on trade there (he had a baker's shop) he was on this account given the name of "Taqí-off "; and as he was one of the Persian Voluntteers who returned from the Caucasus, he was called "Qafqází" ("the Caucasian"). He was Commissioner or *Kad-Khudá* of the Armenistan or European quarter of Tabriz, where the Europeans live and the Consulates are situated. From the beginning of the Tabriz Revolution he was enrolled in the "Caucasian Band" (in the sense explained above) of the National Volunteers, and was one of their leaders. He went into hiding, but Samad Khán found him, seized him, strangled him by night, and near day cast his body out on a dung-heap. He was especially obnoxious to the Russian Consul. He was well-known for the excellence and integrity of his character. I knew him personally.

The dead body of Taqí-off, of the "Caucasian
Band," surrounded by the soldiers and
executioners of *Shuja'u'Dawla.*

(I)

Mír Aqá Khusrawsháhí. (Khusraw-sháh is a village on the
West side of Tabriz, situated at a distance of four parasangs
or sixteen miles there from.) He was one of the Constitutionalists of Khusraw-sháh, who defended that place when
it was attacked by Samad Khán last year during the siege
of Tabriz. They brought him, together with another Sayyid
(whose name may have been Sayyid Muhammad or Mír
Muhammad) of Khusraw-sháh to Tabriz, and there hanged
him. (The variant in the name may perhaps arise from their
having misread "Sayyid" as "Sa'id".) These two were good
men, patriots and Constitutionalists.

The dead bodies of Sayyid Muhammad and Mír
Aqá Khusrawsháhí, lying on the ground and
surrounded by the executioners of *Shuja'u'Dawla*.

(J)

Chapukh Muhammad. He was a well-known National
Volunteer, aged about thirty years. (The word Chapukh
in Turkish signifies "torn", and is applied to a person who
bears permanently on his body the manifest scar of some
wound which has befallen him. And since the face of this
Muhammad was disfigured by the traces of a severe dagger-
wound, he was nick-named "Chapukh"). He was one of the
comrades and followers of Sattár Khán during the Tabriz
Revolution. After the recent catastrophe he was for a while
a fugitive and in hiding, and afterward succeeded in escaping
from Tabriz, but when he sought to cross over into Russia

at Julfa, he was arrested and brought to Tabriz, where Samad Khán killed him.

The dead body of Chapukh Muhammad, with
dagger planted in breast, killed by Samad Khán
Shuja'u'Dawla.

(K and L)

The two halves of the body of Yúsuf of Húkmabád. Huk-mábád is a well-known quarter in the North-west of Tabriz. This Yusuf, or Ná'ib Yúsuf, was one of the chief National Volunteers and leading Constitutionalists of this quarter. There were two brothers, one of whom was killed in the Tabriz Revolution of A.H. 1326 (= A.D. 1908). After the arrival of the Russian troops at Tabriz in Rabi' II, A.H. 1327

(=April, 1909), the first step which they took was that, on the pretext that it had been forbidden to fire shots in the town (although at that time all the National Volunteers were armed, and the war with Muhammad 'Alí Sháh had not yet completely come to an end), and that a shot was heard from the Húkmabád quarter (where, it would appear, a quarrel had arisen between Yúsuf and another person, who, being a Reactionary, went straight to the Russian Consulate to complain and demand redress), a number of Russian troops by order of the Russian Consul, surrounded the Húkmabád quarter, a remote quarter of the city chiefly inhabited by farmers and agricultural labourers, arrested the above-mentioned Yúsuf with several other persons, confiscated his arms and household effects, blew up his house with dynamite, and brought him hand-cuffed to the *Bágh-i-Shímál*, where the Russian camp was situated. After keeping him in prison for two or three months, they let him go.

He was one of the most courageous and influential National Volunteers. On the occasion of the attack delivered by Samad Khán in the month of Safar, A.H. 1327 (= February-March, 1909), on the side of Qará-malik and Húkmabád in order to capture the city, in which he almost succeeded, and indeed actually held Húkmabád for a few hours, Yúsuf offered a fierce defense, and helped Sattár Khán to drive him out of this quarter of the city. Therefore Samad Khán when he re-entered Tabriz seized and killed him, cut his body in two halves like a sheep, and hung up one half on the Gate of the *Bázárcha-i-Gachil*, situated on one of the main thoroughfares of the North-Western quarters of the city, and the other half on the Húkmabád Gate, where they remained for some time.

The above-mentioned Ná'ib Yúsuf was one of the wealthier and more considerable inhabitants of his quarter, and was a land-owner and farmer.

Yúsuf of Húkmabád was cut in two, and the halves of his body were hung up like a sheep's carcass by order of Samad Khán *Shuja'u'Dawla.*

(M)

Yúnus of Ardabíl. He was one of the good and true Constitutionalists of Ardabíl. He was arrested and brought to
Tabriz by command of Samad Khán, and hanged from a
ladder by the *Qári Bridge*. When about to suffer death he
made a fine and courageous speech and gave up the ghost
cheerfully, crying with his last breath, "Long live the Country and the Constitution!"

(N)

Hájjí 'Alí *Dawa-furush* (the Druggist). He was one of the
chief and most prominent leaders of the Constitutionalists
of Tabriz, and was like the Danton of the Revolution in that
city. It is impossible to record in writing all his doings and
sufferings, which indeed, would be tantamount to writing
a history of the Revolution in Azarbayjan in all its details.
Some time ago I wrote an account of his life to (Shaykh
Muhammad Khán), who may have sent it to you. He may
be reckoned, after the *Thiqatu'l-Islám*, the most intelligent,
statesmanlike and intellectually able man in Tabriz.

In brief, during these six years, without exaggeration, he
did not rest day or night, but was always working and striving. As a speaker he exerted great influence. He was prudent,
courageous, upright, intelligent, energetic, and a skilful politician. As I have said, I cannot in this brief summary which
I am writing enumerate his qualities and virtues. The very
soul of the Tabriz Revolution was in his hands and those
of Karbalá'i 'Alí "Monsieur", mentioned above. These two

were, indeed, to a certain extent rivals, and closely resembled Danton and Robespierre.

Hájjí 'Alí was about forty years of age, and from early youth was an admirer of civilization and progress, for the promotion of which he strove for a long while even before the proclamation of the Constitution. He kept a Druggist's shop called *Dawá-Khána-i-Násiri*, and used to obtain drugs from Europe and sell them, though not himself of the commercial class. After the proclamation of the Constitution he was one of the first persons who went to the British Consulate, and he became subsequently one of the chief leaders and guides of the Constitutional Party. On the occasion of the bombardment of the National Assembly and the restoration of Autocracy (June 23, 1908), he took refuge in the French Consulate with three companions, who were also leaders of the Constitutionalist: (namely Mirzá Husayn the preacher, who, poor man, is still a fugitive in hiding, Sayyid Hasan *Sharif-záda*, who fell a martyr during the days of the Revolution, and the seal-engraver Mirzá Mahmúd Khán), and there they remained for two or three months. After the triumph of Sattár Khán he came out and busied himself with the utmost zeal and energy in keeping the Revolution. He founded a Council of War named *Útáq-i-Nízám*, and exerted himself night and day with untiring energy, until, in one of Samad Khán's attacks on the city, he was struck by a bullet on the town-barricades and severely wounded in the wrist. For two or three months after this he was confined to his bed, but finally recovered.

During the Second Constitutional Period he spent most of his time in promoting education, to which he devoted himself with the utmost energy. By his energy was founded the *Madrasa-i-Sa'adat*, which was attended by nearly five hundred students, and was the best, most excellent, most admirable and best organized of all the colleges in Tabriz. The pupils of this college for the most part turned out good, patriotic and capable young men, well instructed and writers. In the last catastrophe the Russians, without any reason, destroyed this college, burned its furniture and fittings, and took possession of the building, which is still occupied by their soldiers.

The late Hájjí 'Alí was one of my own personal friends. His views were moderate, and he always favoured peace, tranquillity and order. He did not approve of the second Revolution. He was prudent and foreseeing. When, after the restoration of the Constitution, the elections to the Provincial Council were being held in Tabriz, his name was included in the list of nominees; and I remember that M. Miller, the Russian Consul, said to one of my friends that in all this list of names only two were really men of merit, one of whom was the late Hájjí 'Alí; and he then proceeded to praise and extol him, applauding his good sense, and expressing a hope that he would be elected on account of his pacific tendencies, and his desire for settled conditions.

After the return of Muhammad 'Alí Mirzá to Persia last year[52] and Samad Khán's renewed attacks on Tabriz, he again rendered great help in defending the city, and was himself the chief of the military administration of the town, but latterly, that is to say two or three months before the final catastrophe, he withdrew from these activities, retired to his house, and took no part in affairs, while in the last events (i.e. the fighting with the Russians) he took absolutely no part. He continued for some days after this quietly in his house,

---

52 In August, 1911.

but subsequently Samad Khán sent men who took him from thence and cast him in chains into prison. Some days later the Russians came and took him away and hanged him with Mirzá Ahmad Suhaylí at *Qúm-bághí*, and blew up his house with dynamite. He leaves two small children, a girl and a boy, aged eight and ten years respectively, who were attending the American College. They had already lost their mother, and now their father too is dead and their house lay in ruins: they have nothing and are beggars.

The late Hájjí 'Alí was guilty of no crime save patriotism, love of the Constitution, virtue and capability. A man who reached Constantinople a fortnight ago and was in Samad Khán's prison relates that Hájjí 'Alí said to him in the prison, pointing to the chain round his neck, "O So-and-so, this chain is the order of merit of patriots and lovers Freedom!"

The late Hájjí 'Alí was one of Persia's greatest losses.

(O)

Mirzá Ahmad Suhaylí. He was about thirty-five years of age, and was a very ardent and sincere patriot, and a devoted Constitutionalist. I knew him personally. In early life he was a tradesman, but subsequently and until the end a broker. He had some practical talent and was a poet. "Suhaylí" was his *takhallus* (poetical *nom de guerre*), and for the last fifteen years he walked in the poet's way. He wrote poems both in Persian and Turkish, and some of them have been printed. In politics he was a Democrat.

During the last siege of Tabriz the Governor of Tabriz sent him to Tiflis to buy uniforms, that is to say stuff wherewith to make them, for the soldiers and National Volunteers who were defending the city against Samad Khán's attacks. Having purchased the necessary materials he had returned to Tabriz only a few days before the final catastrophe, in which he took absolutely no part, took place, and there seemed not the slightest probability of his arrest or imprisonment, so that all the townsfolk were amazed when they heard that the Russians had killed him, for, besides the fact that he was absolutely innocent of any crime, he was not even a person of any particular note amongst the Constitutionalists, but was but an ordinary and little-known member of their ranks. But he was connected and on friendly terms with the editor of the *Shafaq* ("After glow"), and so continually frequented the office of that paper, and it was probably this fact which led to his execution, for the Russians apparently imagined him to be one of the staff of that paper, and in the telegrams of the St. Petersburg News Agency on the occasion of his execution it was stated that the editor of the newspaper *Shafaq* and several members of the staff had been hanged, whereas neither the editor nor any of the regular contributors were captured. We did not know who was meant by "the editor and staff"; until it afterwards appeared that they had killed this poor wretch supposing him to be a writer for the *Shafaq*, whereas he was not a writer for it, and never contributed anything to it.

Of relatives and kinsfolk the late Mirzá Ahmad Suhaylí had only a mother, whose only child he was. The Russians hanged him at *Qúm-bághí* with Hájjí 'Alí *Dawá-furúsh* and the nephews of Sattár Khán, but it appears that the photograph of these two and the photograph of Sattár Khán's nephews were taken separately.

This is what I have been able to put together in a fragmentary fashion concerning the biographies and characters of these twenty-six victims whose photographs are in your possession and Mr. Turner's, either from my own knowledge or from enquiry, but, since I have written in haste, I have not had much opportunity to make full investigation; else most of the fugitive Constitutionalists who are now in Constantinople are acquainted with the circumstances in detail, and, if one should strive at leisure and with ample opportunity to collect their history and adventures, one might compile a far more complete record. Notwithstanding this I have striven, so far as was in my power, to include all that I could remember or which could be verified, and I think that this account is relatively complete. There are people now in Constantinople who were for a long time in Samad Khán's prison, and who relate things which cannot be written down.

Such, at all events, is the brief account of the victims represented in the photographs. But it is strange that there exist no photographs of some of the other well-known and notable victims, such as Agá Mír Karím, Mirzá Mahmúd of Salmas, etc. If you will permit me, I will now write a brief account of the circumstances of the other well-known martyrs. But before beginning to do so, I think it necessary to say first of all that all that you have hitherto heard of the barbarities of the Russians, Samad Khán and his followers, *Rashídu'l-Mulk*, the *Begler-begi* and other local Reactionaries, and various outcast *mullás* and Russian subjects, and all that has reached the Press of Europe, or been represented in photographs, is, as you must know for a certainty, without any exaggeration, not more than one hundredth part of the truth. I do not exaggerate in any way which [when] I say that the sufferings and cruelties to which the Constitutionalists in Azarbayjan have been exposed in the course of this year are a hundred times [more than] what you have heard. Imagine a city most of the inhabitants of which are Constitutionalists, who have been for years at enmity with Muhammad ʿAlí Mirzá and his adherents, and between whom and the local Reactionaries blood-feuds exist; a city, moreover, which, from the beginning of the Constitution, unlike other towns and provinces (of Persia), has not for one single day experienced autocratic administration; and on the other hand imagine the boundless hatred existing in the hearts of the Reactionaries, Russians and Russophiles, which has accumulated, awaiting an opportunity for vengeance, for years. What will these do after the city has fallen into their hands? Besides the hundreds of persons whom they slew, and the hundreds more whom they cast into a savage imprisonment, which would serve as the worst specimen of the barbarities of ancient times, there are the thousands of fugitives from their country, and the many who are still in hiding in the dark places of Tabriz city, in the extreme of a misery worse than death. Those who are exiles from their native land abroad are in many cases almost perishing from poverty. Besides all this there are the financial losses and the ruined houses which are the portion of such as remain in the city, which can neither be described nor set forth in writing, for in truth and without exaggeration they transcend all reckoning, and can neither be described nor set forth in writing. There is not a day on which merchants and tradesmen who sympathized with the Constitution, and even those who were of no party are secure from the hands of Samad Khán's *farrashes*. I take God to witness that in what I am saying there is not one particle of exaggeration, or prejudice, or excess of sympathy, but it is the simple truth. They have exacted fines from and otherwise molested every inhabitant of the city, without exception, except the Reactionaries, and that repeatedly. Without exaggeration I can say that Samad Khán and his followers and the Russians have stripped the people and made more than a million *tumáns* of profit out of Azarbayján, which is no small sum for a city like Tabriz, which has not as much wealth as one single street in Manchester. I will only mention one instance out of ten thousand, one of my Constitutionalist friends of Tabriz, who resided at Rasht, returned some while ago to Tabriz, and after a month's stay there sent a letter here. In this letter he says:

"Since reaching this town I do not walk abroad much, and exercise prudence. During the first days (of my sojourn) a *farrásh* came to our house, knocked at the door, and said, "Give me five *gráns* for this sum is taken from every house." We asked why. He said, "Money to provide a sheep to sacrifice on the road for the return of Hájjí Mirzá Hasan Aqá" (the Reactionary *mujtahid* expelled from Tabriz who founded the *Anjuman-i-Islamiyya* of the Devechi quarter in A.H. 1326 (= A.D. 1908), one of the worst of the Reactionaries, like Mír Háshim and Shaykh Fazlu'lláh, but far worse than them). We gave the money. Two days later the *farrásh* again came to the door of our house and again demanded money – a *tumán* this time – on the same pretext of sacrificing a sheep; and though we told him that it had been already paid, our remonstrances were of no avail. And so in like manner money was taken on this pretext from all the townsfolk."

This incident was recorded not only by the friend above mentioned, but in all letters from Tabriz, and by all those who come from Tabriz; that is but to say it is a matter of common report, uncontradicted and certain. This is one unimportant instance out of thousands.

Hájjí 'Alí *Dawá-furúsh* ("the druggist") and Mirzá Ahmad Suhaylí, a poet and journalist, hanged by the Russians.

The victims of these last seven or eight months are many more than you have heard of or have been photographed. Many nameless and unnoted persons have disappeared of whom no trace remained. They go about by night, and in the morning many corpses are seen in the street, and, as they are those of unknown or little known persons, and the town is oppressed by an autocratic rule, and it is forbidden for people to visit or converse with one another, no one has news of another. Sometimes a headless body is seen, and not recognized. Notwithstanding this, the names of nearly a hundred of those slain in cold blood, that is to say hanged or executed in other ways, are known, and a list of them, would, perhaps, were it necessary, be compiled from those acquainted with the facts. I here append a list of the names of some of those (apart from those who were killed in the fighting, and in addition to those enumerated above) who were executed by the Russians and Samad Khán, so far as my knowledge goes. Here is the list: (1) Mirzá Mahmúd of Salmas; (2) Mirzá Ahmad Khán Binábí; (3) Imám-qulí Khán; (4) Aqá Mír Karím the Orator *(Nátiq);* (5) Mash-hadí Muhammad Usku-i, known as 'Amú-oghlú; (6) Firidún Mirzá; (7) Hájjí Naqi the Jeweler *(Jawáhir-furúsh);* (8) Mullá Ghaffár *Rawza-Khwán;* (9) Mír 'Alí Akbar Qara; (10) Mash-hadí Háshim Kharázi; (11) Mashhadí Ghaffár, the brother of Sattár Khán; (12) Mashhadí Muhammad Ja'far the Bar-ber *(Dallák);* (13) the apprentice of the last-mentioned; (14) Taqí Khán the Centurion, known as Bálá Tagi of Khiyábán; (15) Mohammad Dá'í, known as *Ajúdán;* (16) Mamaw; (17) Petros Khán Andressian; (18) Mashhadí Ahmad the Coffee-seller *(Qahwachí);* (19) Mashhadí Mohammad Charandábi; (20) Yúzbashi (Captain) Ahmad, the brother of Mashhadí Hájjí Khán (see photograph A., No. 3), of which two broth-ers both died martyrs' deaths; (21-23) Ná'ib Ahad of the Márálán quarter, and two other National Volunteers; (24) Mirzá Mahdi Khán, director of telegraphs and his son. These two harmless persons who took no part in politics on either side lived in a house near the *Bagh-i-Shimal.* The Russian sol-diers entered it and killed them both; (26) Hájjí 'Alí Khatá'í, together with several members of his household, including his son, his wife, his daughter, a child six years of age, his cousins and the bride of the latter, whom the Russians killed in his house; (33) Mashhadí Muhammad Aqá *Qannadi*; (34) Nagu the Georgian; and many others.

The houses looted by the Russians those of which they gave the furniture and contents to Samad Khán and those which they blew up with dynamite are very numerous. Amongst the houses so destroyed may be enumerated those of Sattár Khán, Bagir Khán, Hájjí ʿAlí *Dawa-Furush*, Mashhadí Mohammad *Dallák* (the Barber), Mashhadí Ghaffár, the brother of Sattár Khán, Mashhadí ʿAbbas ʿAlí the Grocer, Hájjí Naqi the Jeweler, Hasan Aqá the money-changer *Amir-i-Hishmat*, Mirzá ʿAlí of Wayjuya, Mír Karím the Orator, *Sadiquʾl-Mulk*, Shaykh Salím, Mashhadí Shaker, and Hájjí Mohammad Bálá, besides the fine building of the Provincial Council (that is to say the centre of the Constitutional and Revolutionary movement in Tabriz), the walls of the fortification of the Arg (Citadel) of ʿAlí -Sháh, all the shops, caravansaries and coffee-houses situated near the Aji Chay Bridge, the houses situated round about the *Bagh-i-Shimál*, amounting to some forty in number, numerous caravansaries and coffeehouses by the Devechi Gate, many more in the Ahráb quarter (situated on the West side of the city), etc., and there are many more besides those of which I have knowledge.

In the destruction of these buildings the Russians showed the greatest savagery, using the dynamite in such a way that they injured all the surrounding houses in the street, so much was this the case that before they touched certain houses the neighbors, to the distance of five or six houses, fearing the demolition of the house of such-and-such a Constitutionalist, quitted their homes and migrated with their families from that quarter to another, where they had relatives or friends, until after some days, when their fears had somewhat declined, they returned to their empty and ownerless houses. Such was the case as regards my own house, which it was feared by the neighbors might be destroyed, as indeed was the case.

The worst of all was that neither the deeds of the Russians, nor those of Samad Khán, were regulated by any law or principal, even a savage and merciless one, but, as in the case of the worst forms of autocratic government, no one was secure as to his life and property, and there was no system in what was done, so that anyone could anticipate whether such-and-such a house would be destroyed or not, or whether so and-so would be killed or not.

On the occasion of the destruction of the Castle and fortifications of the Arg (Citadel) of 'Alí-Sháh, one of the oldest and finest monuments of the Mongol period (Thirteenth Century), the dynamite employed for this purpose caused such distress to those who dwelt in that quarter and neighborhood and to the inhabitants of the adjacent houses that they all went to the Russian Consulate and begged that, if it was intended to blow it up with dynamite, but leave it to them to hire, at their own charges, laborers and workmen to pull it down. This request was accepted by the Consulate, and the unfortunate inhabitants of the quarter, who were moreover poor men, collected money by subscription amongst themselves, and sent laborers to pull down and remove the walls.

As for the prisoners of Samad Khán, in whose hands also were the prisoners of the Russians, the guards of his prison were, besides his own *farrashes*, Russian soldiers. All his myrmidons and officers, and all the town officials, even the police in the different quarters, wore Russian arms on their sleeves, in default of which the Russians molested them and would not suffer them to go about their duties. The Russian flag, moreover, is hoisted over Samad Khán's Judgement Hall, as well as over the Citadel, the Government House, and the Revenue and all other State departments. The new offices of the Constitutional period also, such as the Police, Municipality and Justice, and the *Shamsu'l-'Imára*, Arsenal, Magazine and Barracks, are still occupied by the Russians.

The state of the prisoners is the worst conceivable in the world, perhaps even worse than that of the prisoners of the Pharaohs of Egypt, Nero or the Middle Ages, and I am afraid that whatever I write I shall be unable to give an adequate picture of the true state of the case, since it is difficult for Europeans to imagine such a condition of things. Imagine, then, a small, narrow, dark and very dirty space or ground, full of moisture, the whole superficial extent of which does not exceed twenty square meters or a trifle more, on which, on the wet earth, from forty to ninety persons, according to different times, are seated, in chains and bound together, in such wise that it is impossible for them to move or sleep. One of these prisoners who has arrived here, and who is an officer who had completed his studies in the Turkish Military Colleges, and was an officer of artillery, relates that at night, when sleep overcame one of the prisoners, and, losing control of himself, he fell asleep as he sat there, he would fall over against his next neighbor who sat beside him and awake, while his companion would break out into complaints. No food was supplied to these prisoners, but the kinsmen, relatives or friends of each of them had to bring food for him from outside; nor did the jailers readily suffer them to pass, and only did so after exacting exorbitant bribes or money payments so that the food might reach its destination. Most of the prisoners helped one another. All the prisoners were led out twice a day to fulfill the needs of nature, and on these occasions they placed them in a row beside the wall of the garden, still fastened together with their chains, so that they must needs fulfill the needs of nature in presence of one another. In the prison their feet were fettered and placed in the stocks, while some wore on their necks the "yoke" (*du shakha*) which is one of the worst implements of torture, since the victim's hands cannot reach his head. Should anyone be constrained to fulfill a need of nature at other than the time regulated for all, he must needs relieve himself, like a brute beast, where he sat. Amongst the prisoners was a certain Sayyid, a Constitutionalist of the village of Hájjí Aqá, situated about eight parasangs from Tabriz on the road to Tehran, who suffered from dysentery. He used to weep in the extremity of his misery, but they would not suffer him to go out. Lice and other vermins so swarmed on the bodies of the wretched prisoners that description is impossible. The Sayyid above mentioned says: "Since our hands were bound, the lice attacked our faces and heads and even our eyes." The dampness of the place caused the bodies of the prisoners to swell. In such misery were they that some of them used to beg and entreat their jailers to kill them. Another of the Constitutionalists who was arrested and imprisoned for the crime that his brother was a journalist, and who arrived here a few days ago, says that the number of prisoners varied, but that he himself one day counted eighty-six. All these prisoners (who have escaped and arrived here) effected their release by the gradual disbursement of money, and by bribing this one and that one and even Samad Khán himself. Release was impossible until large sums of money had

been repeatedly exacted from each of the prisoners successive occasions by Samad Khán and his satellites, and even
then prolonged bargaining and discussions between the relatives of the prisoners and Samad Khán's staff were generally
needed; while it was necessary that the prisoners should not
disclose the whole extent of their possessions, else all would
have been taken. The Russian Consul and his staff also constantly did wonders in taking bribes to secure the release
of this one, or to take that one under their protection. Of
hundreds of instances of this which are currently reported I
know two of my own personal knowledge. In one of them
200 *tumáns* (= £. 40) was paid to the Chief Munshi (Persian secretary) of the Russian Consulate, while in the other
nearly 500 *tumáns* (= £.100) was distributed amongst the
staff of the Consulate, from the greatest to the smallest, and
the prisoners were then released. A merchant named Mashhadí Rizá, whose son was the editor of the newspaper *Shafaq*
("Afterglow"), was arrested by the Russians for his son's fault
and imprisoned in the *Bagh-i-Shimál*, that is to say in the
Russian camp. Subsequently he was handed over to Samad
Khán, in whose prison he remained for a long while, while
they questioned him as to the place of his son's concealment,
so that they might take him and kill him. Since he really
did not know where his son was, he was at length released,
after paying large sums of money, but in such a condition
that he was utterly ruined and his business destroyed. Then
he abandoned his business, sold his house, and went to Julfa
to practice there the trade of a broker. One of my friends
relates that the household and younger brothers of the editor of the *Shafaq* had been so persecuted, and so harassed by
the constant coming and going of Cossacks and *farrashes* that
the lad's mother, in spite of her extreme affection for him,

used to say to her friends, confirming it with oaths, that if she knew where her son was she would go and point out the place, so that her husband and her other children might be delivered from these intolerable persecutions. Happily the mother also was ignorant of the place of her son's concealment, for she had lost her senses by reason of what she had suffered and was desperate.

There was a harmless old man of fifty-eight years of age, respected by all, who had formerly been the governor of the province of Qára-dágh, and was the leader of the regular troops in Tabriz. His name was Mír Háshim Khán, and he was entitled *Sá'idu'l-Mulk*; and he was one of the Constitutionalists. After the arrival of Samad Khán in the city, [on 11th Muharram (January 2nd) out of fear and on his accord, with his son he goes to see Samad Khan. At their arrival they are both seized and are thrown naked into prison. In the bitter winter cold, that poor man, who was one of dignitaries of the city, is chained and tortured. After twenty-six days in prison and having given some 4000 *tumáns* (= £. 800) is exiled. The old man had suffered so much in the prison that when seven months ago he came here to Istanbul, he was quite sick and he lived in poverty. Last week he died here and saddened us all. He had done nothing at all. Of hundreds people who have been arrested or freed by the Russian since the occupation of Tabriz at the beginning of this year, many are still in prison. According to the news arriving here, the coming of the *Sipahdar* has not changed the situation much, as the Russian insist that Samad Khan should remain as the deputy and *pishkar* of the *Sipahdar*. In fact, Samad Khan is in charge and he rules Tabriz. Even *Hishmat'u'd-Dawla* who had officially come to Tabriz as the deputy of the *Sipahdar*, had to return to Tehran. For the time being, the *Sipahdar* obeys Samad Khan.][53] For instance, one of the *mujahidins,* who with his son, though the Russians had sought for him several times and sent soldiers in quest of him, yet could not catch him, and than whom there was no truer or better man amongst the leaders of the National Volunteers in Tabriz, went of his own initiative to the *Sipahdar's* tent after his arrival, and, according to old custom, took refuge (*bast*), under one of his cannons. The *Sipahdar,* however, seized and imprisoned him, and intends apparently to hand him over to the Russians! [54]

As for the further barbarities of Samad Khán and the Russian Government, I have mentioned some of them in a former letter, and there is no need to repeat them. Yet every day fresh news arrives of Samad Khán's injustice and barbarous punishments, which, in the terminology of the old Despotism, they call *nasaq.* Besides the nose-rope, sewing up of mouths, hamstringing, and cutting off fingers and hands, he has an extraordinary passion for cutting off ears. So often has he done this that the cases in which this has been done are currently reported to exceed a hundred. There is seldom

---

53 This bracketed section was translated by the editor.
54 This man must be Hájjí Husayn Khán Márálání, who was well-known for his piety, and in the time of Samad Khán he took refuge in the village of Kundrúd, that belonged to Mirza Hasan, the *mujtahid,* and for a while the people of this *mujtahid* looked after him. After the *Sipahdár* on his way to Tabriz came to a nearby village Barenj, Hájjí Husayn Khán went to him, but the *Sipahdár* submitted him and another Constitutionalist, Karím Khán *Rashídu'l-Mulk* to the Russians. They took both of them to Khuy and hanged them. [Ed.]

a day on which he does not cut off someone's ears, or nail them to the wall of the bazaar. In the latter case they drive an iron nail through the victim's ear into the wall of the bazaar, and so he remains for a whole day, that the passers-by may see him. One of the people of Tabriz said in jest that they would, if they liked, raise a regiment of earless soldiers in Tabriz!

As regards the barbarities perpetrated by the Russians, such as the stripping and plundering of men, shops, houses, and passers-by in the street during the early days after the catastrophe, of all of which you have already heard, the following is a curious detail which I have lately heard. After the body of the late *Thiqatu'l-Islám* had remained for a while on the gallows, and no one dared to go and remove it and give it burial, one of the disciples of the deceased, a certain merchant named Hájjí 'Alí, of the Laylábád quarter, went and took away the body, wrapped it in a winding-sheet, and buried it. In truth the strength of his affection prompted him to so bold a deed, and it was an act of self-sacrifice. Two or three months later Russian Cossacks one night entered the house of this merchant from the roof and stole his things. And since his house was situated at the end of a blind alley, so that the Cossacks must have passed by several other houses in order to reach it, and it was not situated in a thoroughfare, the people guessed that it was in this manner that he had been punished for burying the body of the *Thiqatu'l-Islám*.

Of the horrible cruelties of Samad Khán one was as follows. He sent his *farrashes* to the house of one of the National Volunteers named Mír Husayn Cháwush to find him. Being unable to find him, they seized his little son, aged ten years, so that he might tell them where his father was. He declared that he did not know. When they had bullied and tormented him a great deal, so that he might tell them (though he did not know), they seized his arm to take him before Samad Khán. The boy was very much frightened and cried out in the extreme of terror. Thus they dragged him to the end of the street, and after a while let him go; but he was so terrified that on returning to the house he was seized with haematuria and shortly afterwards died.

I will now, as I promised, pass to the account of some of the other victims, and I will endeavour to obtain their photographs also and send them to you.

The following six persons were hanged by the Russians on the Citadel (*Arg*) of 'Alí -Sháh: (1) Mír Karím the Orator; (2) Mashhadí Mohammad '*Amú-oghlú* of Uskuya; (3) Mashhadí Ahmad the Coffee-seller; (4) Mashhadí Muhammad of Charandáb; (5) Yúz-bashí Ahmad, brother of the well-known Mashhadí Hájjí Qafqázi (see photograph A., No. 3); (6) Another, whose name I do not know.

(1) Mír Karím the Orator *(Nátiq)*. He was about forty years of age, and was a very sincere, much beloved, unassuming, simple-minded, upright and self-sacrificing Constitutionalist, a disinterested patriot, saintly, religious, devout and full of faith; comparable to the martyred Aqá Sayyid Jamálu'd-Dín,

the Preacher of Isfahan,[55] but more sincere, more innocent and purer in motives. The late Mír Karím was the orator of the common people, and had a great influence amongst shopkeepers, labourers, and the humbler guilds of the bazaar, and exerted himself greatly to stir them. When he was led to the gallows, many of the people wept. From first to last he was a tradesman, a dealer in cloth. From the earliest days of the Constitution until the end he labored and strove without ceasing to promote its triumph. He used to go up into the pulpits of the mosques and speak to the common people in their own idiom. During the First Period of the Constitution, he came to Tehran, and worked there to secure the arrest of Rahim Khán of Qaraja-dágh in the month of Rabi' II, A.H. 1325 (= May-June, 1907). He strove amongst the people to protect the National Assembly. He went through the Tabriz Revolution from beginning to end. The common people cherished an extraordinary affection for and devotion to him, and almost worshipped him. During the Second Period of the Constitution he was a Deputy and Member of the Municipal Council, but still worked at his speaking. After the final catastrophe he was for a time in hiding somewhere, but after some days he came by night to his house to obtain news and then return to his hiding place.

The *Kad-Khudá* of the quarter appointed by Samad Khán got news of this and arrested him, and he was cast into Samad Khán's prison. The Russian soldiers who guarded the prison were furnished with a list of the proscribed, and whoever's name was on this black list they carried off to the

---

55 He was killed shortly after the *coup d'etat* of June 23, 1908. An account of him will be found, with his portrait, on p. 113-117; 165-7 and 204-8 of my *Persian Revolution*, Cambridge, 1910.

Russian camp. So they took Mír Karím and brought him to the *Bágh-i-Shimál*. On the following day they placed him on a tumbril, or wagon for carrying goods, and so brought him to the place of execution. Of all those who suffered martyrdom he showed the greatest enthusiasm, ardor and firmness of faith and conviction, and kept continually crying to the people in the streets and thoroughfares through which he had to pass, making impassioned and moving speeches, reciting poetry, and shouting, "Long live the Constitution! Long live Persia!" Every time he stood up the Russian Cossacks struck him on the head with the butts of their guns: and drove him back into the middle of the tumbrel, but again he would rise to his feet and cry, "I am Mír Karím: behold, they are leading me to the slaughter, and I go gladly, for I have known all along that the end would be this, and such an end we have always had in view and expected. O people, the slaughter of me and thousands of others like me for the sake of our Country, and its Freedom and the Constitution is of no consequence! I am not worth the little finger or even the finger-nail of the martyred Mirzá Jahángir Khán, the editor of the *Sur-i-Israfil!*"[56] "The Persian Constitution will not perish!" and so forth. And he continued to cry, "Long live the Constitution!" He was hanged on the Citadel (*Arg-i-'Alí-Sháhí*), and just as he was about to die he shouted, "Long live Hájjí Shaykh 'Abdu'llah of Mázandarán!"[57] According to

---

56 He was one of those who were put to death by Mohammed 'Alí Mirza after the *coup d'etat* of June 23, 1908. See my *Persian Revolution*, p. 208.

57 One of the three great *mujtahids* of Karbalá who strongly supported and worked for the Constitution. Their portraits are given on p. 262 of my *Persian Revolution*.

another account he cried, "The Turkish Sultán will come and take vengeance for our blood from the Russians!"

I knew him personally and we were friends.

(2) Mashhadí Muhammad Usku'í, called *'Amú-oghlú*.

He was about forty years of age, and was one of the best of the National Volunteers, amongst whom, indeed, he was incomparable. Alike in morals, true self-sacrifice, love of his Country and the Constitution, honesty, integrity, zeal and ardour he was one of the best. Before the Constitutional Period I saw him at Bákú, and knew him personally, and from that time dates his membership of and work for the Committee of Persian Social Democrats (*Ijtimá'iyyún-i-'Ámmiyún*), known as *Mujáhid* (i.e. one who strives, fights for faith, or renders personal service). It was through this body that the name *Mujáhid* (afterwards applied to the National Volunteers) first came into use in Persia, for the name *Mujahid* was applied not only to this body, but to the individual members of it, who played a great part in the Persian Revolution and Constitutional Movement.

Well, after the establishment of the Constitution Mashhadí Muhammad Uskú'í came to Tabriz and also for a while to Tehran. During the Revolution of Sattár Khán (i.e. of 1908-9) he was one of the leading National Volunteers, and after the Restoration of the Constitution he was made the *Kad-Khudá*, or Commissioner of the Devechí (Shuturbán) and Surkháb quarters. Not only did he take no part in the recent catastrophe, but he took into his house several Russian soldiers who were fugitives and gave them refuge, thus saving their lives, and I believe that he also saved a Russian officer from death. According to one account he also took care of two or three Russian women. After the conclusion of the fighting he took these refuges to the Russian Consulate and handed them over. For some days after this he was left in peace, and the Russian Consul gave him assurances of safety, while even Samad Khán made him a Constable (*Shahna*) of the city, that is to say appointed him superintendent (*dárúgha*) of the bazaar and conferred on him this office, of which he discharged the functions for some days. But as soon as they had thus reassured him, one day all of a sudden he was arrested and cast into the prison of Samad Khán, who afterwards handed him over to the Russians, who, as I have already stated, hanged him with Mír Karím the Orator and four others at the Citadel. On the scaffold he made a speech and added a few words in Russian. When the executioner approached him to put the noose round his neck as he stood on the stool and then withdrew the stool from under his feet, he kicked him on the chest from above and threw him backwards. Then, with the utmost courage, he himself put the rope round his neck and kicked away the stool.

(The Russian executions in Tabriz are carried out exactly like those of the Russian military tribunals, where they place the political offenders on a stool or chair, put the rope which hangs over his head from the gallows round his neck, and then withdraw the stool from under his feet. In the Citadel (*Arg-i-'Alí-Sháhí*) ten of these Russians gibbets were erected, with stools placed under them all ready, and these still remain today as they were.)

Before Mashhadí Mohammad Usku'i was executed he exclaimed, "We showed mercy and dealt generously with the Reactionaries when we were in power, not knowing that they would show us no mercy." Then he cried, "Long live the Constitution."

Before the Constitution Mashhadí Mohammad was a tradesman in Tabriz and Baku. He was a native of the village of Usku, situated at a distance of four parasangs from Tabriz. He was well known for the rectitude of his morals and character. I was personally acquainted with him.

(3) Mirza Mahmúd of Salmas. He was about forty-five years of age, and was one of the *'ulamá* and *mujtahids*. He was originally a native of Salmas, a town in the neighbourhood of Tabriz. In his youth he was a student of theology, and studied at the College of Hájjí Safar 'Alí at Tabriz, where he was my fellow-student, and we were personal friends. Having finished his studies at Tabriz, he went to Karbalá and Najaf to complete his education, remaining at the latter place several years. After the establishment of the Constitution he returned, settled at Urmiya, and became the *mujtahid* (chief ecclesiastical authority) of that place. In the elections for the Second National Assembly he was elected in the first degree to represent Urmiya in that Assembly. He then came to Tabriz to join those similarly elected in other districts to choose from amongst themselves deputies to represent them in the National Assembly. He was not himself so elected, but *Mukhbiru's-Saltana*, the Governor of Tabriz, would not allow him to return to Urmiya, but requested him to accept the presidency of one of the Courts of Justice, to which proposal he acceded. He was a quiet and inoffensive man.

In the late catastrophe he in no way participated. Samad Khán sought him out and, as it would appear, they found him in a water conduit, and cast him into prison. He was a very pious and God-fearing man, and even while in prison and in chains was regular in his prayers. Samad Khán demanded a thousand *túmáns* (£. 200) for his release, and some of his fellow-citizens succeeded in reducing this demand to

400 *tumáns* (£. 80), but, as they were a little late in bringing it, he was compelled to drink the cup of martyrdom. He was slain with all manner of savage torments and tortures: they plucked out his eyes and cut out his tongue while he was still alive, and then killed him.

(4) Mír 'Alí Akbar Qara,

(5) Mashhadí Háshim *Harráj-chí* (the Auctioneer), and

(6) Imám-qulí Khán were all leading National Volunteers, and the two first-named were both Captains of Volunteers in different quarters of the city during the first siege of Tabriz (1908-9) and the war with Mohammad 'Alí Mirzá's troops.

(7) Mashhadí Ghaffár.

He was a cobbler, and brother to the celebrated Sattár Khán, and was killed in order to take vengeance on his brother. He was arrested in the bath, dragged naked to the prison, and subsequently executed.

(8) Taqí Khán *Yúz-báshí* (the Centurion) of the Khiyábán quarter, known as "Bálá Taqí" (Tall Taqí).[58]

He was about forty-four years of age, and was one of the most notable leaders of the National Volunteers during the first Revolution, a defender of the Khiyábán quarter, and one of the adjutants of Bágir Khán.

He was a very brave and gallant man. He took no part in the recent fighting with the Russians. After the arrival of Samad Khán he first surrendered to him, but afterwards, seeing how he took one after another and slew them, he was afraid, and took refuge in the Turkish Consulate. After a while he

---

58 Browne has incorrectly translated Bálá as "Tall" in the text; whereas it means "Little." [Ed.]

came out from thence, and earned a livelihood by working in the gardens in the surrounding villages. Samad Khán sent a body of his men who shot him at Zarana, a village distant two or three parasangs from Tabriz to the East, took him prisoner, and brought him to Tabriz, where they hanged him head-downwards from a ladder by the Qárí Bridge, after they had cut open his belly. When his bowels fell out and hung down to the ground, they tied them up with a cord to his belly so that they might not fall out. I knew him personally. During the Second Constitutional Period he was *Kad-Khudá*, or Commissioner of the Khiyábán quarter.

(9) Muhammad Dá'í, known as Ajúdán.

His father was a cotton-carder (*Halláj*), whence he was called *Halláj-oglú*. He was one of the leading National Volunteers of the Khiyábán quarter; for five or six months he was in hiding, but latterly, in the month of Sha'bán (= July-August, 1912), he was found and thrown into prison. He was a man of some wealth, and so, besides seizing his house, they inflicted on him many barbarous torments, at the mere recital of which the hair stands on end, such as branding with hot irons, burning with fire on the breast, etc., in order to extort money from him. By holding out hopes of his release from death they finally wrung from him all his wealth, and finally hanged him before the eyes and in the presence of his sister, wife and children. Thrice the rope broke and he fell from the gallows to the ground, and was wounded by the fall, but they hanged him a second and a third time. I knew him personally.

(10) Hájjí 'Alí Khatá'í and his children.

I wrote a detailed account of their fate in a former letter, and there is no need to repeat it here.

(11) Petros Andressian.

He was one of the most respected of the Armenian Liberals in Tehran. He was in the Public Administration, and was in charge of the "three imposts" (*dawá'ir-i-thalátha*) in Tabriz and the whole of Azarbayjan. (The "three imposts" are the offices controlling the sale of opium, the taxes on alcohol and intoxicating liquors, and [weigh-bridge][59] from which were derived the revenues of the Police). For a time he worked at this in the most earnest and systematic manner, until, in the last catastrophe, he was executed by the Russians. The reason for his execution is unknown until today, for he took no part whatever in the recent fighting (with the Russians), and was in no sense a fighting man, but merely a servant of the State employed in a certain branch of the administration. The cause of his execution can, then, only have been his Constitutionalism, or else the desire to terrorize the Armenians. At his execution in the Citadel he shewed the utmost courage. His wife and children were present. He made a splendid speech, said goodbye to his wife and children, walked with the utmost courage and bravery to the foot of the gallows, and said, "Fear not, nor grieve! I am dying in the cause of Freedom." All the people of Tabriz, even the Reactionaries, and all the dwellers in the city, Europeans, Armenians, and Musulmáns alike, were deeply affected and moved to pity, and his martyrdom had a great effect on men's hearts, the more so as he was guiltless of any crime.

(12) Karbalá'í Muhammad Ja'far the Barber (*Dallák*) and his apprentice.

---

59 Browne has omitted translation of the words "máliát-i-qapándárí" which refers to the weigh-bridge tax. See Willem Floor's *A Fiscal History of Iran in the Safavid and Qajar Periods* (New York; Bibliotheca Persica, 1999), p. 400–04. [Ed.]

This was a godly and faithful man who practiced the trade of a barber. The poor man was very quiet and inoffensive and belonged to no political party, and was not even a Constitutionalist. A fight took place in the street wherein he dwelt between the National Volunteers and the Russians, and it would seem that the body of one of the Russians who were killed was thrown into his house. Subsequently he himself went and gave information of this at the Russian Consulate, so that they might come and take away the body. Then they came and took him and an apprentice of his from his shop. The 'ulamá of the city, the merchants and others of the inhabitants went and testified to his innocence, but to no effect, and both he and his apprentice were hanged. This event grieved the people, even the Reactionaries, more than almost any other, and even some of the Reactionary *mullás*, such as Hájjí Mirzá Hasan and others, did their utmost to save his life, but failed.

The names of the victims recorded thus far are those of only the best known and most celebrated, but, according to statements made by my comrades, those who were slain secretly, or were persons but little known were many more. Those so far mentioned form but one class, and they, moreover, were such as suffered at Tabriz only, while many were slain and executed in other districts of Azarbayjan, and in the villages and smaller towns, and in little hamlets, whence no news transpired, no less injustice was wrought. Thus the accursed *Rashídu'l-Mulk* strangled seven Constitutionalists at Saráb, a village near Ardabíl, in one day, and hanged those others head downwards until they died; and this instance which has lately come to our knowledge gives but an inkling of his villainies. So, too, in Urmiya the Russian Consul acting directly or through the instrumentality of the Governor

Ijlálu'l-Mulk, who simply carries out the Consul's orders and does whatever the Consul bids him, killed several of the National Volunteers, such as Mashhadí Isma'íl, the leader of the Urmiya Volunteers. Other prominent Constitutionalists of that place, being homeless fugitives, have in some cases arrived here, while others, artisans and merchants, to the number of about fifty, took refuge in the Turkish Consulate, until finally the Russians and the Government insisted on their expulsion, and they went to Ván. The Russian Consul also, by means of his Cossacks, dragged from his house and from the side of his wife Mirzá Mahmúd Khán Ashraf-záda, the chief editor of the newspaper *Farwardín,* and tied him up and flogged him in the public square, as I formerly wrote to you. Ashraf-záda himself is now here, living in extreme poverty. In Khuy, Salmas and Ardabil also they did many cruel deeds. At Shabistar, a little town situated eight parasangs from Tabriz, where I have relatives and kinsfolk, Samad Khán perpetrated such cruelties that the people nearly emigrated *en masse.* For instance, I myself know that Samad Khán's agent set one of his men at the post-office to open and read all the letters which came for people, and someone from Tabriz having written a letter to a certain merchant in which the phrase "the Constitution will come all right again" occurred, they hanged this merchant, in Shabistar, in the winter cold, from night-fall until dawn, head-downwards in a stable, and in the morning let him go after exacting from him a fine of 500 *tumáns* (£. 100). It is a wonder that he did not die! And this they did in spite of the fact that not he but another had written the letter in question. From this incident judge [the] others.

Amidst all these barbarities the only thing which affords any consolation or hope is that most of these martyrs went to the scaffold with the utmost courage and intrepidity, and, face to face with death, uttered words full of enthusiasm, and died in full belief of the Life of Persia and her future salvation. The speeches of these were in many cases not recorded, but according to all reports they certainly exhibited great courage which merits admiration and appreciation.

The barbarities of the Russians and the slaughterings, plunderings and other aggressions of Samad Khán continue until today, but since the arrival of the *Sipahdár* no one has been executed.[60] The throwing of his victims into watertanks and beating them on the head from all sides, which is one of the inventions of the accursed Samad Khán, continued almost daily until the beginning of Ramazán (August 14, 1912). Yesterday a letter came from Tabriz from one of the Constitutionalists who was in Constantinople and has now returned to Tabriz to one of his friends here. In it he writes that latterly the Russian soldiers have again begun to behave in the same way as they did last year before the Ultimatum (*i.e.* at the end of 1911). "I do not know," he continues, "why they have thus increased their cruelty and aggressiveness. They molest people in the thoroughfares and bazaars and strike them with their whips. Two days ago a Russian soldier, who was walking in the bazaars with a number of his comrades, stretched out his hand and took some grapes from a fruiterer's shop. The fruiterer caught hold of his arm and followed him to recover his property. Thereupon the soldier drew a dagger and struck him so fiercely that he cut through his wrist, and his hand remained hanging only by the skin.

---

60 Mr. G. D. Turner in his letter in the *Manchester Guardian* of September 3, 1912, says that a fugitive Constitutionalist was executed two days before he reached Tabriz, on August 5, 1912.

Last night likewise several Russian soldiers entered the *Chol Bághí* and wounded four persons, one of whom, Mashhadí Ibráhím the pea-parcher (*nukhúd-paz*) lies at death's door." (*Chol Bághí* is a large garden in the South-east of the city in the Márálán quarter.)

This is what, in a fragmentary manner, has come to my knowledge concerning events at Tabriz and the biographies of its martyrs. Anything which I may subsequently learn I will write to you, I have found here a number of the (illustrated Turkish magazine entitled) *Resmli Kitáb* containing a photograph of the martyrs of *Qúm Bághí*, namely, Hájjí 'Alí *Dawá-furúsh*, Mirzá Ahmad Suhaylí, and Karím Khán and Muhammad Khán, the nephews of Sattár Khán. I am forwarding it to you by this post. Farewell!

The Russian gallows decorated with their colors.

The two nephews of Sattár Khán (the hero of the
Siege of Tabriz in 1908–9) were hanged by the
Russians in January, 1912. The one on the right is
Muhammad Khán, "Amir-Tuman" ("Commander
of Ten Thousand") and the one on the left, his
elder brother, Karím Khán.

No. 21

Biography of the *Thiqatu'l-Islám* published in the Persian *Hablu'l-Matín* (Calcutta) on September 9, 1912.[61]
(A portrait of the *Thiqatu'l-Islám* precedes the biography, and under it is the following inscription.)

"Deem not those slain in God's Way dead, but rather living, provided for by their Lord"[62]

That Martyr of the Path of the Freedom of Islam, that faithful servant of Islamic lands, who preferred the Faith to the things of this world; that famous man of Learning and profound philosopher, that eminent man of letters and distinguished writer, that Leader of the Nation and of the Faith and Guardian of Islam and the Muslims, Aqá Mirzá 'Alí *Thiqatu'l-Islám,* the *mujtahed* of Tabriz, who, as a recompense for his patriotism and service to Islam, mounted the Russian gallows on the afternoon of the *'Ashurá,* A.H. 1330 (= Janu-

---

61 In 1999, Iraj Afshar published a collection of letters of
Thiqatu'l-Islám to *Mustashár ad-Dawla* under the title, *Namehá
yi Tabriz: az Thiqatu'l-Islám bi Mustashár ad-Dawla (dar ruzgar-i
mashrutiyyat)* (Tehran: Farzan) which covers the period January
1907 through May 1911. In this collection, *Thiqatu'l-Islám*
discusses in a cryptic manner the political and social affairs of
the time. The letters describe in detail the social and political
events of Tabriz in these critical years and reveal an amazing
liberal-mindedness and tolerant views of this eminent cleric.
[Ed.]
62 *Koran,* 3, 169.

ary 1, A.D. 1912) in the city of Tabriz, and thus attained to the lofty rank of martyrdom.

Mirzá 'Alí *Thiqatu'l-Islám*, son of Mirzá Musá *Thiqatu'l-Is-lám*, son of Mirzá Shafi' the *mujtahid* of Tabriz, was accounted one of the celebrated scholars and men of learning of his age, and belonged to a distinguished family of Azarbayjan. He was connected with Hájjí Mirzá Rafi', the famous *Kálantar*, and was born in the month of Rajab, A.H. 1278 (= January, 1862). His martyrdom took place on Muharram 10, A.H. 1330 (= January 1, 1912).

The *Thiqatu'l-Islám* was one of the philosophers of his age, and famous amongst lovers of Liberty and men of letters. He had a good command of the Persian, Arabic, Turkish and French languages. His philosophical articles, published in the *Hablu'l-Matin* and the Egyptian *Hilal*, etc., were numerous, and he was the author of other works and treatises. He was the head of the Shaykhí sect in Azarbayjan, being a follower of the late Shaykh Ahmad Ahsá'i, and, even beyond Tabriz and Azarbayjan, his disciples were numerous throughout the Caucasus and at Erivan, Nakhjuwan, Qara Bágh and Ganja (now called Elizavetpol). The quarrel which formerly arose in Azarbayjan between the Shaykhí and Úsulí sects was entirely composed by this holy man, who put an end to the mutual recriminations of Úsulís and Shaykhís, and brought about a sincere reconciliation between them, so that now for many years they mix together like milk and sugar.

Since the late *Thiqatu'l-Islám* was cognizant of the news of the time and had an adequate acquaintance with the modern sciences, he, unlike the majority of the *'ulamá* of Azarbayjan, from the very beginning of the Constitutional Revolution in Persia, grasped in his hand the banner of Freedom.[63] The late Muzaffaru'd-Din Sháh was particularly devoted to him, which even Mohammad 'Alí, the ex-Sháh, ostensibly professed a similar devotion. Thus it was that during the conflict of the Nationalists and Royalists in Tabriz, the late *Thiqatu'l-Islám* enjoyed the confidence of both sides, and all the negotiations for peace which passed between *'Aynu'd-Dawla*, Tehran, and the Nationalist leaders in Tabriz were carried on through him. He repeatedly went to Básminch as the representative of the people to Prince *'Aynu'd-Dawla*, and took part in negotiations for peace.

Although the *Thiqatu'l-Islám* was a Liberal, yet he favoured moderation, and constantly counselled the people against violent measures and in favour of pursuing the end in view in a manner conformable to the requirements of the time. About two years ago the Russians, on the pretext that one of their soldiers had taken refuge in his home, sent an officer and several privates to make a domiciliary visit. They found no traces there of the missing man, who, at the very time they were hunting for him, was calmly walking about in the bazaars of Tabriz. In consequence of pressure exerted at Tehran on the

---

63 Kasravi in *Tarikh-i Mashruta-yi Iran* (p.348) writes: "The only one of the great *mullás* of who remained with the Constitution was *Thiqatu'l-Islám*. Although he did not show very much enthusiasm and fervor, he stood firm in his commitment to the progress of the country and its people." Then referring to the incident of the expulsion of Mirzá Hasan *Mujtahid* from Tabriz in which *Thiqatu'l-Islám* also left Tabriz, he says that there was a difference. "Since there had always been hostility and rivalry between [*Thiqatu'l-Islám's*] family and that of *Mujtahid*, he showed sympathy in order to stop the tongue of slanderers." Kasravi's reference is to the *mullás* of Tabriz that while most of them turned away from the Constitution, *Thiqatu'l-Islám* remained steadfast in his liberal ideas. [Ed.]

Russian Legation, the Russian Consul-General at Tabriz was obliged to make a formal apology to the late *Thiqatu'l-Islám*, and he cherished this grudge in his heart until, when an opportunity arose, he was able to gratify his revenge.

During the last revolution at Tabriz the *Thiqatu'l-Islám* made the most strenuous efforts and endeavours to reconcile the two conflicting parties. The proclamations, both written and verbal, issued from him to the *fidá'ís*, and the correspondence conducted by him on this subject with the British and Russian Consuls prove that his ideals were entirely pacific end conciliatory; while that he remained boldly and steadfastly in his house, devoting himself without fear or apprehension to the furtherance of a peaceful solution, shows that he relied completely on the innocence of his conduct and actions; nor, indeed, did anyone imagine that any could, without any cause or reason, meditate evil against him. The letter which the Russian and British Consuls wrote to him some days before his martyrdom, and which are still in existence, clearly demonstrate his peaceful and conciliatory disposition and his complete detachment from politics antagonistic to the Russians, and, indeed, as some of the *fidá'ís* assert, had it not been for his strenuous efforts to secure peace and tranquility on the part of the people, the Russians would not so easily have overrun Tabriz and the whole of Azarbayjan. But as soon as the Russians were reassured as to their occupation of Tabriz, had set up their cannons to command every street and quarter, had posted guards, and laid low the loftier buildings, and the townsfolk, unwarned from any quarter, were busy some in (the Muharram) mourning for the Imam Husayn, some in weeping and lamenting over the innocent slain, while others were occupied with their own sufferings from hunger and destitution, and a few filled with fear for the future, the following proceedings took place.

On the afternoon of the *Tásu'á* (or 9th of Muharram, A.H. 1330 = December 31, 1911) the Russian Consul sent several persons with a special message to the late *Thiqatu'l-Islám*. In this letter he wrote: "A meeting for consultation and the conclusion of peace is being held in the British Consulate with the other foreign Consuls, at which your presence is urgently required." The *Thiqatu'l-Islám*, without any sort of fear or apprehension arose and accompanied them. As soon as he had left his house, the messengers took him to the Russian Consulate. On meeting the Russian Consul he said, "Your message was an invitation to the British Consulate: why have they brought me here?" The Russian Consul roughly addressed him in unseemly words. The *Thiqatu'l-Islám*, with a courage which demonstrated the perfection of his faith, replied, "Such unconstrained speech is not fitting on the part of the respected representative of a great Power, nor am I willing to defile my mouth, as you have done, with vituperation and unseemly words." Then the Russian Consul placed a sheet of paper before the *Thiqatu'l-Islám* on which was written: "the *fidá'ís* in Tabriz first fired on the Russian troops, who behaved in the most humane and civilized manner, and killed no one unjustly," and the document concluded with the words, "We, the people of Tabriz, are not willing that the Russian troops should withdraw from Tabriz, for fear that fresh occasions of disturbance may arise in the city; and we are extremely pleased with the good conduct and discipline of the Russian troops in Tabriz."

The *Thiqatu'l-Islám* gently observed, "This declaration is contrary to the truth, nor can my pen defile itself by making such an affirmation." At these words the Russian Consul blazed out in rage, and he and two other members (of the Court-Martial) who were present fell to vituperating, reviling and abusing him to the utmost of their powers, to such a degree that he fainted from his sufferings. Then, in the bitter cold weather, they carried this martyr for the sake of Islam's freedom into an uncarpeted room and inflicted on him every suffering they could compass.

At twelve o'clock on the night of the 'Àshúrá (*i.e.* just about the entry of the New Year of 1912) Mirzá 'Alí Akbar Khán, the *Munshi* (Persian Secretary of the Consulate) again came to the *Thiqatu'l-Islám* on the part of the Russian Consul-General and requested him to sign the above-mentioned declaration. "Alas! Alas!" he replied: "say to the Consul that I, in imitation of my Master, will not put forth my hand to do wrong, even though I should (in consequence of this refusal), be sent to join my Master Abu 'Abdu'llah al-Husayn." Then he turned to Mirzá 'Alí Akbar Khán, the *Munshi*, and said, "Since thou wert born in Islam, I beg of you a little water to perform my ablution, so that I may engage in my Devotions." Mirzá 'Alí Akbar Khán promised to send the water, but broke his promise, so that the *Thiqatu'l-Islám*, like his Master (the Imam Husayn) had to be content with the dry ablution (with sand), after which he betook himself to Divine Worship.

Until after midday on the Àshúrá, repeated attempts were made on the part of the Consul to induce him by threats, promises, inducements and menaces to sign the document in question, but, in reply to all their importunity, the *Thiqatu'l-Islám* persisted in his refusal, and finally said, "Never by my pen will I sanction the triumph of Infidelity over Islam, or justify the infidels!" They several times so cruelly entreated him in the Russian Consulate that he lost his senses and fainted away.

At length they brought him to the foot of the gallows. A watch was set on the environs, sentries were posted at the ends of the streets and passages, and traffic was stopped on every side. When they were about to suspend him from the gallows, they again demanded of him that he should sign the declaration, but he again refused. Just as they were hanging him, he turned his face towards the *qibla* and said in a weak voice: "I bear witness that there is no god but God, and I bear witness that Mohammad is the Apostle of God! O Apostle of God, bear witness for me that I have not fallen short in the way of guarding thy Faith, and that I have not been led astray by the deceit of this world, nor confirmed with my pen the triumph of Infidelity over Islam!" As he said these words, his saintly spirit winged its way to the groves of Paradise: and "they shall know who have wrought injustice with what a turning they shall be turned!" [64]

(*Hablu'l-Matin*'s Note)

If we look closely into the circumstances accompanying the martyrdom of the *Thiqatu'l-Islám*, many obscure matters will become plain to us. According to what writers who enjoy the confidence of this office have written during the last few years, the late *Thiqatu'l-Islám* had no aim save to compose the differences between the conflicting parties, and the Russians had no legal pretext for compassing his death. Several reasons appear, however, which explain their action

---

64 *Koran*, 26, 227.

in this matter. One of these is his refusal to sign the false declaration prepared by the Russian Consul-General; but the chief object of the Russians was to show the present political and religious apathy of the people of Tabriz, which for several years had filled the world with zeal, courage and awakening political and religious sensibilities. Moreover the Russians, having secured their conquest by the quiescence of the people of Tabriz, realized that, so long as the *Thiqatu'l-Islám* existed, they would be unable to find any fresh pretext (for intervention) on the ground of national or religious ferment for pursuing their aggressive aims more than before. For the same reason they publicly hanged the late *Thiqatu'l-Islám* on the afternoon of the Day of the *'Àshúrá*, which is accounted the most holy day of the Mohammedan year, in order to increase the agitation of the Muslims.

This view of the execution of the late *Thiqatu'l-Islám* is nowhere more clearly set forth than in the White Book, from which we subjoin some extract in translation.

(Here follow two columns of translated extract from the White Book.) The article then continues:

From the official correspondence cited above it clearly appears that the execution of the late *Thiqatu'l-Islám* was chiefly due to several causes, to wit, first, to gratify the Russian soldiers' desire for vengeance; secondly, to excite the Persian people against the Russians and so afford a pretext for seizing Tehran; thirdly to avenge the death of a Greek priest who was killed in Macedonia,[65] as the Russian Foreign Minister himself explained to the British Ambassador at St. Petersburg. How admirable a thing is "Civilization"! In putting to death the *Thiqatu'l-Islám* the Russians were

---

65   See page 131 for more about this incident.

themselves even more apprehensive than the English, as is shown by a Reuter's Telegram of that time stating that the Russian Government was increasing the number of its troops in the Caucasus, the reason for which apparently was lest the Musulmans (of the Caucasus) might be goaded into revolt on hearing of the catastrophe of Tabriz and the execution of the *Thiqatu'l-Islám*. According to a despatch of Sir George Barclay, the British Minister at Tehran to Sir Edward Grey, which appears on p. 74 of the White Book, No.5, the Persian Cabinet censored all telegrams which it was feared might excite the people, and prevented their publication, which precaution on their part was the principal reason for the absence of excitement amongst the Persians at the execution of the *Thiqatu'l-Islám*. Even so the *Revue du Monde Musulman* of Paris writes: "the Russians increased the number of their troops in Ganja, Qara-Dágh, Persia, Baku, etc., on the occasion of the *Thiqatu'l-Islám*'s death because of the number of his disciples in those places, lest some popular movement should take place against the Russian troops."

To prove the savagery displayed by the Russians at the execution of the *Thiqatu'l-Islám*, Shaykh Salím, the *Ziyá'u'l-'Ulamá*, *Sádiqu'l-Mulk*, and four other Members of the Provincial Council of Tabriz, whom they hanged on the afternoon of the *'Áshurá*, there is nothing more convincing than the photographs...published in some of the English papers, and we will quote here, in a somewhat abridged form, what the Editor of the *Manchester Guardian* says about them in the issue of August 13 of that paper:

"The death of the *Thiqatu'l-Islam* is a historical murder, and one may say that from the beginning of Islam until now such a thing has not happened to the Muslims, that is to say that an eminent divine and leading *mujtahíd* of the Muslims should be publicly hanged in broad daylight by the Infidels. It is for the Muslims of the world not to forget this epoch-making catastrophe, and to commemorate everywhere and always the illustrious name of the martyred *Thiqatu'l-Islám*, who, after the martyrs of Karbalá, Badr and Hunayn,[66] is the greatest of those who gave their lives for their country, for Islam and for the Islamic Constitution."

Mirzá 'Alí Thiqatu'l-Islám with
his father Mirzá Musá

---

66 Badr and Hunayn are two of the great battles of the Prophet
    Muhammad.[Ed.]

EUROPEAN ACCOUNTS

Apart from the official despatches and communications contained in the White Book (Cd. 5, p. 17) published on [the basis of] the only printed accounts in English of what happened at Tabriz in the winter of 1911-1912 and subsequently embodying information collected on the spot are, so far as I know, those of Mr. G. Douglas Turner and Mr. Morgan Phillips Price. Of these gentlemen the former visited Tabriz early in August, 1912, collected a great deal of information from residents in that city, and published some of the facts, which he had gleaned in the *Manchester Guardian* of September 3 of the same year. He also brought back a collection of 19 photographs illustrative of the horrible events described in this book, of which 12 had already reached this country by another channel somewhat earlier. Some of these photographs appeared in the *Graphic*, the *Sphere*, *Egypt*, the *Anglo-Russian*, etc.; and almost the entire series, with explanatory letter-press, was published in the form of a pamphlet entitled *The Reign of Terror at Tabriz: England's Responsibility (with Photographs and a Brief Narrative of the events of December, 1911, and January, 1912)*. Mr. Turner was fiercely attacked by the Russophile *Pall Mall Gazette* and replied with great spirit. Mr. Phillips Price visited Tabriz later, in October,

1912, in the course of a journey through Turkey in Asia to Tehran, and published his observations first in the *Gloucester* and afterwards in a paper read before[1] and subsequently printed by the Persia Society under the title of *A Journey through Azarbayjan and Persian Kúrdistán*. Both travelers were very disagreeably impressed by what they saw and heard of the Russian methods. European residents in Tabriz are either Consular officers, whose information to their respective governments, if published at all in Blue Books, White Books, Yellow Books and the like, is only published in part and in a carefully expurgated form; or merchants, traders, professional men, missionaries, and the like, whose position compels them to avoid offending the Russian officials, who really rule Azarbayjan, and who are able to expel them or render their lives intolerable. But the testimony of European residents, so far as it is obtainable, entirely confirms the Persian narratives printed above. From a collection of letters from such I will now subjoin a few extracts; but in many cases, for the reasons indicated above, it was expressly stipulated by the writers that their statements should not be published, so that I am obliged to withhold many of the more forcible passages, while in all cases I have been compelled to avoid giving any indication which might lead to the identification of the writer. The first extract (undated) is from a letter written in January or February, 1912, and describes "the terrible destitution now existing in this city."

"I have never seen anything like it," says the writer; "*Shujá 'u 'd-Dawla*, fighting to restore Mohammad 'Alí Sháh to the throne, held all the roads leading into the city, except the one to Julfá, from the month of August, preventing the

---

1   It was read on March 7, 1913.

entrance of food and fuel and completely stopping all traffic. He thus produced an artificial famine, the price of all
the necessities of life going up to three and four times the
normal rate. They were already so high as to make it very
difficult for many to live, and now this stoppage of business,
which threw many out of work, and the frequent closing of
the bazaars made it very hard. This man (*i.e. Shujá'u'd-Dawla*)
allowed some wheat to come in at a high price or toll, which
went into his own pocket. When people would naturally be
laying in supplies for the winter, they were unable to do so.
Many persons who were well off have been reduced by the
disturbances of the last three years to deep poverty. They have
sold off everything they could part with and are face to face
with starvation. Everyone is in a state of terror and many
in hiding. There is no work going on, and the cold winter
adds to the distress of the situation ... We find people without
fire when the temperature is some degrees below freezing,
without anything but the hard earthen floor to sleep on, and
sometimes with no covering for their bodies at night and
very insufficiently clothed, also with no food... Prices still
continue high, and there is no prospect of relief."

Another resident wrote towards the end of January or
beginning of February, 1912:

"Houses have been looted and blown up, and there has
been a great deal of robbery pure and simple, also false accusations. Instead of law and order, as we were having it, and
security, there is lawlessness and extortion, such as I never
knew of in existence, even under the old *régime*. The number
of executions is between sixty and seventy, still going on, and
every case is the pretext for the most shameless and heartless
extortion. The city is given into the hands of the *Shujá'u'd-
Dawla*, whose aim seems to be to wreck it ...I know you

have been watching all that has gone on here with much interest, and you will appreciate the reasons why I do not write fully ...You have had plenty of information and some misinformation in the telegrams sent to England, especially to the *Times*."

Another resident, writing on January 21, 1912, says:

"The decrees of the Russians that all men in any way connected with the recent troubles should be hanged, and that all houses from which any shooting had been going on should be razed to the ground are being fulfilled, and our hearts are heavy for our friends ...Yesterday they began with the Armenians, and Petros Khán (Andressian) was hanged. Some say there are twenty-five Armenians in all to be hanged, some a hundred...The dynamite explosions keep us jumping. It is all so ruthless and heart-rending.You, who are so well acquainted with Russian methods of terrorizing, can probably understand much of the situation without all the painful details."

Another resident, writing about the same date, tells of the closing of a Persian school, the shooting of a Muslim woman who came to the door of her house to look after her son, and other such things. "And for this state of affairs," adds the transmitter of this letter, "England is partly responsible!" He further adds:

"It is to be borne in mind that it is not safe even to send letters through Russia, on account of what is called "the Black Cabinet", which makes it its business to open letters. "What was that tobacco smoke in your letter?" wrote a Russian correspondent to me — a hint that my letters were being opened."... Certainly the holding back of important information on grounds of prudence is a great drawback in the way of arousing general interest. There are times when it is necessary to risk everything, and then again there are times when such a course would be unwise. It is not always easy to know which is the right course."

The following extract is from a letter dated Tabriz, March 8, 1912:

"The city seems quiet, but prices are higher than ever, and we are thronged with half-starved humanity. You know what ordinary conditions are here. Crops were poor last year. The city has suffered three sieges, and there has been much devastation of the surrounding country. The bread-winner has been taken away from many families, while in others the man of the house is in hiding, and at heavy expense to preserve the secret of his refuge. It is costing one man, who can ill afford the expense, about 125 *túmáns* (£. 25) a month to keep his head in a safe place. One person I know of, a man in good circumstances, after having a large sum taken from him, was sent in chains to Marágha, and there money is demanded constantly. His family [members] are at the end of their resources, and are afraid it will cost him his life if he does not continue to pay out money. Some of the men that have been hanged were poor men, but their families had to pay to get their bodies, after having all the money extorted which it was possible to wring out of them. One member of the *Anjuman* (Provincial Council), it is said, had ten thousand *túmáns* (£ 2000) taken from him before he was executed. As I understand, he paid it, supposing he was buying his life, but, after the money was raised, he was arrested and executed, his house stripped, doors, windows, beams, etc. carried off, and the walls blown up with dynamite. I do not know what the family had left, but of course such a family has friends, and they are not likely to suffer for common necessaries as poorer families do, but there has been a great impoverishment of the people. Then, of course, many lives are lost in fighting. Business is paralyzed, and men willing to work, with families to provide for, are unable to obtain employment. Between the Russian army and the hordes of Samad Khán – mounted men who have been brought in – there is a great consumption of food-stuff that ordinarily does not have to be provided, and this tends to keep prices up and the supply down. I never expected to live through such a reign of terror as the last winter has been."

The following is from another letter from the same writer, dated March 9, 1912:—

"I want to add another word in regard to the situation here. We keep seeing in the papers that the situation is improving in Persia, and that Russia is withdrawing her troops. Troops are being massed on the Turkish frontier and some have been sent over from Tabriz, but if the Russian troops should be withdrawn the city would, be entirely in the hands of Samad Khán. The city is full of his horsemen. Not only the fighting men but the citizens have been obliged to give up all arms, the barricades and defenses have been pulled down, and the leaders of the people killed or dispersed. There is no representative of the Tehran Government, for Samad Khán is not recognized by the Government. It would seem as if conditions could not be worse if Russia should withdraw, but there have been no indiscriminate looting and massacres so far. The *Ark* (Citadel) is being leveled. A good deal of the walls has now been taken down, and this week the *Bálá-Khána* was dynamited."

The following is from another letter written on March 23 by one of the correspondents already quoted: –

"With regard to matters here, they are better in one respect. The daily arrests and public executions have come
almost to a standstill. But one man has been executed lately in public, but there is just as much extortion of money
and oppression going on as ever. Business is quite dead. The
self-constituted governor, who has never been officially
appointed or recognized by anybody except the Russians,
continues to rule with a rod of iron. The old Government
chastised with whips, but he is chastising with scorpions.
People are dying with hunger, and he is the principal wheat-
merchant. I have heard that he fined a baker twenty *tumáns*
(=£.4) lately for a slight reduction in the price of bread. We
don't know what is going to occur, but the Russian troops,
instead of being withdrawn, are being increased, and are being sent to different parts of Ázarbayján. There are vague
rumours of apprehended trouble, and many think that an
artificial outbreak will be produced to justify the annexation
of the province. The poverty and distress are very great."

The following is from a friend familiar with Tabriz and in
correspondence with residents there:

"A letter of July 13, 1912, from Tabriz speaks of the *Near
East* as much more reliable than the *Times* about Persian
affairs and says that the silence of late in regard to Tabriz
and Ázarbayján does not mean that nothing is going on:
that for some months there has been fighting in the Ardabil
and Saráb regions, the Russians attempting to disarm the
Sháhsevens, who have given up Mohammad 'Alí Mirzá and
accepted his son; that they are contending for the independence of Ázarbayján, which the writer evidently fears
is hopelessly lost; and that they are against Samad Khán,
who is acting Governor by his own appointment, who
has neither conquered the city nor been appointed by any

recognized authority, and who is a tool in the hands of Russia as long as it serves her purpose, and can be disowned at any time. He says that it is strange if England is really fooled by Russia's saying that she is withdrawing her troops from this place and province. A few whose time has expired have gone home but other soldiers are coming all the time. The *Times* not only suppresses the truth, but tells that which is false and misleading. Many new men and cannon have just come in today (July 13, 1912), and others went last week against the Sháhsevens."

The Tabriz *Ark*, or Citadel with the Russian flag
hoisted over it.

Explosion in the *Ark*, or Citadel, caused by
careless handling of shells by the Russians.

AFTERWORD

HASAN JAVADI

Letters from Tabriz ends in July 1912, when the Russians are in control of Azerbaijan, and the attempts of the second *Majlis* to put the finances of Iran in order by bringing Morgan Shuster to Iran have not been realized. Devoted and sincere in his mission, Shuster tried to help Iran, but right from the beginning he was convinced of the unjustness of the Anglo-Russian Convention. He ignored the two legations and tried to retain the support of the *Majlis*, which was badly divided and had no power. Even if he had had a broader understanding of the politics in Iran, his problem with the Russians would not have been resolved. He tried to understand the Russian position, but it was very unclear and furthermore, because the Russians did not want him to succeed, they were not forthcoming with information. He similarly failed to grasp the fear of Sir Edward Grey of Germany in backing the Russians in Iran. Right from the beginning the Russians and their sympathizer, M. Mornard, Iran's Belgian chief of customs, frustrated his efforts of financial reforms. Within a short time Shuster had not only become engaged in the dangerous showdown between the British and the Russians, but was badly mired in the internal factional politics of Iran. Shuster's relations with the British dissenters of Grey's foreign policy, particularly Browne, as well as the Democrats in Iran were extremely cordial. Shuster was bitterly opposed to the bid of the ex-Sháh to the throne and his attempt to return to Iran. Soon after came Shuster's decision to form a treasury gendarme force under Major Stokes, whose sympathy with the Iranian nationalists was well known. Stokes wrote to Browne: "The Russians are doing their best to hamper Shuster and to encourage Reaction and it will be interesting to see what line Grey takes with them about the Shuster affair and about the appointment offered to me."[1] Stokes' four-year appointment in Iran was nearing a close and the Indian government had asked him to return to India. It was from this time on that Russia started asking for the dismissal of Shuster. In spite of the campaign of the British dissenters in support of Stokes' continued stay in Iran, Sir Edward Grey again sided with the Russians in their fight with Shuster. At the end of the year Shuster was dismissed and thus ended the attempt to reform Persian finances with American assistance. It can be said that the fight between the Russians and Shuster was the last phase of the Constitutional Revolution and despite general growing fear of Germany, Grey's unquestioning support for Russian demands produced much bitter criticism of him.

The Russian atrocities in Tabriz had prompted the Persia Committee to further action and Browne wrote and spoke about them in every possible publication and venue. Pictures of their brutality, in some of which Russian soldiers were shown posing beside their victims, were widely circu-

---

1   July 17, 1911, Letters from Persia 1910-1911, Add Mss. 7604, f. 58, quoted by Bonakdarian, *op.cit*, p. 252.

lated and published in his *Russian Reign of Terror in Tabriz*[2] in October 1912. Shuster, returning from Iran, spoke to the Persia Committee at the end of January and gave a scathing account of British and Russian actions. In a letter to Browne on December 6, 1911, he wrote: "I can assure you as a man that the spectacle now presented to us here of the strangling of the national spirit of a people who have lived for centuries under the most frightful despotism and tyranny, and who only recently have begun to enjoy even the sentiments of liberty, though without many of its practical benefits, is a most sickening and melancholy one." He continues that *The London Times* called Browne a "dreamer and sentimentalist," but "from their smug editorials I take it they consider any man who dares to look further than his own pantry or larder as stamped with his seal," (and an idealist). "While I am no student of England's political problems, I cannot help but believe that if the British people permit themselves to be carried along these lines to the inevitable conclusion, their prestige and even the integrity of the British Empire itself will before many years have suffered a series of surprising shocks."[3]

Although Sir Edward Grey had given public assurances that once Shuster was dismissed the Russian forces would pull out of Iran, there was no sign of it. They committed more such atrocities in Rasht, Anzalí and Gilan. The people of these cities in protest to the crackdown of the Russians closed their shops, and Nekrasov, the Russian

---

2   Browne in a letter to Taqí-záda (Nov. 15 1912) says that 7000 free copies of this pamphlet had been distributed, *Nameh-haye Browne beh Taqí-záda*, p. 59.

3   Shuster's letter to Browne from Tehran, of which I have a copy.

Consul in Rasht, on the slightest pretexts, and sometimes without any excuse, ordered the killing of sympathizers of the Constitution. Unlike the Russophile British consul in Tabriz, Shipley, who denied any wrongdoing on their side, H. L. Rabino, the British vice-consul in Rasht, saved some Constitutionalists by allowing them to take refuge at the consulate. He was one of Browne's informants and a Persian scholar in his own right. When in September 1912 the Russian foreign minister traveled to London, the public demonstrations against him made him aware of the extent of the British antipathy towards St. Petersburg's policies in Iran. Sir Edward Grey, who was constantly criticized for the Russian actions, asked for some moderation on their part. Meanwhile, the Persia Committee, one of whose members had been detained protesting against the Russian foreign secretary Dimitrovich Sazanov, issued an appeal to the two powers, asking them not to divide Persia, and to observe the terms of the 1907 Convention regarding her territorial integrity. Persia officially protested as she was excluded from a conference in which her fate was discussed.

Pressure from every side and the demand of the people of Tabriz induced the Iranian government to send a governor to Azerbaijan and oust Rahím Khán, who had become the virtual governor of the province under the Russians. It was not easy to find a strong and effective constitutionalist who could be acceptable to the Russians. Eventually, after months of deliberations Muhammad Valí Khán *Sipahsálár Tunkáboní* was chosen and persuaded to go to Tabriz. He was one of the conquerors of Tehran, a former prime minister, and had somewhat good relations with the Russians. On July 27, 1912 Samad Khán forced a number of merchants and dignitaries of Tabriz to sign a petition that they wanted Samad Khán as the governor. In order to show his defiance to the central government, he hanged Imám-qulí, a close friend of Sattár Khán and Yuzbáshí Taqí, one of the leaders of the Constitutionalists. On August 4, the Russians notified Samad Khán that they had accepted Sipahsálár as the governor and he had to cooperate. Although outwardly respecting Sipahsálár, Samad Khán did not stop creating tension between him and the Russians. In a letter published in the Blue Book[4] by Sazanov to the British ambassador in St. Petersburg, Arthur Nicholson, Sazanov complains that Sipahsálár had secretly allowed 900 *mujahids* to enter the city. Although the Tabrizis regarded Sipahsálár as their hero and hoped he would save them from Samad Khán and the Russians, he could not effectively stand up to them. In one instance, he even handed over to the Russians Husayn Khán Márálání, a well known leader of the Constitutionalists who had taken refuge with him. From the start Sipahsálár knew full well that without having a proper army he could not put an end to the rule of the Russians and Samad Khán, but he tried and relatively succeeded in stopping their atrocities. He managed to negotiate the departure of a number of Constitutionalists who had taken refuge in foreign consulates in Tabriz. After a few months, he asked for a leave of absence and left Tabriz for Europe. The government wanted to send the crown prince, Muhammad Hasan Mirzá, to Tabriz, as had been the custom throughout the nineteenth century, but there was no chief of staff or *pishkár* to be found for him. Eventually the crown prince went to Tabriz and Samad Khán was chosen as his *pishkár!* As the Persian saying goes, "This time the thief

---

4   Quoted by Mehdi Malekzadeh, *Tarikh-I Mashrutiyyat-e Iran*, vol. 6–7 (Tehran, 1974) 1584.

came with a royal edict!" Samad Khán was so much a vassal of Russia that on March 5, 1913, he forced the people to celebrate the 300th anniversary of the Romanov dynasty in Tabriz and to decorate the city.

In October the elections for the *Majlis* were underway. Though outwardly Samad Khán pretended to comply with the government order, in reality he prevented it and stirred reactionary *mullás* to send a telegram that Tabriz did not want to participate in the elections. Furthermore, he killed two more Constitutionalists. The first of July 1914 was the coronation of Ahmad Sháh, who had come of age and was taking the responsibilities of a monarch. Less than a month later, the First World War broke out and within short intervals all sides declared war against each other. Emboldened by the new situation, the Iranian government asked the Russians to agree to a different *pishkár* for Azerbaijan, and they chose Rashíd al-Mulk for this position. Samad Khán's reign of terror was finally at an end. Under the threat of the Ottoman army and because of the war, the Russians had changed their position and wanted to appease the people. Samad Khán retired to his sumptuous mansion that he had built in Ne'matabad, not far from Tabriz. Later fearing for his life, he went to Tiblisi under Russian protection.

The Russian occupation of Azerbaijan as well as some parts of northern Iran continued until after the 1917 Revolution, when the Russian army disintegrated. In October 1912, the Turkish troops that had already occupied some parts of the Western Iranian border were called back. In December of the same year while the forces of Anwar Pasha[5]

---

5   For an account of these days see the book of the German consul in Tabriz, W. Litten, *Persiche Flitterwochen*, Berlin 1925. See also by the same author *Persien von der "pénétration pacifique" zum "Protektorat"*. It is translated into Persian as

were threatening the Russian army in the Caucausus, some Kurdish groups were sent to Azerbaijan, and the Russians withdrew from Azerbaijan between December 27, 1914 and January 6, 1915. Two days later Ahmad Mukhtár Beik Shamkhál entered Tabriz with his Kurdish troops, but the occupation did not last long and on January 31 again the Russians occupied Tabriz. The Constitutionalists that had fled from Tabriz and lived the hard lives of exiles in Turkey returned with the Ottoman army, and were an important force in the fight against the Russians. The Kurds, who under the pretext of *jihad* or "unity of Islam" were fighting under the Ottoman banner, were mostly after plunder. The Assyrians and some Armenians, who had sided with the Russians, were moving along with them. Urmiya suffered more at the hands of the Kurds and the Assyrians than any other city in Azerbaijan. On February 22, 1915, the Kurds took out sixty Assyrian notables from the French mission in Urmiya and shot them in cold blood. Mar Shimon, the religious leader of the Assyrians, who tried to find alliance with the Kurdish chief, Simgo, was murdered with fifty of his companions. The Assyrians reciprocated and massacred the innocent citizens of Urmiya. According to some accounts the number of victims was nearly 10,000.

During the war the German influence gained momentum. In 1913 the Ottoman government gave command of its army to German Liman von Sanders to be trained in modern warfare. By November 1914 the German consul in Tabriz,

Írán az nufúz-i musálamat ámiz tá taht al-himáyagí: asnád va haqáyiqí dar bárah-yi nufúz-i Urúpá-íyán dar Írán (1860-1919) by Maryam Mír Ahmadí, Tehran : Mu'ín, 1367 [1988 or 1989]. Also look for a very interesting article by Rahim Raisnia "Tabriz et l'intervention des armées étrangèrs 1915-1919" in *La Perse et La Grande Guerre,* etudes rèunies et présentées par Oliver Bast, Institut Français de Recherche en Iran, Tehran, 2002. pp. 293–316.

Litten, was arming the tribes. The German propaganda went so far as declaring that the Kaiser had become converted to Islam and had also made a pilgrimage to Mecca. In the tribes of the south the famous Wassmus was active against the British, who were going to form their South Persian Rifles in 1916. For most of the remainder of the war Azerbaijan and Kurdistan saw a back-and-forth campaign of the Turkish and Russian forces attacking and counter-attacking each other. In the south the British were after German agents, and battled them throughout Iran. At the insistence of Winston Churchill the ships of the Royal Navy had started burning oil, and the Anglo-Persian Company (which later became BP) was on its way to becoming the cornerstone of British policy in Iran. Therefore, the southwest was becoming exceedingly important for the British. Although the oilfields were in the neutral zone according to the 1907 Convention, the British made a secret agreement with the Russians to have free access to these areas. Meanwhile in Tehran the governments came and went, and they were so weak that they could not take any stand against the foreign powers. The Iranian people, who had suffered the atrocities of the Russians and were disappointed with the British, were becoming increasingly inclined towards the Germans.

At this time the Gendarmerie was under Swedish officers, who were very much pro-German. The third *Majlis* was even weaker than its predecessors. Some of its Democrat members as well as Gendarmerie officers, and a number of mujahidin, who had returned to Tehran, were urging Ahmad Sháh to move the capital to Isfahan. The Russian forces that had reached Qazvin had further increased the fear of the occupation of Tehran. On November 15, 1915, a large number of notables and politicians left Tehran, and Ahmad Sháh was preparing to leave the following day. The Russian and British ministers met with him and reassured him that the Russians would not come to Tehran. Furthermore, if Iran chose to side with Germany, the two powers had no choice but to change their "friendly" policy with Iran. Thus Ahmad Sháh was dissuaded not to leave his capital, and a number of *mu-hajirin* (exiles) returned. Another group did not return and formed a "Defense Committee," which was in fact a government in exile. This was in Qom, and already Hamadan had been taken from the Russians. Though Isfahan was in the hands of *mujahidin*, Bakhtiyaris and German agents, the forces of General Baratov, after taking Qom, Savah, Kashan and Hamadan, occupied Isfahan. Meanwhile the gendarmes were fiercely fighting the Russians near Kirmanshah and were reinforced by the Ottomans who had already defeated the British in Kut al-Amarah in Iraq. Baratov wanted to help the British by forcing the Ottomans back, but could not do so. In the end of June 1916 the Ottoman forces after occupying Kurdistan took Kirmanshah. At this time, Nizám al-Saltanah and other members of the "exile" group reached Kirmanshah and under the name of *Tudeh-e Iran* (The Persian People) formed a new government.

For a while there was a stalemate between the Ottomans and the Russians. Hamadan was evacuated by the Russians, but they were still facing the Ottomans in Malayir, Kurdistan and Loristan. On February 24, 1917, General Stanley Maud retook Kut al-Amarah, which General Townshend had so disastrously lost a year earlier, and had freed 18,000 Ottoman troops to invade northwestern Iran. Thus the road to Baghdad was opened and the Ottoman troops gradually gave up the towns that they had occupied as the Russians took them back. Nizám al-Saltanah and some of the "exiles" went along with the Ottoman army to Turkey, and some even went as far as Berlin. The Russian army joined the British in Iraq and the Iranians despaired of any German or Ottoman help.

The Russian Revolution was a god-sent relief for Iran. The February Revolution in 1917, which resulted in the abdication of Tsar Nicholas II, the collapse of Imperial Russia and the end of the Romanov dynasty, was celebrated not only by the Iranians but amazingly also by the Russians themselves. The unexpected news of the demise of the Russian empire coincided with Naw Ruz celebrations. The Iranians after six years of hardship and incredible atrocities were looking foreword to the spring of freedom, and strangely enough the Russians had joined in as their "companions in liberation." Kasravi, who as a young man lived through the Constitutional revolution in his sequel of *The Persian Constitution*, describes these days in Tabriz:

> "In Tabriz the Russians continued to woo the Iranians, and asked the *kárguzár* to appoint a day for them to go along with the Iranians to the graves of the *Thiqatu'l-Islam* and other victims and in this way gain their affection and undo the wrongs of the past. This was a very good gesture. Everyone accepted it with joy and the Democrats and others rose to the occasion. A joint committee of Russians and Iranians was formed for this purpose, and another of the Iranians was formed to prepare the shrines. On May 26, 1917, freedom-lovers from many groups as well as students gathered and printed songs and poems in Turkish and Persian, and distributed them everywhere...."

On that day the governor, *kárguzár*, consuls, chiefs of government offices, and leaders of the Constitutionalists gathered in the army barracks. The place was decorated with flags and even in the memory of the 'Ashura of 1330 (December 31, 1911) gallows were raised. Then the Russians and Iranians marched in with flags and music, singing songs:

ملته دار اوسته ویرن امتحـــان   ای وطنه بذل ایلین نقد جـــان

محو اولا، مشگلدی بو نام ونشان   قانیله صفا تاپدی بهـار وطن

O you who sacrificed your lives for this land
And in this test of valor were so grand.
Your blood has replenished afresh our springs,
Could such names will be gone? Hard it seems.

Here Khiabani [6] gave a speech and Qanbarov, the head of the Russian Committee talked of the injustices done by the despotic Russian government in Iran, and on his own behalf, and on that of his colleagues, asked for forgiveness.

> "From here they went to Sayyid Hamza shrine, where
> *Thiqatu'l-Islam,* Prince Amanullah, *Sádiq al-Mulk* and
> Hájjí 'Alí *Davá-Furush* were buried. The Russian
> commanders bared their heads, knelt and laid wreaths
> on the graves. Here, also, many speeches were given
> and then different groups went to the cemeteries of
> Devechi, Amir Khiz, Ermanistan and Lailava....."

---

6   Shaykh Muhammad Khíábání was the leader of the democratic movement of "Azadistan" in Azerbaijan that was started soon after these events and took over the rule of Tabriz. But he was treacherously murdered by the government troops of *Mukhbir al-Saltanah*, and his movement was destroyed.

The corpse of *Ziyá'u'l- 'Ulamá* had been sent to Iraq, and his mother had written a heartrending letter:

> "I am a mother who has seen her son hanging from
> the gallows, and in my old age, with bent back has
> not taken out the mourning dress in the memory of
> my son and my brother. I as a misery-stricken mother
> can only take out my mourning dress and those of
> my orphaned children when the colleagues of my
> son would remember me in my deserted home and
> give condolences to the daughters of *Ziyá'u'l- 'Ulamá*
> continues: "As a response to her request everyone came
> out from Sayyid Hamza and visited her home and gave
> their condolences to that poor mother…"

After the October revolution the Russian consul in Khuy, Karl Bravin became the representative to Tehran, but could not establish relations with the government, and was recalled by Moscow. The second envoy was Ivan Kolomitsov, who was sent by Stephan Shaumian, head of the Bolshevik Committee of Baku, but as a result of the intrigues of the Tsarist ambassador, Von Etter, could not be accepted by Vusugh al-Dowleh. Furthermore, in November 1918, a group of officials from the former embassy of Russia invaded the residence of Kolomitsov and put him to flight. He returned to Russia, and came back for a second time with two companions and a large amount of diamonds and cash. Although he was officially empowered to cancel all of Iran's debts as well as many of Russia's other claims and the 1907 Convention, Iran did not pay any attention to him. Kolomitsov and his two friends were arrested in Sári by gendarmes, and after a telegraph to Tehran, they were summarily tried, and shot.[7] The Iranian government took all the money and diamonds, and continued to treat Von Etter as the Russian representative for a time after which there were no relations between the Soviets and Iran until the third ambassador Rotschin came to Tehran and a comprehensive friendship treaty was signed in 1921.

---

7   For the tragic life of Kolomitsov see Ghaffar Bakhtiyar, "Ivan Kolomitsov, dovomin ferestadeh rusiyeh-e shuravi beh Iran", *Tarikh Ravabit-e khariji*, vol. III, No. 12, Tehran, Fall 2002, pp. 82-90.

INDEX

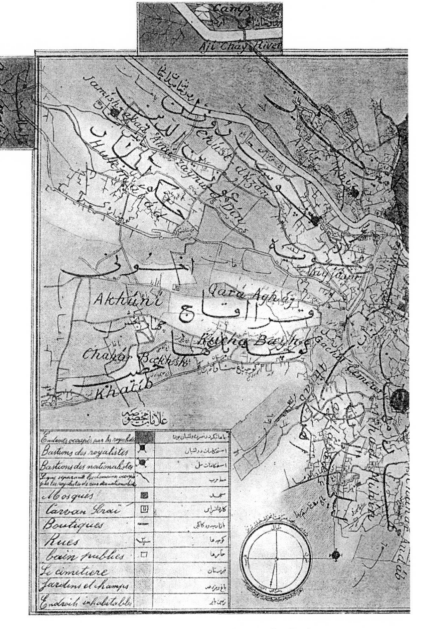

A map of Tabriz showing the districts.

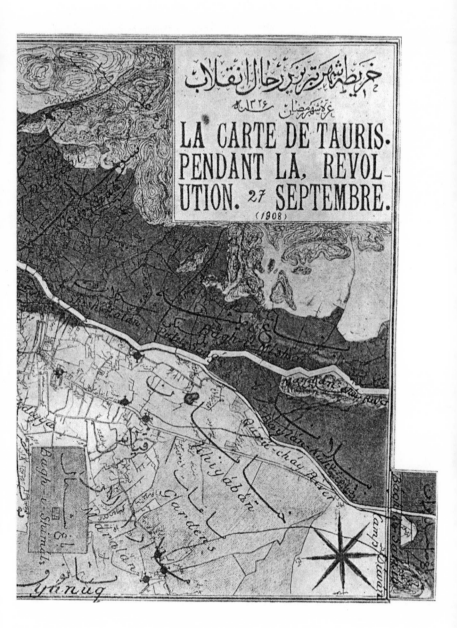

LA CARTE DE TAURIS.
PENDANT LA, REVOL-
UTION. 27 SEPTEMBRE.
(1908)

SOME OTHER MAGE TITLES

Obeyd-e Zakani: Ethics of the Aristocrats
and Other Satirical Stories
Translated and Edited by Hasan Javadi

The Strangling of Persia
Morgan Shuster

The Persian Revolution of 1905–1909
Edward G. Browne / Introduction by Abbas Amanat

Crowning Anguish: Taj Al-Saltana
Introduction by Abbas Amanat / Translated by Anna Vanzan

Agriculture in Qajar Iran
Willem Floor

Public Health in Qajar Iran
Willem Floor

The Persian Gulf
A Political and Economic History of Five Port Cities
Willem Floor

The Persian Gulf: The Rise of the Gulf Arabs
The Politics of Trade on the Persian Littoral, 1747-1792
Willem Floor

The History of Theater in Iran
Willem Floor

Travels through Northern Persia, 1770-1774
Samuel Gottlieb Gmelin / Willem Floor

Titles and Emoluments in Safavid Iran:
A Third Manual of Safavid Administration
Mirza Naqi Nasiri / Willem Floor

The Persian Garden: Echoes of Paradise
Mehdi Khansari / M. R. Moghtader / Minouch Yavari

Printed in the United States
203614BV00002B/112-129/P